CONSTITUTIONAL EXPOSURE

Constitutional Exposure
A Postulation for Democracy to Come

Pablo Ghetti

COUNTERPRESS
OXFORD

First published 2017
Counterpress, Oxford
http://counterpress.org.uk

© 2017 Pablo Ghetti

Rights to publish and sell this book in print, electronic, and all other forms and media are exclusively licensed to Counterpress Limited. An electronic version of this book is available under a Creative Commons Attribution-NonCommercial (CC-BY-NC 4.0) International license via the Counterpress website: http://counterpress.org.uk

ISBN: 978-1-910761-04-5 (paperback)

Typeset in 10.5 on 12 pt Sabon

Global print and distribution by Ingram

ACKNOWLEDGEMENTS

This book and its main topics consumed so much of my attention in the past 15 years that it would be unwise to attempt an exhaustive list of acknowledgements. Wholehearted thanks go to my contemporaries in the postgraduate programme and to the staff who made all the difference to my PhD research at Birkbeck, University of London, and to Peter Fitzpatrick, my diligent and generous supervisor. I also acknowledge important funding and guidance provided by the Brazilian Higher Education Training Coordination (CAPES) and research undertaken at the Pontificate Catholic University of Rio de Janeiro, at the British Library, and at the École Normale Supérieure. The memorable Latin America/Global South reading group at Birkbeck, the Adieu Derrida seminars, and the Critical Legal Conferences (2004–8) deserve high praise for their contribution to the ideas in this book. I am also indebted to the staff and students of the School of Law and the Politics Department at the University of Exeter for their patience and critical engagement with my work. The very conceptualization of this book owes a great deal to Johan Van der Walt's studies in legal and constitutional theory. As viva examiners, Johan and Denise Ferreira da Silva provided key insights.

I also thank Chantal Mouffe and Jean-Luc Nancy for invaluable correspondence during the early stages, and for giving me the opportunity to translate some of their work into Portuguese—another formative experience. My gratitude further goes to my colleagues at the Brazilian Ministry of Foreign Relations with whom I have had the opportunity to discuss aspects of my work. Evidently, however, the ideas developed here do not necessarily reflect their views nor those of the Ministry.

Despite having rewritten a number of sections, I should thank Jeremy Langsworthy for his sound copy-editing of an earlier draft and Richard Joyce for his patient reading of early drafts and for his thought-provoking observations. Moreover, the final text would not have the same readability if it were not for the gifted editorial comments offered by Gilbert Leung, through whom I also thank all the dedicated Counterpress team.

I would like to acknowledge the extraordinary intellectual companionship of my sister Paola Ghetti, who has joined me in the unchartered territories of Jean-Luc Nancy's thought, and the ethical and political inspiration drawn from our parents.

And to my wife, Paula, without whom nothing makes sense. All this time has made us stronger and more committed to the struggles in which we believe. And I dedicate all these efforts to our adored children, Lucas, Heitor, and Olívia. Being exposed to and with them has changed everything.

CONTENTS

INTRODUCTION 11

1. 'DEMOCRACY TO COME' 20

   1.1 Approaches 22
   1.2 'Democracy to Come' Comes to Light 26
       Democracy Today 26
       Democracy and 'to Come' with(out) Europe 29
       An Institution to Come 32
   1.3 Common Sense: Irruptions 34
       Universalizations 34
       Common Sense 39

2. DEMOCRACY 47

   2.1 Ruins of Law 48
   2.2 Democratic Licence 52
   2.3 Forces: Sovereign, Democratic, Deconstructive 58
       Sovereignty and Democracy 58
       Force of Deconstruction 61
   2.4 Inviting the Exposure of Dominant Discourses 65
       Autonomy and Autoimmunity 66
       Democratic Autoimmunity 69

3. LAW 74

   3.1 Derrida's Law 76
   3.2 Beyond Strict Law 84
   3.3 Strategic Predicament 91
   3.4 From Acknowledgment to Exposure 97
   Excursus I: Composing Rights 101
   Excursus II: Right Carnival of Democracy 107

4. 'TO COME' 113

    4.1 Future and 'to Come' 114
        Futures 116
    4.2. Two Unconditionalities 120
        Sovereignty and Unconditionality 125
    4.3. Towards Another 'to Come' 128
    4.4. Encountering Fears 134
        Courage 138

POSTULATING FORMALIZATIONS 146

        Exposure 147
        Law and Constitutionality 148
        'To Come' 149

BIBLIOGRAPHY 151

NOTES 165

INDEX 221

Elections are an excellent procedure, and democracy entirely justified as the only desirable form of government, precisely because it constitutes the condition of veracity for the consciousness of the community.

— Álvaro Vieira Pinto, *Consciência e Realidade Nacional*

We have to reinvent language if willing to develop democracy.

— Luis Alberto Warat, *Manifesto of Legal Surrealism*

Why does one so often pretend [*feindre*] (a fiction of democracy) to ignore the violence of this dissymmetry [given the absence of the right to respond], and what can or cannot be reduced [*se laisser réduire*] in it? Why such hypocrisy, the denegation, or the blindness before the all-too-evident? Why is this 'all-too-evident' at once as clear as the light of day, and the most nocturnal face of democracies as they are, presently?

— Jacques Derrida, *The Other Heading*

Exposed, thus: but this is not the coming to light of what had initially been hidden, enclosed. Here exposure [*exposition*] is being itself (this is how it is called: existing). Or even better: if, as subject, being has autoposition for essence, here autoposition is itself, as such, in essence and structure, the exposure. Auto = ex = body. The body is the being-exposed of being.

— Jean-Luc Nancy, *Corpus*

INTRODUCTION

This book addresses Jacques Derrida's postulation of democracy to come. It aims to contribute to Derrida's postulation by interpreting it as 'constitutional exposure,' and then by intensifying the call to democracy to come as constitutional exposure.[1] I maintain that the latter means the theory and practice of exposing democracy's fundamental laws, or the exposure of the orientating distinctions and divides that shape democracy (constitution–ruin, public–private, general–particular, near–distant, visible–invisible, etc.). In this regard, I propose two organizing discursive layers, which are not immune to each other. In the first (prevalent in my first two chapters), I put forward an interpretation of democracy to come in which constitutional exposure comes to the fore. In the second (prevalent in my final two chapters), I seek to intensify such an exposure, and consequently democracy to come itself.

This exposure can be disorientating. And, in fact, with democracy to come, Derrida seeks to destabilize the settled and self-satisfied orientation of democracy its quotidian exposure. That is, democracy is already a practice of exposure, where the lines of what is public and private, lawful and unlawful, similar or foreign are constantly being negotiated or transacted. Such an exposure, though, can be encapsulated or exploited by constitutional regimes in which situations of exclusion, hierarchy, and exploitation are condoned. The form of democracy should not thus allow any condescension or contentment. This entails, I argue, the necessity of an overexposure, which involves the intense pursuit of the transformation of existing democratic practices. It requires a more radical sensitivity to the limits of democracy, to exposure itself, and the chance, albeit fragile, of engendering other forms (in theory and practice) of organizing social life. All this, I shall argue, can be found in Derrida. And my work here belongs to the domain of interpretation, the first layer of my argument on constitutional exposure, prevalent in my first two chapters.

However, in Derrida's work there are also instances of writing hardly compatible with overexposure. That would not necessarily be a problem for this book if such instances were not relevant to democracy itself. As already mentioned, constitutional exposure is to some extent the exposure of fundamental laws—putting them in question and often re-energizing them. Furthermore, the 'to come' (an openness to the future 'here and now' that is not predetermined) is an unavoidable term within any discourse that addresses the transformative potential of democracy, for it raises both the problems of time (the promise of another democracy or another struggle for democracy yet to come) and space (the difference and distance of the people in relation to political power and among themselves). So, the understanding and the discourse of law (fundamental or constitutional laws in particular) and 'to come' are inextricable from the practice of democracy itself.

Democracy to come requires an approach to law that takes into account its complexity and democratization, and does not reduce it to the domain of strict and unexposed distinctions typical of modern traditions of jurisprudence. In spite of its richness, Derrida's approach to law needs to be radicalized so that a strategy similar to that of democracy can be articulated. Thus, law should not be seen as a domain opposed to justice, for instance; law is rather the very articulation of justice and rule. So the question, for democracy, is not the coming of justice, but a new articulation of justice and rule in which justice is not exploited by the few and in which the rule is not socially and politically stifling. In other words, the task in hand is not akin to a binary distinction itself but the clash of two or more different forms of bringing together distinctions, divides, or orientating lines of sociability (note that the problem here is not only terminological, even if I adopted Derrida's terminology (law–justice) I could still claim that it is necessary to think in terms of a different articulation of law–justice, rather than the coming of justice itself).[2] Bearing that in mind, and integrating gestures found in the works of Jean-Luc Nancy and Johan Van der Walt, I postulate a groundwork for a democratic understanding of the law, for an overexposure of the law, or, for reasons of simplicity, an 'expositivism.'

Another problem, similar albeit less evident, pertains to the promise of another democracy (constitutive of democracy) encapsulated in the phrase 'to come.' Derrida distinguishes the unconditionality of the 'to come' from an unconditionality with power: sovereignty. Yet democracy, as that negotiation of opposed drives, can neither side entirely with 'sovereignty' nor with the 'to come' (in the sense of an exigency), neither with power nor with lack of power. Both are inextricable to democracy. More than that, I argue that it is problematic to conceive of sovereignty and 'to come' in a separate way. The 'to come,' in fact, may be more promising and more apt to support social change if it includes in itself a dimension of power; that is, if what is to come is another way—less hierarchical, less exploitative—of enjoying the movement between conditionality and unconditionality. The strategic question is again not one of the necessity to reactivate the pure 'to come' (like justice, or exposure before), but to think other articulations of the 'to come' itself that can face up to a certain sovereignty and sovereign democracies, that is, against a system in which the 'to come' is mobilized in favour of social exploitation and hierarchies.

I shall now clarify a few terms used or implied so far before I move on to the next section on the methodology of this book. This is a preliminary explanation since these terms will often appear throughout this work, and their meaning will be enriched as the text progresses. The relevant terms are the nouns *postulation*, *strategy*, *exposure*, the adjective '*constitutional*,' and *theory*.

Derrida himself uses postulation to refer to his approach to unconditionality and to the plural and complex heritages of the politics of friendship.[3] Postulation is used instead of principle, 'in order to avoid the princely or powerful authority of the first, of the *arkhé* or *presbeia*.'[4] He also says that postulation avoids the axiomatic, and thus the comparable, 'scale of values and evaluations.'[5] Moreover, postulation 'gesture[s] toward the demand, the desire, the imperative exigency.'[6]

In my use of postulation, however, I do not aim at a clear-cut discarding of power, or the authority of the 'first.' A postulation cannot avoid power, despite Derrida's attempt. When one postulates, in both French and English, one speaks on the basis of a premise upon which one can start reasoning. Derrida is correct to the extent that, etymologically, postulation (Latin *postulatio*) refers to a demand, a call, a request, either to a law court or to a representative of a god. It implies the position of the weak, of those under the law or the authority of a god. In French, in particular, the etymological sense is still current. But so is the sense of the premise, the first element in a chain of arguments. I consider it important not to neglect this risk.

Thus, in my usage, postulation follows these two aspects of its meaning. It is situated between the pure ethical demand or exigency, on the one hand, and the pure power that posits an idea as invariable in order to be able to proceed. It does not mean a pure sense of exigency without power, condition, or calculation. It involves an attempt to address the order of power; to speak to it in whatever ways available; to appeal to a higher law—to a power even higher than the currently dominant—before a situation of injustice. And it means not eschewing to define, albeit provisionally, a premise upon which to discern a course of action, a call to thinking, struggling, resisting.

Postulation certainly does not mean that all power, authority, and hierarchy will have an end.[7] This for Derrida is not in question. What is in question is the position of the weak, and those who suffer; that is, the opportunity of political-ethical-legal action, the chance of an event that destabilizes a given hierarchy,[8] in the face of suffering, exploitation, and exclusion.[9] And in many ways, I shall demonstrate in this book that in the practice of his writing—sometimes despite his stated aim or meaning—it is precisely such a postulation that Derrida puts forward.

There is in this book such a postulation for democracy to come against current forms of oppression including, most importantly, those condoned in or by democracy. Because of that, it is possible to think strategically. And in a way, it is because of that, of a premise, a position, albeit a precarious one, that it is possible to think at all (for otherwise it would not even be possible to choose what to write about, to be passionate about a topic, to engage in something that matters). All writing is in part strategic. Certain strategies must be devised in order to conform to patterns of writing, to an agreed readership, to current socio-political conditions. A strategy implies the recognition of a correlation of forces, which must be addressed at all times.

However, there must be scope equally for a radical absence of strategy, that is to say openness to the demands of writing and thought that are foreign to a pre-established goal. Without that, university and academia as relatively autonomous spaces would make little sense, and writing would be perceived purely as a cunning art of persuasion (rather than a tireless pursuit of truth). The actual meaning of strategy in Derrida's work, and its consequences for my understanding of law and sovereignty will be addressed in a more sustained way in chapters two and three.

The democratic exposure put forward here should not be equated with transparency; nor should it be reduced to the revelation of an essence, a hidden reality and a hidden ground. On the contrary, in many ways it is the discourse that privileges transparency, essence, and grounds that needs to be exposed. But exposure also suggests the frail possibility of remaining within the surface itself, dwelling at and revelling in the constituted and constituting limits of democracy and law. This resolute outward position of exposure (the impact of the prefix 'ex') is also a strategy to disrupt the order of legitimacy that arises from the hidden–apparent and inside–outside divides. There is also a sensitive issue in play here: it does not mean an invocation of sense as opposed to reason, but the irruption of sensing from sense itself, as if it were possible to conceive of, in the utmost situation of exposure, a touching of/on the evanescent point where something moves beyond the control of dialectics, and conceptual and transcendental schemes.[10]

Yet, it is not possible to depart entirely from the traditions that inform legal thinking and research. Even though such traditions are often marred by problems and bound to existing power relations, it is necessary to find elements or currents within the legal tradition that can help initiating new paths of thought. Often indeed, it is the most problematic current of that tradition that is most interesting and thought-provoking. That is the case of constitutional law: the legal tradition that desperately seeks to find a legal way of describing and, sometimes, proscribing the ultimate source or ground of legality from legal practice. By choosing the adjective 'constitutional' in relation to exposure, I aim to refer to this legal tradition; constitutional—rather than constituting, constituted, or deconstituted—for it signifies something that relates to the realm of grounds, but is not reduced to the ultimate ground, or the ultimate lack of grounds. The suffix '-al' allows exposure to refer and relate to constitutionality without being reduced to one of its manifestations.

'Constitution' has a dual meaning, active and passive: constituting (forming) and constituted (formed, established). Deconstitution too has these two meanings, if not tendencies: deconstituting (dismantling) and deconstituted (dismantled). The adjective 'constitutional,' in turn, refers to all of these. Yet, as this book progresses, it will become clear there must be a strategic privileging of 'deconstitution' for the sake of the struggle against settled practices of exploitation, exclusion, and hierarchy. Even then, in a radical exposure, in an overexposure, it shall be argued that this very privileging is a choice, a decision, and a law that this work does not fail to embrace and to expose.

'Theory' is a term often used to describe a wide range of research approaches in the humanities. My reading of Derrida, contrary to what might be expected, has made me increasingly suspicious of this use. It implies that there is a distinct domain of theory that could inform all practical research, a domain that is at the same time foreign to practice and capable of governing that practice. It is thus difficult to describe what I have been doing as theory, be it legal, political, or ethical. It is almost equally suspect to bring practice and theory together in terms like 'theoretical practice,' for the same problems are simply brought to another level of abstraction.

It must be acknowledged, though, that this book can be read as theoretical research, mainly because it partly conforms with what is expected of 'theory.' It addresses Derrida's work, that of an established author. My coherence is thus initially assured, and constantly reassured, by the coherence of his signature and mark of his style. Moreover, it proposes the task of reading texts, interpreting, and contributing to them; it is not an investigation into Derrida's life or time. And it sometimes crafts new terms, when confronted with new and fundamental problems. In this way, it makes use of the poetic space that is to some extent authorized and even, in some corners of the world at least, de rigueur in theoretical texts. It is difficult to deny this work's theoretical stance.

At the same time, the author who supposedly reassures this book as theoretical is not exactly a reassuring author. Derrida does have a signature and he does have a unique style—and some security can always be found in that consistency—but he also troubles the orders of meaning, authorship, and scholarship that are part of the theoretical domain. He can hardly be said to have followers, for he rarely generalizes. His vocabulary is firmly attached to the texts that he discusses; and he has always avoided the spirit of a School.[11] Moreover, his books problematize the very idea of a book; the received ideas of book and of thesis require a totality, which can only be crafted by an outside that guards a pre-existing and originary whole.[12]

I also attempt to avoid the contemplative aspect of the theoretical domain. The etymology of theory, from Greek *theoria* (*thea*, namely spectacle, plus *horeo*, namely to see), indicates something that has a social cogency. The domain of thinking, writing, and addressing fundamental questions is sanitized, kept at bay in restricted circles. It is not open to general observation, scrutiny, questioning, and kept within the functional logic of a university or research institution. On the contrary, the practice of theory—of all the practices of a university—would benefit from, and at the same time greatly enrich, social life. This is precisely because good theory should indeed address fundamental issues that extend beyond the university. As Derrida has eloquently argued, life cannot be neatly extricated from writing and philosophy.[13] In some respects, indeed, Derrida's life experience and commitments ground in part my willingness to articulate his thought with experiences of suffering, inextricable from my own commitment to taking his thought, his 'theory' one step further.[14]

As mentioned, I put forward two combined arguments: I interpret democracy to come as a radical advocacy of constitutional exposure, and I seek to intensify such an exposure in certain problematic instances of Derrida's writing, namely law and the 'to come.' The first two chapters put greater emphasis on the first move, whereas the following two privilege the second one.

Yet, there is another structuring way of understanding the book. The first chapter proposes a close reading of Derrida's first approaches to democracy to come. It offers an initial engagement with the term and with my overall argument. Subsequently, each chapter tackles one of the several constitutive elements of 'democracy to come.' Two of them are explicit elements: 'democracy' (ch. 2) and 'to come' (ch. 4); and another one is implicit, albeit equally relevant: law (ch. 3).

In the first chapter I provide an initial treatment of democracy to come and put forward my overall argument out of careful textual analysis of Derrida's texts. I argue that Derrida proposes an exposure of the self-satisfied and self-contented image of democracy that gained purchase towards the end of the cold war. In addition, I argue that Derrida claims a universalizing role for democracy, beside its concrete and contingent manifestations. Yet, this universalization is not settled and colonizing; it thrives through sensitivity to the transformative opportunities of the democratic discourse, when taken up by those who are excluded or exploited. In all, 'constitutional exposure' is put forward and the call to another experience of democracy from within modern democracies is presented for the first time in this book. I achieve that by first situating Derrida's discourse on democracy to come and my own approach to it in relation to key contemporary authors. I then address key early texts in which Derrida presents or comes near to presenting democracy to come. I conclude by discussing an instance of Derrida's writing which shows how he clearly avoids the traditions, akin to democracy, that engender social hierarchy, exploitation, and exclusion.

In chapter two, I interpret further Derrida's postulation of democracy to come. I show in a more direct way that this postulation means a radical constitutional exposure, that is, exposure of constitution and ruin, and constitution and deconstitution, which are integral to democracy. I further demonstrate how democracy itself is crucial for Derrida, and not only democracy to come (because the 'to come' is already inscribed in the democratic tradition). I achieve that by addressing the problem of constitutional ruin, which is richly embraced by Derrida. In addition, I focus on the aspects of the democratic tradition that already praise the plurality and restlessness of ruin; with the distinction between liberty and licence being crucial here. I then address the question of force in relation to democracy—a constitutive element of its etymology—with resonances regarding sovereignty and the role of deconstruction itself in tackling dominant discourses. I finally use an important framework of Derrida's thought, autoimmunity, to question the modern 'democratic' emphasis on autonomy and the dominant discourse of democracy as a whole.

The third chapter places more emphasis on the intensification of Derrida's postulation of democracy to come. This intensification happens in two main ways: by means of an intense interpretation of Derrida's key texts on law—particularly his institutional analyses—and by means of a critique of his Kantian starting point, which I deem to be a strategic predicament. I argue generally that Derrida's take on law, if that predicament is overcome, can be invaluable to the intensification of constitutional exposure and, consequently, democracy itself. My argument unfolds in four stages. I first address Derrida's main framework in relation to the interplay between law and justice, and I identify a problematic starting point. I then maintain that this interplay is more complex than it may appear, involving inseparability between the two terms. I subsequently maintain that, in spite of the latter point, a strategic predicament persists with regard to Derrida's starting point in light of current legal theory that includes without true democratic implications various forms of appeals to justice and flexibility. Finally, at a faster pace and in a more tentative mode than the rest of the book—and following gestures from philosopher Jean-Luc Nancy, legal historian and philosopher Michel Villey, and legal theorist Johan Van der Walt—I seek to point to the thinkability of another thought of law for democracy.

The final chapter continues the intensification of Derrida's postulation of constitutional exposure. I approach another constitutive element of the phrase 'democracy to come,' namely the 'to come' itself. I argue that the 'to come' should not be construed in a way that is strictly opposed to sovereignty, that is, if these terms mean, respectively, unconditionality without power and unconditionality with power. This opposition is not strategically sound. And by putting this forward, Derrida saps his own democratic discourse. Democracy as such is understood by Derrida in complex, rich, and undecidable ways. It is a key task of thought to articulate precisely such undecidability in relation to the 'to come' itself. Legal-political-ethical research will then be more apt to counter the drives towards exploitation and exclusion that can be called sovereign, that is, an exploitative form of organizing the restless 'to come.'

I sustain my argument in four moments. First, I argue that Derrida's distinction between 'to come' and future is possible, albeit always fragile. Secondly, I seek to problematize and complicate Derrida's second distinction between two unconditionalities. Despite the innovative side of this distinction, I maintain that it cannot be sustained as such, not to speak in relation to social experiences of democracy. Thirdly, I argue that there is a chance of another 'to come,' one that is more pervasive and restless. Like law (within its social domain and in a more implicit way) the 'to come' provides a reminder to democracy about the paradox of what it actually means. Fourthly, the novel 'to come' intervenes radically in sovereign democracy by addressing its politics of fear. It engages here in an exposure of exposure (what is already a democratic task); but for that to be possible, it must neither be pure nor independent: it must itself be *exposed*.

With this set of arguments, I seek to intensify the discourse of democracy to come and develop a new postulation—with and beyond Derrida—of democracy itself as a radical exigency, inextricable from actual political and social struggles for equality, freedom of expression, participatory governance. To that end I take particular care in devising an apt vocabulary to make sure that the starting point of such struggles cannot exclude the collusion of democratic models themselves. This is a vocabulary for thinking democracy to come in ways that are more concrete and more directly political, perhaps towards a radical, a true, an exposed democracy.

— 1 —

'DEMOCRACY TO COME'

It is always problematic to classify any of Derrida's ingenious terms. They have been created precisely in a way that evades such facile classifications. It is hard to say straightforwardly what democracy to come properly is, for, in the still Aristotelian academic and theoretical environment we live in, saying what it is means to classify it, to put it in a settled frame. Yet, Derrida's writing cannot entirely evade a certain economy: the discourse of democracy to come can be addressed with regard to the internal economy of 'his' writings, writings united by the signature Jacques Derrida. That is, the term could be understood with regard to the role it plays in building up an interrelation amongst the pieces where it appears. Such an interrelation is both constituted by the signature, but also necessary to the credibility of the signature.

This is not entirely dissimilar from the role of jargon or from the creation of a vocabulary. Certainly, one would have to assess key moments of this appearance and discern the specific problems in relation to which the term has been used. When assessed in this way (with regard to its problems, its addressees and non-addressees) one realizes that democracy to come is more than jargon, even though, unavoidably, also jargon. For it is rich in sense (beyond common sense), in space for further thought, and pregnant in ambivalence (like democracy, whose radical semantic plurality could be pushed to the extreme).

Highly praised by Derrida, this richness and ambivalence of democracy supports the argument regarding constitutional exposure. Derrida seeks to expose the plurality of grounds of democracy, and its lack of an overarching ground or constitution. Without turning exposure into an absolute, Derrida exposes democracy's own limitations and incompleteness in a very careful way, one that does not simply posit the way forward, but raises a number of specific issues that engender a subtle coherence. What emerges is a careful exposure of the orientating distinctions that underpin the quotidian democratic space.

These considerations lead one to a careful textual-historical reading. Fortunately this enterprise has already commenced. Only a handful of authors, though, discuss Derrida from within his very premises; and even fewer without *legislative* (not to say sovereign) intent.[1] With regard to political theory and democracy in particular, one finds powerful arguments in the work of Alex Thomson.[2] Besides a broad survey of Derrida's political writings, with an emphasis on *Politics of Friendship*, Thomson offers a compelling diagnosis of the origins and 'place' of democracy to come in the economy of Derrida's writings.

My approach is different. First, this is because my point of departure is democracy to come itself, and does not focus on deconstruction or politics in general in relation to democracy (Thomson's book). Moreover, my interest is democracy itself and not politics in general. Secondly, this is because I privilege the question of the law, or the extent to which democracy to come is pervaded by 'law' (what brings to the fore constitutional exposure). There are textual grounds, as I argue, for that emphasis.[3] In doing so, I bring to the fore a crucial question in contemporary legal and political theory: the relationship between law and democracy.

I intend to make two integrated points. On the one hand, I argue that Derrida's early concern with democracy involves a rejection of the self-satisfied and self-contented notion and practice of democracy. Especially in light of the imminent dismantling of the 'communist' bloc, Derrida tried to warn against facile appraisals of democracy. Even more radically, he rejected, at least implicitly, a crucial aspect of the widely well-regarded work of Claude Lefort on democracy. He did not embrace Lefort's demand to pose a stark contrast between democracy and totalitarianism. I argue one can start to see here Derrida's discourse of exposure of settled distinctions (which is not to say that democracy should not be rethought and practiced as distinct from totalitarianism, authoritarianism, and dictatorship). On the other hand, and in spite of his resistance against democracy, a democracy of his time (evocatively of 'the day,' as he puts it), Derrida also claims a universalizing role for democracy, one which can be identified in its concrete manifestations, but which is often obfuscated in these manifestations. Democracy is not the apodictic opposite to totalitarianism, and yet there is in it an experience of universalization and exposure that is worth fighting for, that is worth intensifying.

This chapter presents the first instantiation of my argument on constitutional exposure. Yet, it does not posit absolutely that interpretation of Derrida's discourse of democracy to come. Rather, it builds its case carefully, with Derrida's texts, and what emerges is indeed a constant work of exposure and self-exposure of the constitutional orientations of democracy, and an interpretation of democracy itself as the pursuit of an ever more radical exposure of its grounds and lack of grounds.

1.1 Approaches

Derrida's work in no way underwent a shift from the philosophical to the political, nor indeed from the political to the ethical.[4] Certainly, political-ethical-juridical questions became directly thematized in Derrida's later writings, where a certain boldness can be found in areas with respect to which he might have been otherwise more careful.[5] In his later writings, though, one easily notices a great anxiety and impatience with his readers, which, in any event, does not deny its fundamental postulations.[6] Amongst these claims, the one levelled against Derrida by Claude Lefort (briefly discussed by Thomson) deserves particular attention.

In a 1984 text (prepared in the context of the Centre for the Study of the Political, set up by Jean-Luc Nancy and Philippe Lacoue-Labarthe) Lefort produced a strong defence of political philosophy—against political science—and a strong critique of Jacques Derrida and, by extension, of those who worked along his lines. This text is '*La question de la démocratie*.'[7] Without entering into the field of Lefort's rigorous broader work, I shall discuss specifically this text to the extent that it touches upon Derrida's work. There is no longer any point in arguing that this critique is mistaken since Derrida's work has always been pervaded by legal-ethical-political concerns (and we shall incidentally notice, throughout this book, that Derrida's work did have such a dimension since its inception).[8] There is no point any longer for Derrida has extensively treated these matters directly in subsequent writings. And yet, it is evident that the nature and authority of such a critique required some type of response from Derrida. In part at least, Derrida's directly legal-ethical-political writings respond to Lefort (and more broadly to the context of scholarship at Nancy's and Lacoue-Labarthe's centre for studies on the political).[9] My principal argument here, though, is that Lefort's main assumption—that the great task of political philosophy is to propose a discourse on the 'good society'—is not acceptable from a Derridean perspective.

Let me allude briefly to Lefort's critique of Derrida, inextricable in fact from Lefort's notion of the *judgemental* task of political philosophy. This rhetorical question should suffice to make sense of the picture: 'is it possible to manage ontological difference with such subtlety, to rival the greatest prodigies in the combined exploitation of Heidegger, Lacan, Jakobson and Levi-Strauss, and to fall back onto the crassest realism when it comes to politics?'[10] What exactly Lefort means by this realism is elusive. Yet, if he means a certain crudity of analysis of social forces and insistence on not taking definitive sides (perhaps in contrast to idealism) then he may be correct.

Derrida indeed could not accept, and has never accepted, Lefort's 'restoration of political philosophy.'[11] Lefort's requirement that every political philosophy should concern 'always ... the difference of essence between a free regime and a despotism or tyranny' would have to be met with qualifications by Derrida. To be sure, Derrida claimed never to have wished to 'disqualify' the great emancipatory discourses of the enlightenment.[12] Yet, a difference of essence between a 'free regime' and a 'despotic regime'[13] would import the type of naturalization of political regimes against which Derrida has always striven. What one learns from Derrida after this critique is that the great value of democracy lies not in the self-congratulation of institutions, but in the critical—in the sense also of bringing up a crisis—input of the democratic drive.

What, though, is Lefort's point of departure; from what Archimedean point will he be able to assess all other regimes? This text is also illuminating in that regard:

> Incorporated in the prince, power gave body to society. From this fact, there was a latent but efficacious knowledge of what constituted *one* for the *other* in all the extension of the social. In light of this model, one can designate the revolutionary trait of democracy. The place of power becomes an *empty place*. ... What is essential is that it prohibits those who govern from appropriating power and incorporating themselves in power.[14]

This is Lefort's 'ground': democracy's capacity to encompass this empty place. Lefort adheres to this purportedly historical experience as fundamentally opposed to the fulfilment of such a 'place' in totalitarian regimes.

As one will see extensively in this book, Derrida embraces democracy in many different ways. He claims to be a democrat and not to forsake that tradition (or only to forsake that name, democracy, in name of the democratic tradition).[15] However, that type of overconfidence in the powers of philosophy that one sees above is something that Derrida lacks (many will recognize in him the student of Foucault that he was. The timing of Derrida's reception in Anglo-American academia was so precocious that one often loses sight of Derrida's indebtedness to authors like Foucault and Deleuze).[16] Committed to investigating all aspects of the metaphysics of presence, Derrida realized the resilience of subtle legitimating mechanisms and technologies of power surrounding so-called empty places. Yet, in contradistinction to Foucault, Derrida is often praised for engaging in what Lefort considers to be political judgement, for taking the responsibility not to *posit* the law, but to practice it in writing patiently delimited interventions.[17]

Another two interrelated important aspects of Lefort's text are his emphasis on 'taking the risk of judging,' and his understanding that all work in philosophy in France during his lifetime depended on the democratic experience.[18] If Derrida were willing to embrace each of these ideas, if he were to provide a frontal response, he would have to make some qualifications. Derrida never abstains from discussing, in a sense 'judging,' and providing his fragile postulations on a whole range of legal-political-ethical matters. As I sustain later, this is possible by not asserting the law, by not leading the way forward, but by raising the questions, difficulties, and complex informative elements that are crucial for an independent legal-ethical-political response.

On the other hand, Derrida has been careful, since long before Lefort's critique, to stress that his work as a philosopher and his capacity to critique were indebted to democracy.[19] Derrida is on Lefort's side against positivist political science, but this should not obscure the necessary 'critique' of one's own society. The only true critique that remains for Derrida is a critique of one's own involvement in the tracing of the social texture, one that may rightly resemble Derrida's own attempt at a creative translation, 'deconstruction.'[20] (In this sense, a critique that takes as its point of reference 'another society' tends to dismiss the actual problems that one society poses for itself uniquely.)

As one shall see, Lefort's work anticipates many of the issues that positively or negatively influence Derrida's ethical-juridical-political trajectory. It will be noted that Lefort's critique can often be heard in the background of Derrida's work. Yet, it would be unpersuasive to encompass all of Derrida's contribution in this field as a response to Lefort. Derrida, we shall see, was a prolix writer with a passion for democracy, and his allegiance is paid in delicate ways—to guard against possible and risky power-based appropriations of an emancipatory discourse. First, let us see now how a much more recent political-literary theorist characterizes Derrida, which will assist in explicating the type of model of writing that I attempt here.

Thomson's main suggestion with regard to the philosopheme 'democracy to come' is that it has to be read in the context of a particular period in France, the 1980s, and the reception of Derrida's work by friendly and less friendly political theorists (Thomson's more general claim is that Derrida's work provides a significant political contribution, and is not a 'refusal of politics').[21] As Critchley has done before, Thomson equates expressions such as democracy to come, justice, and *aimance*, and finds their distinction in the different contexts in which they appear, and their similarity in the affirmation of 'the possibility of something else happening.'[22] It is certainly not only a matter of different contexts, for these notions betray a certain fidelity to Derrida's mode of writing, to Derrida's autobiography and signature. Yet, the emphasis on context is strong, and can be given expression in Derrida's work itself. Thomson's conclusions can be found in a passage of *Politics of Friendship*, even if not avowed as such:

> Saying that to keep this Greek name, democracy, is a matter of context, of rhetoric or strategy, of polemics even, reaffirming that this name will last as long as it has to but nothing longer, saying that things speed up singularly in these fast times, is not to give in to the opportunism or cynicism of the antidemocrat that hides his game. Completely on the contrary, one keeps this indefinite right to the question, to critique, to deconstruction. [23]

Here, Derrida suggests that his recourse to democracy is to some extent a matter of strategy. Thomson's point in emphasizing this issue is to avoid turning Derrida's terminology into new political fetishes. It is not democracy to come (neither is it the democracy of 'democracy to come') that is 'coming.' It could be something entirely different, indeed something worse than current democratic institutions. There is no programme of action in democracy to come; it is the affirmation of a non-closure at the height of the most settled legal-political-ethical closures. For Thomson, it is an invitation to further action and thinking, to further scrutiny of our institutions, and to further reflection on the conditions of possibility and impossibility of the political. This is illustrated by his subtle rejection of Bennington who would have forgotten the actual necessity of deconstructing 'political thought and politics as such.'[24] Thomson emphasizes the political indeed, suggesting that democracy to come would be playing a fundamental role to reshape the political, and is itself a political enterprise (he does remark on the inner tension between politicization and de-politicization, but in a delicate progression towards a reactivation of the political). The whole emphasis of Thomson's careful work is on the contours of the political, rather than any major clarification of the specific role of democracy.

Not against Thomson, but more radically, I argue that in the economy of Derrida's writing, the fundamental role of democracy to come is to displace the political and even the fundamental practices and laws of the polity as such, its constitution; that is to say, to dislocate a 'polity' as such, the exclusionary practices of the polis, and the very antagonistic structure of 'the political.' Yet, in my appreciation that is not exclusively for the purpose of dislocation (as I shall discuss extensively, there is in Derrida a clear commitment to *exposures*, to non-hierarchical rearrangements of 'constitutional' experiences). In this process, Derrida admittedly chooses an expression that is part and parcel of contemporary political conditions: democracy. But he emphasizes the dimensions of democracy that have not been entirely integrated into the 'political' system and that in fact threaten its law of reproduction. Most importantly, for Derrida, it is because of these marginal dimensions that democracy itself is worth fighting for. It is not only in the 'to come,' but also in 'democracy,' as practice, as an unsettled term, that a transformative dimension of social life comes to the fore; and as we shall see, it is democracy indeed that caters for the right 'to come,' for the struggle against the coalescence of power, abuse, and exploitation of the 'to come.'

1.2 'Democracy to Come' Comes to Light

The very fact that Derrida chose to engage robustly with democracy and always with an element of praise is prima facie evidence of a degree of belief in and allegiance to democracy. Let us see how this expression comes to light in the early hours of his reference to democracy and to a type of temporal disruption of some of its structures.

Democracy Today

Before using the term 'democracy to come' directly, Derrida employed another very similar expression in a text entitled '*La démocratie ajournée*,' 'democracy adjourned' or, as in the English translation, 'Call It a Day for Democracy.'[25] This text may be seen as the earliest formulation of Derrida's engagement with democracy.[26] Derrida's commentators seem not to have grasped the full implication of this title and the deep connection between this and the 'main' text of *The Other Heading*, in French *L'Autre Cap*, where democracy and the 'to come' are directly formulated and discussed in some length (even if not there yet as democracy to come).

At first sight 'democracy adjourned' means simply democracy postponed or delayed; a democracy that has not yet arrived, still to come. Thomson has remarked that democracy here can be seen as a threat that has to be deferred for a time yet to come. This would be so when one is not yet ready for it today. Yet, what makes the writing of Derrida's interpreters entirely elusive is the absence of any reference to the centrality of 'today' and within it, the 'day' itself (further highlighted by the fact that Derrida wrote the text in a newspaper or, in French, '*journal*,' in the press that brings issues to the light of day, instantly, and constantly—*jour* [day], *aujourd'hui* [today], and *journal* [newspaper] recurring ceaselessly in the text in an almost alliterative fashion).

The evident tone of the interview published in January 1989 is one of admiration and praise for democracy on the one hand, and concern for the dangers of self-praise and stabilization of democratic institutions and systems on the other. Derrida praises especially the freedom of the press—'democracy's most precious good'—but also freedom of opinion, the instability of public opinion, and even, by implication, representative democracy as a system.[27] Yet, in all these settings, Derrida raises suspicions as to the 'today' and the day of democracy, that is the 'present' day and the public portrayal and manifestation of democracy. Derrida is concerned that democratic institutions may indulge themselves in their success without paying due regard to new challenges and new forms of censorship, manipulation, accumulation, and marginalization.[28]

It would be necessary to reinvent democracy, and a readiness for democracy to reinvent itself constantly. This can be illustrated with the problems surrounding the freedom of the press: 'this fundamental "freedom" is yet to be invented. *Every day* [*Chaque jour*]. At least. And democracy along with it.'[29] Derrida adheres to the principle of democracy, to a postulation of democracy, inherent in existing democratic institutions, without ever renouncing the countering of its shortcomings, without ever renouncing vigilance for democracy ('democracy shall guard [*une démocratie doit veiller*]').[30] Yet the question of the 'day' does not come entirely to light here.

For the 'day' does not entail only a concern for innovation and novelty; the day is also, in its abrupt breaking of night (a *daybreak*), an index for the manner in which democratic institutions come to 'light,' how they are formed. With regard to public opinion (this unfathomable and unstable 'ghost'), Derrida explains that it can only be formed as it comes to light, through the processes that make it come to light: 'public opinion does not *express itself*, if one understands by this that it exists *before* manifesting itself in broad daylight, as such, in its phenomenality.'[31] Taken radically, this political philosophical notion of the inexistence of an opinion or of a will prior to its manifestation would have far-reaching consequences, coming to threaten the very notion of representation and representative democracy itself.[32]

Derrida requires us to guard the day; that is, to guard the manifestation of democracy, and to guard against the conceptions that mask the phenomenality—and its immanent power relation—of democracy. For this phenomenality, radically understood, entails its own unsettlement: the 'today,' as what brings about and not what represents or portrays, requires the 'non-presentable' at the very moment that it is invoked. When invoking this movement of protracted coming of the day (*ajournement*: complex to render properly in English, but something in the vicinity of a non-ordinary 'coming of the day'), Derrida invokes also what is neglected, excluded, and often exploited and concealed in that coming of day and to daylight. All his concern for novelty and the problem of the 'settlement' of democracy is not just for the sake of novelty. Rather it is because the manifestation of democracy, in its triumphalism, disregards that which is constitutive of itself: the interdependence between the ordinary (*quotidian*) and the non-ordinary (*non-quotidian*).

More specifically in this setting, Derrida is concerned with the extent to which the 'day' of democracy is determined by those who control the means through which it can manifest itself ('day' as the present and the vitality—the coming to light—of democracy). Derrida is concerned with the press (with regard to public opinion), but also, by extension, with the organized forms of representation (tied to those who exercise power here and now, with the allegation that they give expression to un-presentable voices). These conditions of manifestation of democracy bring to light the very 'day' of democracy. A right to respond is here the great example of how these conditions determine and complicate the public and general right to respond to all abuses that can be performed under the daylight of democracy.[33] For Derrida, this complication or difficulty in responding epitomizes the problems of democracy even at the height of its public exposure (that is, in spite of this stark visibility). These abuses say something about the lack of care, the irresponsibility of democracy.[34] And, perhaps, such abuses anticipate the language of later texts and so crucial for us here, a certain roguishness:

> Why does one so often pretend [*feindre*] (a fiction *of* democracy) to ignore the violence of this dissymmetry [given the absence of the right to respond], and what can or cannot be reduced [*se laisser réduire*] in it? Why such hypocrisy, the denegation, or the blindness before the all-too-evident? Why is this 'all-too-evident' at once as clear as the light of day, and the most nocturnal face of democracies as they are, *presently*?[35]

'Presently' in italics, for it is precisely not a question of a settled present, but of the day, the visibility and publicity of the to-day. In other words, it is the question of how the present comes to light, comes about; it is the event of to-day itself. It is this event of to-day that is entirely elusive, and, for Derrida, needs to be rethought. For now, the to-day is measured by the fake light of day. This is a light of symmetry and equality, representation and responsibility that settles itself and renounces the realization and the joy of the spark that brings itself to light. Rather than a scrutiny of its conditions, this light refers back, as we have seen, to a presence, a ground, the will of the people, the substance of public opinion, or its own regularity; or, as we shall see in the next section, it could refer to a future, yet again without enjoying the non-presentable as constitutive of the to-day (this is not to say, however, that terms such as 'people,' 'public opinion,' ground, presence, or appropriation must be somehow banned from emancipatory discourse; quite the contrary, provided they are *exposed*).

An incisive and disruptive epistemic move is expressed in Derrida's final words of the text: 'Has the day ever been the measure of all things, as we pretend to believe? In its first edition [of the newspaper brochure for which he was writing], this opinion, I painstakingly dare to say this fiction, remains the most shared thing in the world.'[36] Our predicament, the predicament of the political 'today' as a self-satisfied *daily* manifestation is not only a fiction. For Derrida, our predicament is also a shared fiction, a shared practice of pretending. Those who pretend need not be presented with the truth, unless, perhaps, with the truth of one's own dissimulation. The radical possibilities and impossibilities of democracy are already clearly within our cognitive and sensible reach. With the practice of this text, what Derrida suggests more radically is that democracy is already, but could be much more, the experience of the sensibility to an inevitable fate of 'fiction'; or more than that, fate of imagination and creation, since the opposition between reality and fiction would not endure. 'We' seem to share the quasi-overt 'fiction' of democracy. What we can and cannot do with that very sensibility is to be seen below.

Democracy and 'to Come' with(out) Europe

Within this context (the context of the pretension of a 'today' settled by its present and self-satisfied enlightened day) Derrida discusses a range of issues that throw him very near the expression 'democracy to come.' The book *The Other Heading* (where 'Call It a Day for Democracy' appears) is prefaced by a short text called simply 'Today [*Aujourd'hui*].' This word, 'today,' is also extensively discussed in the main text: 'The Other Heading: Memories, Responses and Responsibilities.' It strongly links the two pieces and reveals a rich significance for democracy in a context of what could well be called a democracy in gestation, a certain democracy to come: the European context of integration.

Derrida addresses Valéry's use of 'today,' what it represented in 1939 and what it could mean in 1990 (the time of Derrida's first presentation of the text).[37] Valéry wrote 'today' in capital letters: 'AUJOURD'HUI.' These capital letters, for Derrida, represent the challenge of the times, the 'pressure' of imminence. At the time of Valéry's writing this would be the pressure of war and of a possible and extremely violent European unification. Even with the defeat of a certain idea of Europe, the post-war period also resulted in a fixation of European culture and 'quasi-naturalisation of borders.'[38] At the time of Derrida's writing, he claims, it is again necessary to scrutinize the 'today,' and indeed, even then, the today in capital letters. It would be necessary to assess the pressures of the day, the dangers and hopes of a new Europe, inasmuch as it adheres to a new unity of the today, capitalizing on the manifestation of itself 'today' (yet, as we shall see, such a unity is not only an issue for Europe).[39]

'Today' this new Europe has to reckon with its memories, its responsibilities, and the responses and lack of responses to itself. Europe has to deal with its own memory of identity, with the role that it has constructed for itself in the world with others. This memory is not simply plural and diverse, as goes the platitude of our times. Derrida rather tries to think in terms of the memory of the universalization of singularities, the memory of accumulation of experiences and knowledge and power, the language of capital, heading, leadership, and exemplarity. He expatiates over the polysemy of the French word *cap*, meaning both heading and cape, but also serving as a written index to capital (wealth, accumulation) and the geographic capital (a city), and capitalism itself. It is a complex call, and one that would have to be discussed in an unheard-of political economy. That would be one in which the role of masters and slaves, oppressors and oppressed is not so clear-cut;[40] in which, if one can speak of suffering, anxiety, and despair, one cannot simply attribute them to peremptorily defined social groups (the legal and political struggles that can be sparked from the experience of suffering must be thought in contingent terms, albeit still in terms that may articulate the universal).

What is crucial for us is Derrida's attempt, 'today,' to reckon with the paradox of universality. Derrida takes issue with Valéry's treatment of it. For Valéry it is paradoxical that the very specificity of the Frenchman may be to have a sense of universality. Derrida does not deny that this may constitute a paradox but he is rather unimpressed with it, for in fact it constitutes a general law. A few pages earlier Derrida had indeed explained this very paradox, albeit not avowed as such, as a law. I refer to the identification between exemplarity and universality. Let us examine this rich passage:

> The value of universality here capitalizes all antinomies, for it must be linked to the value of exemplarity that inscribes the universal in the proper body of a singularity, of a language or culture—be this singularity

individual, social, national, state-like, federal or confederal ... the self-affirmation of an identity always intends to respond to the call or to the designation of the universal. There are no exceptions to this law. No cultural identity presents itself as the opaque body of an untranslatable language, but always, on the contrary, as the irreplaceable inscription of the universal in the singular, the unique testimony to the human essence and the proper of man.[41]

What is implicit in this passage is a very simple but meaningful tautology: the universal is universal. That is why Derrida is impatient with Valéry. The great paradox is not between the universal and the particular, but the encounter of incommensurable universalizations (the encounter of the two paradoxical processes of universalization—a paradox of the paradox). That is why Derrida refers always to singularity rather than particularity; a singularity, as he came to state much later is universalizable.[42] For Derrida 'the feeling of being 'men of universality' [*homme d'univers*, Valéry's term] is not reserved for the French. Not even, no doubt, for Europeans.'[43] This is Derrida's greatest wager here: that Europe may realize that it is not alone in claiming universality, that the other is not another to itself (Europe), but another in its own right. Perhaps, moreover, a radical otherness irreducible to the self-referential process of becoming Europe could arise from within Europe.

This is the fundamental meaning of democracy to come when applied to Derrida's address to France and Europe: to seize the tradition of democracy and encourage Europe to experiment with the coming of the whatever other, and with a true otherness within itself (unresolved by itself, and not originating from itself).[44] Ultimately, this is an attempt to unsettle 'the day,' so as to ward off Europe's fiction of triumph with its own political institutions, its 'day.' Moreover, this is an attempt to proceed without relinquishing an aspect of that very fiction, that is, its very chance of coming to light, its event, and its spark. This should expose all 'parties' involved in this process to a different experience of sensing the other.

Returning to our theme of democracy to come, it is worth noticing that these terms (and not this phrase) appear together in this text in a rather oblique way. They appear as one of the several duties that European memory calls forth, a memory that should include the memory of its complex paradoxes. Derrida implies that democracy is neither practically nor conceptually fully realized, and that its structure is precisely that of a promise; a promise, in fact, like that of a new Europe 'today.' For Europe's memory today has to include its very promise of 'something that remains to be thought and to come.'[45] Such a memory invites a 'democracy that shall have the structure of a promise—*and thus the memory of that which bears the future, the to-come here and now*.'⁴⁶ In other words, democracy implies the memory of a fissure that opens up the present to the event, to the unforeseen, and wards off the fixation of time (which should include the problem of the fixation of the event as absolutely novel, for the novel and unanticipated event has to relate to a series of iterations, to coded and programmed memory).

We have so far privileged *The Other Heading*. Such a text not only inaugurates Derrida's sustained approach to democracy, but also proposes a concrete rendering of democracy to come. The expression is born concretely out of the experience of Europe's coming to terms with itself in/and otherness. And yet, this experience cannot be entirely determined by this specific instance. Indeed, as we have seen, this writing, within the European context, already contains the seeds for much broader concerns. I have noted that Derrida employs democracy within a context and alleges that one must heed one's tradition and put in question the way its institutions come about. In raising such questions as to the present and the 'day' of democracy, Derrida also indicates the chance of something or someone entirely other *to come*. Yet, the phrase 'democracy to come' as such still eludes us. Let us see how Derrida employs it directly in another key context, but now applied to his own activity as a philosopher.

An Institution to Come

The expression 'democracy to come' appears in Derrida's discussion of the philosophical institution; of philosophy as a teaching institution, philosophy in its condition of discipline of State (funded and regulated by the state, and crucial for the self-understanding of the modern State). It is remarkable to see a democracy to come entering the stage as a way of accounting for Derrida's 'own' attempt (Collège International de Philosophie ['CIPh']) at intervening/reforming the institution of academic philosophy.⁴⁷ Democracy to come is here a form of addressing the problematic question of the self-foundation of CIPh. The *Collège* aimed at exposing its own fundamental choices, a philosophical college, willing to be open to the most unheard-of and innovative formulations within and beyond the field of philosophy. To achieve that, CIPh wishes to be independent from the constraints of being state controlled or state funded, and especially independent from a philosophy of State.

Derrida explains that in spite of its apparent independence there are several academic and societal conditions that show that the foundation of CIPh was at least authorized by the State.⁴⁸ In fact, Derrida continues, there is never absolute self-foundation, and certainly not with respect to an institution that is so troubled in determining its own identity. This institution was founded on 'an open and still gaping question of the subject of [*au sujet de*] founding power and its self-founding power.'[49] In spite of the impossibility of self-foundation (and perhaps one could add, of foundation, originary and present, in general), this self-foundation happens. It happens as a promise: 'The self, the *autos* of legitimating and legitimated self-foundation *is still to come* [*reste à venir*] … as that which will always retain [*gardera toujours*] the essential structure of a promise.'[50]

Derrida later relates this project with a 'democracy in philosophy.'[51] This is one in which the question of the plurality of languages in philosophy is brought to the fore. In addition, this project brings to the fore that plurality of the codes that underpin relationships amongst these languages (and the difficulty of translating between them and, most radically, of translating within the several registers of each language). Here democracy seems to ground philosophy itself, as a discipline *to come*. However, 'democracy, the democracy that remains still to come' is said to be 'also a philosophical concept.'[52] The inclusion of a crucial 'also' here saves democracy and 'democracy to come' from being entirely encircled by the 'logic' of philosophy. In any case, and in spite of not going any deeper into the theory of democracy, Derrida proposes here that there is a homology between the concerns of a certain philosophy and those of a certain democracy ('this concern, which is also that of the democracy to come').[53] We shall come back to other aspects of this text in the third chapter, especially with regard to law.

So far, we have seen how democracy to come pertains to a fundamental openness and call for the other. One notices here openness to an irreducible time of events, and the coming of another that cannot be subsumed by the one. And this call is not extricable from the social experience of democracy itself, as inspiration for Europe and for philosophy. Thus the call to democracy to come takes place in both temporal and spatial-manifesting terms, that is, in openness to both the non-present and the non-manifested in democracies. One notices here that democracy is spacing and timing that overflow settled legal and political positions. One could add that affirmations take place, threatening positions.[54]

Derrida in later works pursues more extensively his interest in law, fleshing out the positions, oppositions, limits, and distinctions that make up the elements that democracy aims to expose. But Derrida's democracy is not simply an imperative of the time; his allegiance to the democratic tradition is bound to his engagement with the politics of friendship, in other words, with politics itself. We shall see that Derrida wishes *another* politics and democracy to come, for good historical and conceptual reasons. One can see below how exactly Derrida identifies the traditions that hinder the coming of democracy, and how he wishes to *make sense* of them.

1.3 Common Sense: Irruptions

As we have seen with regard to *The Other Heading*, Derrida is not simply advocating a novelty. He is concerned with several forms of accumulation, capitalization, exploitation, and marginalization that occur 'today.' They are complicit with the phenomenal manifestation of the day as a self-legitimating presence. There is another book, in fact a collection of seminars, where this concern with the actual injustices of political life comes to light. This is not a direct reference to theories of democracy, but it does refer to one classical theme that underpins democracies, and polities in general, and that is friendship in *Politics of Friendship*. Many authors have critiqued Derrida for not putting forward a clear institutional analysis in that book (and indeed even commentators favourable to Derrida have agreed that such an analysis is in some sense lacking).[55] Others have praised *Politics of Friendship* as an expression of personal taste and creativity, more like a work of art, and without major political implications.[56]

I argue that Derrida is precisely not doing 'institutional' analysis, for this would imply that very distinction between public and private, singular and universal, concrete and abstract that he wishes to problematize. His work could not possibly be a retreat into private matters of self-realization, since what he is remarking on is exactly that mistake of rigidly demarcating these domains. I argue rather that Derrida is working at the deep structure of common sense and common-sense formation; interested as he is not only in the disruption of common sense, but also in its very irruption, in making sense, in postulating, in affirming, in stimulating thought through the very aporias otherwise deemed paralyzing. In order to get there, though, I need an initial detour around the thematic of the book (around a thematic of universalization that is itself indispensable to the sedimentation common sense).

Universalizations

Derrida's main question is not the concept of democracy; nor the concept of friendship; nor, more generally, the history of Western political thought, even though all of them play a crucial part in the text. For Derrida, the canons of philosophy and literature are the clues, the historical and testamentary inscriptions of determined legal-political-ethical relations whose cogency can still be felt today. What Derrida addresses is a type of social process (in Derrida's language, a surface of coding and de-coding), one that he calls a 'logic of universalization.'[57] This 'logic' articulates those singular forms of affinity and affection (such as friendship, fraternity, and love) to expressions of universality, in different degrees of intensity (such as ethics, law, justice, and democracy). Derrida writes alongside a long-standing tradition of authors who have strongly associated democracy with an expansive form of affection. This affection in expansion, this 'logic of universalization' should not be perceived in a seamless way; it is highly aporetic. A restless movement pervades relations between the singular and the universal (and between different singular–universal articulations), and no final decision can be made about where to locate them.[58]

What Derrida discerns in the logic of universalization that leads from friendship to democracy (imprinted in democracies, and in the social realities of democracy today) is a constitutive and hegemonic alliance between two logically conflicting orders: that of the number and the name (we shall see that Derrida himself comes to relativize the internal certitude of this distinction). Democracy resists the infinite calculation of the number via the name, and the finite incalculability of the name via the number. Yet, one continues to 'see' such an opposition, which is so constitutive of political formations. Furthermore, it is constitutive in a particular way, one that Derrida deems not to be acceptable. Let us briefly pursue this treatment of the question of what is, after all, wrong with democracy and its concepts. Followed then by the question of what is still promising (what is of the order of the promise) in that very political practice and practice of thought. This explanation should help in the clarification that we pursue here of what democracy to come means in Derrida's writing.

Number and name are here inextricable. It may appear that Derrida begins with the question of number, the number of friends. Can one be a friend of many? How many, according to Aristotle and early Greek democracy? There would be a privilege of the small number, of the few; or, at least, a rejection of the great many, of the crowd.[59] In order to be a friend one would have to endure time together. One would have to choose he with whom one wishes to spend time, and such time allows for knowing, for an active engagement with the other and the other's merits (the masculine pronoun is chosen here because of the necessary singularity of this choice, and because the model of friendship upon which Derrida dwells and critiques is a masculine one).[60] It is always necessary to prefer certain friends; a choice, a decision, an election appears here.[61] Yet this very choice raises the question of name.

The choice for one friend rather than the other comes down in this tradition to the chosen one's merits, a matter of virtue. Virtue introduces a hyperbole amidst the number. One's affection is not directed to a number, the calculated number of one's possible friends (a few), in one's lifetime. One's friendship, the 'object' of friendship, in following the lesson of Montaigne, is not a person, but a name.[62] He means a name in all that it entails: permanence and endurance, on the one hand, and reputation, an example of virtue, on the other. A name is a line and a lineage, a genealogy to which one adheres according to the rules and protocols of the always reconstructed (never simply natural) process of filiation and memorization. In such a lineage, and in this tradition, the name of women is evidently subjected. Furthermore, the name entails feats and virtue, a reputation that is the precondition of exemplarity. When brought together, the lineage and the reputation (or its pursuit) carve out the name by virtue of one's action within a fraternal reciprocity. The number (the uncertainty and/in the many) can now be putatively settled by the name.

If the name serves to suggest settling, within a certain narrative and social-historical framework, it also contains the seeds of friendship's very unsettlement. For the name, and virtue especially, import also the introduction of an absolute into the calculation, into the arithmetic of numbers.[63] In Derrida's reading of Aristotle, virtue is not calculable, not even the number of those who are virtuous.[64] There is no certainty in determining how many friends or how many virtuous friends one might have. Moreover, there is no certainty in determining the amount of good or the deeds that one may need to perform to deserve to be a friend. This issue may seem awkward from the perspective of quotidian relationships, but indeed Derrida is concerned to show that quotidian relationships are not the model of friendship here. Following Cicero's rejection of vulgar or ordinary friendship (and Montaigne after him), the friendship that calls forth virtue is a true friendship.[65] This is the one that can be cited, remembered, and turned into an example.[66]

That true friendship (of the proper name and of the right number) will provide the examples needed in the polity, the model of affection, collective belonging, and reciprocal relations. As Derrida suggests, this is a model of friendship marked by reciprocity, which praises reciprocity. In this process it privileges a logic of the same, a universalization of sameness, which may be said to exclude or marginalize differences. Marginalization is one way of seeing this trajectory; that of women, children, foreigners, and even perhaps animals. Such existences are apart, therefore, from those 'properly' belonging to the matter of commonality. Yet, in fact, every time 'the same' is invoked, every time 'a virtuous' is chosen, 'the other,' the 'marginal' is logically in play. For the very differential code that excludes 'something,' also includes it by means of setting it as a negative element of that very code. An element of dissymmetry is thus always present.

Moreover, such is not simply a by-product of sameness and symmetry; in fact dissymmetry inhabits the heart of friendship, there where it cannot be properly extricated from love. This is clearly discerned in the whole tradition of the funeral oration, particularly in political friendships.[67] True friendship between two must include one's capacity to endure the death of the other, to be a friend at that ultimate moment, and even to anticipate the death of the other. In Cicero, especially, it is the moment of the funeral oration that shows true virtue, for it makes the absent present; it enables those who are dead to live.[68] This is a scheme very much debated in political philosophy, whereby the polity provides immortality in its very temporal endurance. Nonetheless, the phenomenon of the funeral oration portrays the micro-universe of this process and the very spark of universalization out of the voiding of friendship. True friendship is so intense, and to use Montaigne's term, so sovereign, that it commands affection for ever fewer friends, to one friend only and, ultimately, to no friend—to the dead friend.[69]

Derrida further explains this process through Aristotle's hierarchy within love. For Aristotle, it is honourable to love, but less so to be loved.[70] Being loved is also part of love, but in an accidental way. The essence of love is here an action. A true lover need not be loved; the joy of being loved would be here a selfish sentiment. There should be love, the very true one, even if the loved one is not aware of the lover's affection. Derrida pursues this in Aristotle's *Ethics to Eudeme*, and in his praise of those who continue to love in spite of the death of their loved ones.[71] Derrida shows that there is a distinction in the tradition between friendship (symmetrical and reciprocal) and love (dissymmetrical and non-reciprocal), and yet he tries to show that they are intertwined, each requiring the other in a complex of affections. Here, on the funeral oration, this interdependence between love and friendship is well pronounced. But what is the real problem of democracy here?

Democracy is perceived as the contemporary name of this form of universalized affection.[72] This name speaks for a certain heritage, and that is a heritage of what Derrida chooses to call here 'phratrocentrism.'[73] Universalism is obtained through a binary machine that brings together and sets apart. That is most conspicuously laid bare in the legal-political-ethical centrality of the family and the brother. Hence one speaks of the male son; of a certain filiation that grounds equality and reciprocity, and the exclusion/exploitation of whoever or whatever embodies otherness, emptiness, and the immeasurable number.

Derrida's engagement with Schmitt plays a fundamental role here. It plays a role in that it suggests that modern democracies are also based on this intense rejection and affection (the friend–enemy distinction for Schmitt is the very ground of all political unities).[74] Contra Schmitt's grounding of friendship in autochthony, territory, and proximity, Derrida shows that political affection, and the process of universalization that it entails, must involve voiding, making itself empty of proximity or family.[75] But this, in a sense, also happens in Schmitt, who is aware of the modern recreated notion of political proximity and political familiarity. What Schmitt never acknowledges is the fragility and the commonsensical nature of his über-distinction between friends and enemies, as we shall see shortly.[76] All universal fraternity is thus a type of fraternity without fraternity.[77] It must have the form of a *'familiarity of election.'*[78] It must open itself to this election, to this possibility of a plurality of decisions. Indeed, to deserve a universalizing name, it cannot be merely natural.

This is, however, still a type of fiction, the fiction of enjoying the universal, in self-congratulating institutions (in their light, in their vision, and splendour). Admittedly, it is a very effective fiction; it enlists so many supporters. Yet, in this very process of universalization, in the promise of universal fraternity, one can discern the 'profound strategy of all nationalisms, patriotisms and ethnocentrisms.'[79] As we have seen with regard to *The Other Heading*, 'we' are all commonly involved in the process of forging our universalizing images. The problem in fact lies not with those images themselves, but with the process of promising them in a type of experience of exploitative belonging. The promise is still often, as we shall see shortly, programmed and determined by a certain belonging and a certain delimited calculation that denies the possibility of an equal exposure to the promise. 'We' pretend to be bound universally, we fake that universality when in fact we 'know' that our bond is a much more indigenous one (as we shall come to see, 'to know' that, to be aware of one's exposure to a logic of exploitation is insufficient; one needs a more radical process, a form of double exposure, that is, exposure to one's own exposed involvement in binary structures complicit in subjugation).

All those instances of dissymmetry show that the logic of universalization cannot survive without them. It has to be nourished by them, even if, purely logically, universality and singularity may be deemed incompatible and opposed. However, they are still perceived and experienced as subordinated to the reciprocity and equality hailed in the current constitutional settlement of world democracies; that is, to a certain type of universality. Moreover, that is why Derrida refers concretely to a logic of universalization, but not one taken, or likely to be taken, to its extremes; the crowd, the numerous are foreclosed.[80] As we have seen, there is effectively no universality if not through its *forging*, which cannot be achieved without the structure of the promise, the example, and the intensity of the singular. The promise lies at the heart of the 'logic of universalization.' It allows the universal to happen, and yet it is not subsumed by it. It cannot be measured nor quantified. One cannot find out in advance if the promise will be successful, if it will reach a great number; if it will reach the right, plausible, or necessary number. The act of promise, its effect, here and now, and not only its content, are unforeseeable.

Common Sense

Derrida perceives a chance for democracy to come precisely in the experience of threading the line of the promise, undoing the subordination of the promise to a binary structure of society. What this intense experience of promise does is to help in reshaping the lines of sociability.[81] Derrida's emphasis on intimacy, friendship, and love serve to highlight how these instances are crucial to democracy in spite of the formal equality, generality, and neutrality of the polity. They are non-presentable elements that are at work in any presentation of democracy. There would be no democracy without singular examples of dedication to the polity, the image of the intensity of friendship and love to be further replicated.

Yet, Derrida is not praising the private, the sentimental, and invisible, as opposed to the public, rational, and visible. Rather, Derrida is striving to set aside or suspend oppositional logics itself (as we shall see, that is not to do away with differences but to intensify and disseminate them; differences are not necessarily oppositions). Derrida strives thus to suspend the 'logic' that sets up the binary and hierarchic machines of sociability, with regard to which ethical-juridical-political judgement is passed everyday: universality–singularity, autonomy–heteronomy, clarity–obscurity, visibility–invisibility, proximity–distance, familiar–unfamiliar (and one could include, even if not so explicitly in these writings we have seen so far, male–female, human–animal, white–black, etc.). He tries to show that the number cannot be shaped without the name; by virtue of this the number becomes incalculable, pervaded by incommensurability. He does not say that one is merely excluded; he says rather that both are articulated and settled in a certain way, and often this causes suffering, exploitation, and anxiety.[82]

On the other hand, Derrida cannot deny that all singularity also takes place in the space (or spacing) of a thin sharing.[83] This is what always remains regardless of any will or contract, the very experience of being near one another. More than that, it is a living, a sensing-being often forcefully pressed together, hence 'being-huddled-together' [*être-serré*], and even 'being-pressed' [*être-pressé*] against one another.⁸⁴ And this is an experience that can be equated with that of language, inasmuch as a sort of passivity is here pronounced, even if not devoid of activity either: 'a type of minimal community—but also incommensurable to all others—speaking the same language, or praying for translation against [*dans*] the horizon of a same language.'⁸⁵ This can only reinforce my recurring reference to an always uncertain boundary between each and every dichotomy employed (wittingly or unwittingly) to orientate sociability.

The great challenge for Derrida is precisely the elevation of fundamental orientations, which coalesce in common sense or good sense. Yet such a challenge calls for another form of orienting oneself, away from good sense. In combating the factual grounding of orientations, Derrida mobilizes a discursive practice, not unknown, but uncanny: that of the grammar of the 'perhaps,' which can hardly be avoided in the discourse of the humanities. It becomes hard to say 'perhaps' when one is expected to take a side.⁸⁶ A 'perhaps,' and Derrida's use of it, speaks precisely to this restless inappropriateness to any given side. And indeed, even the possibility of reshuffling dichotomies and common-sensical orientations is itself pervaded by the fragility of the 'perhaps.' See it for instance in relation to the dichotomy autonomy–heteronomy (one we have pursued in relation to the creation of the international college of philosophy):

> The same good sense opposes autonomy, even autarchy, to heteronomy. That is the epitome of good sense—the irrefutable in its incontestable authority. However, perhaps one *fails and needs* [*faut-il*] to distort [*déformer*] that oppositional logic and prepare, from afar, the 'political translation' of what one thus *fails to do and yet needs* [*faut-il*].⁸⁷

Good sense and common sense are a recurrent theme in Derrida's work, and most clearly in *Politics of Friendship*. Good sense is said to be the premise for the justification of a friendship based on active affection and self-awareness;⁸⁸ it is prone to providing a retrograde analysis based always on the possible and the real (where the possible and the real speak to the unavailability of the radical novelty and the spectres of non-presence);⁸⁹ and it deeply pervades philosophizing.⁹⁰ Most noticeably, it is nourished by an oppositional 'logic,' and that is why Schmitt's model of the political (based on the distinction of friends and enemies) is not foreign to common sense.⁹¹ Even though Schmitt manages to mobilize the energies of the people and to envisage the entire transformation of the polity, this is proposed through a very strict binary distinction that obeys a common-sensical distinction, in which the 'perhaps' is by definition precluded. Derrida recognizes Schmitt's descriptive power; indeed this distinction is cogent and has a practical impact, but he cannot at all embrace it, not even to use it in order to depart from Schmitt's more conservative world views. More than merely reshuffling the political order and re-energizing it, Derrida subtly threatens (in turns, not directly, one by one) the common assumptions of political formations and political philosophy as a whole.[92]

The intriguing aspect of common sense rests in a certain sharing. This means sharing in the practice, and theoretical practice that ignores—or pretends to ignore—violence, exclusion, exploitation, and massive accumulation; whereas the experiences ignored here are at the same time intimate to the political and legal institutions that shape most of the world 'today' (see 'Call It a Day for Democracy').[93] Accordingly, Derrida is not interested in revealing the obvious; not simply because one cannot reveal what is already current, but because what is current is this practice of revealing and concealing. This is the rule of the game, and not only the game of 'theory.' A new revelation, the vision about what things really are or what they shall turn into, is part of the game of antagonisms that may bring one or other groups to the fruition of certain goods or benefits in a given society. Part of an economy of the plea or of the claim—common sense can certainly accommodate that.

Yet, deconstruction has to start from somewhere, and that starting point often has to be the oppositional logic itself. In the strategy of deconstruction, a good starting point has always been to reassess the role of the marginalized term in a dichotomy. However, a subsequent move is to show how they are mutually contaminating in a way that overturns that very opposition that helped the discussion to start in the first place.[94] (What one may start wondering is whether this strategy is always invaluable, a theme to which we shall return. If it is a strategy it must involve its own social-historical conditions and may have to be dislocated in different contexts, different rhythms, times, and settings).[95]

With respect to democracy in *Politics of Friendship*, Derrida shows how the incalculable, the heteronomic, the intimate belongs to the heart of the construction of the calculable equality of 'autonomous' democracy. Throughout the text, though, the dissemination of aporias accentuates the different instances of this strange belonging. Such dissemination starts to draw a framework in which there is calculability and incalculability in democracy, friendship, intimacy, and publicity. In addition, Derrida does that without renouncing the aporia. He does that without renouncing the radical undecidability, and the lack of an assured way forward. What this brings about is not a picture, if ever there were such a thing, of a thesis-made world (thetic world), but that of a differential world-making (the aporia is not a binary distinction, which has an orienting purpose, whereas the aporia points out only the non-way).⁹⁶ There are rarely generalizing extracts in Derrida's writing; they are always thought in relation to specific issues. But they almost always also extrapolate these issues (in a tension between a context and what is beyond the context). From this passage we can extract some interesting resonances:

> The singularity/universality divide has always divided the experience, the concept and the interpretation of friendship [*le partage (singularité/ universalité) a toujours divisé l'expérience*]. It has determined other oppositions within friendship. Schematically on the one hand the secret-private-invisible-illegible-apolitical, ultimately without concept; on the other the manifest-public-testimonial-political, homogenous to the concept.⁹⁷

One can reflect on this in relation to the issues that I have raised. The structural divide of friendship is certainly not only *of* friendship, but also of the democratic, the political, the ethical, and the juridical. Derrida is not claiming to do away with these oppositions. Yet, it is not a matter of simply doing away with them, but of a new sensibility to that which within them already disrupts the opposition. In the French version, one reads that there is a type of 'partage,' of sharing between the two terms; they share something in dividing together, and they make experience 'divided' at bottom between division and sharing.

As to singularity and universality, they are dependent upon each other. Without the singular, no universal will be formed nor enduringly sustained. Without the universal, the singular will not be able to be a singular; for it to be a singular, it has to be a singular in relation to something that surpasses its own limitation and reaches a wider degree of generality, towards universality. However, in Derrida's approach, their relationship is not seamless either; one cannot decide precisely when one turns into the other.

§

Is it thinkable, though, to dwell on a space where these exigencies are articulated? A spacing where they are mutually contaminated and never settled, safeguarded by knowledge, without privileging one or another term or an artificial middle term (or to use indeed an artificial term without 'privilege,' or without recourse to sublation)? Is it feasible to think of a 'differential contamination' of these exigencies? Can these exigencies be treated and interact as different forces? In *Politics of Friendship*, Derrida has several passages on democracy and 'democracy to come.' They seldom refer to democracy to come in relation to any tradition of democracy, and rather dwell on its constitutive demeanour, on the opportunity to challenge the existing constitutional settlement, or indeed on how the presentation of this settlement is always rotten from within. Here, towards the end of the book, the question of presentation returns: 'it [democracy] will always remain, in each of its future times, to come: even when there is democracy, it never exists, it is never present, it remains the theme of a non-presentable concept.'[98]

Equally, much could be said of this process in relation to the autonomy and heteronomy of democracy that appears in *Du droit à la philosophie*. Derrida shows irrefutably that there is a differential alliance between singular and universal, presentable and non-presentable, autonomy and heteronomy. It is necessary to expose oneself to it and to dwell in that drawing of lines. As I have shown, in *The Other Heading* it was not the conflict between the singular and the particular that posed a challenge to this model, but the conflict between processes of universalization, which may bring about the 'the paradox of paradox.'

Yet it is only later in Derrida's work that this law of negotiation between two exigencies will be spelled out explicitly, in relation to this strange presentation; opening up a new space of mutual differential contamination and variation of exigencies, requiring a certain presentation of democracy:

> Is it not also democracy that gives right to irony in the public space? Yes, for democracy opens public space, the publicity of public space, by granting the right to a change of tone [*Wechsel der Töne*], to irony as well as to fiction, the simulacrum, the secret, literature, and so on. And, thus, to a certain non-public public within the public, to a *res publica*, a republic where the difference between public and non-public remains an undecidable limit. There is something of a democratic republic as soon as this right is exercised.[99]

Now one has a clearer picture, if it is a matter of picture, of what Derrida resisted with democracy to come (a democracy that is already 'to come,' but resists its always recurrent 'constitution' as common sense). One has a sense of his deeply entrenched allegiance to democracy as a space opened to the constant negotiation of the singular–universal divide, and indeed to the negotiation of democracy's very lines or boundaries and major institutions of representation and decision-making. In addition, we notice that such a divide is not overcome in a higher order of unity. The divide exists, and it exists in a process of making-sense, of constituting the guidance for action and practice in the world. This process, however, tends in different degrees to stabilize itself, to satisfy itself in a structure of knowledge-possibility that suppresses its blind spots, incidentally causing suffering.

In this way, I have established that a certain self-satisfied celebration of democracy is problematic and unsustainable. I have explained how the process of universalization appeared early in Derrida's work on democracy, and how this leads to a notion of struggle and resistance that is not prone to facile categories of power and oppression, and hardly to any pre-defined political project (*The Other Heading*).[100] One realizes how democratic affection, private and public, plays a significant role in the discourse of democracy; and indeed how this affection is itself aporetic and inescapable. Democracy was perceived as the very space where the divides of sociability (the aporias of sociability that inform sense and common sense) can be constantly negotiated. The performative effect of Derrida's work is to indicate that democracy, as a form of living together–apart, insists on an aporia that is otherwise not well *exposed* (there is a problem in the intensity of exposure).

I say not well exposed, or underexposed, instead of concealed, because Derrida is not in the business of revelations (not willing to keep within the business of strict dichotomies).[101] Even if one could say that there is a strange concealment, the task of thought is not to reveal it, but to experiment with that wide participation in 'concealment,' or in the resilience of underexposure. As I highlighted in my discussion of 'Call It a Day for Democracy,' it is a matter of shared dissimulation, or even *forgery*. This forgery need not be revealed, but more radically exposed to those who are already possibly aware of it or even involved in it. Yet, in order to insist on that 'participation,' on that radical self-exposure (what I will later call an overexposure), Derrida also goes through the stage of cognitive exposure. In the following chapters, I shall argue that these moments constitute the fundamental postulation of Derrida's discourse of democracy to come, a postulation of exposure, and with the 'to come,' to constitutional exposure.

Do I mean that one is always already involved in the forgery of sociability, and that either through exploitation and exclusion one is always caught in this process, in the binary machine of societal orientation? Yes and no. On the one hand, this involvement is, as we have seen, pervasive and one cannot easily escape it, certainly not by merely opposing it. The logics of exploitation (self-capitalization) and exclusion (de-capitalization of others) are, by definition, complementary and colonizing, and an outside is, by definition, precluded from within their operations. On the other hand, by proceeding patiently, by writing contingently but rigorously, Derrida proposes an *exposure* that sustains a careful distance from exploitation and exclusion; it enjoys the exposure (by definition at least non-hierarchical) to the undecidability of all the binary terms that 'make sense.'

The key to Derrida's writing rests in his style. But in his style rests something related to the law. As I alluded with regard to Derrida's resistance to Lefort (and that could be applicable to Bennington's interpretation of Derrida), Derrida does not aim to posit or impose the law. Derrida's *postulation* of exposure is akin to the law, but embraces a different approach to the law—to the existing rules of sociability, to the existing codes, regularities, and irregularities of living-together— which themselves always already involve a process of dissolution. His postulation is akin to the law because it does not shy away from taking positions (and indeed taking radical and persistent positions as to the patience of his writing). But more than that, as we shall see, Derrida's postulation of exposure (and democracy as such) is indissociable from a certain understanding of law (although I shall be strategically critical of Derrida's starting points in relation to law).

Yet, already one can find certain contours of Derrida's radical postulation, his form of playing, enjoying, and intensifying the experience of making use and creating law: democracy. One may wonder, for instance, where exactly is the *other* universalization to which Derrida alluded in *The Other Heading*. It is worth advancing that the democratic discourse includes a form of universalization; it attempts to depart from phratrocentrism, fraternization, and all other forms that deny a radical share of exposure to the universalizing process. In my appreciation, what the logic of the father, the brother, and the sovereign friend do is still universalizing; it involves 'the many' and 'the crowd,' but denies to them the right to enjoy the traces of their very coming together–apart. In Derrida's *other* universalization, one may still find a subtle postulation of a tentatively non-hierarchical experience, an egalitarian experience of enjoyment of the universalizing process.[102]

Yet, this egalitarian experience is not rooted in a simplistic call towards abstract equality, but in a practice of exposing and intensifying the singular–universal; that is, one that is already happening, tentatively to be sure, in the overarching drive of existing laws. Derrida does not strive against the universalization of a 'universal' nation, France for instance, but he strives to move along that drive towards expanding it to a point of rupture, a point that exposes a fragility that universality always had, the otherness inherent in universality itself. This practice one may call an epistemic practice, to the extent that it attempts to know the law of sociability. Yet, in the practice of Derrida's writing, this knowing becomes such an ethical and political experience, a postulation of democracy, that it explodes any containment within the sphere of knowledge.

One could still even argue that democracy is not the best name for this process of insistence on the dividing lines, the laws of sociability, and radicalization of the (un)common experience of knowing (at the limits of knowledge) the law and one's role in a society. One could as well call it 'politics,' or 'republic.' However, in the next chapter I shall argue that democracy appears for Derrida in a way that is 'positive'; but also in a way that is creatively reformulated. It has a long-standing historical-philosophical bearing. It speaks to a philosophical heritage very close to the core of Derrida's work, one whose relation to the 'to come' is internal and not at all the arbitrary result of Derrida's crafting. So Derrida does not simply critique the phratrocentric, male-centric, underexposed, exploitative and excluding contours that democracy may have, he also attempts to find that which is liberating, non-hierarchical, radically expositive within the democratic discourse; in a way that could invite, perhaps, its own dissolution, but not without a relation to its tradition.

As the first contours of constitutional exposure have now emerged, the cross-fertilization of law and democracy can take place, and we can proceed with an interpretation of Derrida's postulation for democracy to come, which will later become an intensification, so that another law, another 'to come,' another democracy may be thought and experienced.

— 2 —

DEMOCRACY

Democracy can be reread as the *exposure* of the constitutional experience of law, which involves constitution and deconstitution: democracy as constitutional exposure. This *exposure* is what Derrida most highly praises in the democratic tradition, the moment when the *powers* of law fail; the moment when the common sense of structuring dichotomies is challenged; when the more than one arrives. This is when democracy *arrives*. And the arrival of democracy means also the struggle against forms of constitutional ruin (deconstitution) that potentialize hierarchic and exploitative institutions. A more radical work of exposure must be undertaken in order to bring about an overexposure and a fuller deconstitution. Thus Derrida emphasizes the moment of deconstitution, even though constitution, albeit minimally, cannot be avoided; both constitution and deconstitution should be enjoyed. Indeed the call itself, the postulation of democracy is already a constituting moment: the constitution of deconstitution, the constitution of democracy.

The argument in this chapter (democracy as exposure of the constitutionality of law) unfolds on four levels or moves. First it focuses on law and democracy themselves, and the love of ruins that can be found in them (see ch. 2.1). Secondly, there is a focus on that which, within the democratic tradition, imports the praise or enjoyment of deconstruction itself or, better, the exposure to an existing exposure. In that way, one allows for the overflowing of the containment of power formations. The place where this first move is most explicitly articulated is in Derrida's treatment of Benjamin in 'Force of law,' but also in more recently in *Rogues*. The second move is clearly articulated in *Rogues*, but with a much earlier indication in *Dissemination* (see ch. 2.2). My third move involves the question of force in relation to democracy. Here democracy qua force is brought together with its putative rival pertaining to force in Derrida's work, sovereignty. And this question has interesting resonances with the strategy of deconstruction itself as operating amidst social forces, and in particular amidst a dominant discourse of democracy, which can be exposed by employing a Derridean framework (see ch. 2.3). Finally, this dominant discourse is more finely scrutinized with some examples of allegedly emancipatory or transformative theories. The Derridean framework of analysis is brought to bear on that dominant discourse, showing the paradox of the modern emphasis on autonomy and its incapacity to tackle the pervasive problem of autoimmunity (see ch. 2.4).

2.1 Ruins of Law

Derrida does not reject the 'corruption' of law, which is characteristic of democracy for Benjamin, and for which Benjamin is suspicious of democracy. In fact, Derrida elevates that very corruption as democracy's great role, and that permits, within the democratic space, a more differential encounter of social forces. Admittedly these forces will have to live together, and that raises the question of the new law; how new forms of regulation and normalization, and new patterns of differentiation emerge through other forms of law. Democracy becomes thus a reflexive sphere upon the condition of elaboration and utter openness of the 'corrupted' law; a law that can no longer sustain the unity of the mores, the common sense of the polity, in other words, uphold indisputably the structuring dichotomies of sociability. In fact, the idea of a 'corrupted' law can only be sustained if something like an integral or pure law is also kept. But the emphasis on corruption permits the emergence of a less stable notion of law in democracy, which in turn can be better enjoyed with constitutional exposure, or 'democracy to come.' Let us understand Derrida's point first in relation to Benjamin.

Derrida takes issue with Benjamin's distinctions between lawmaking (*rechtssetzende*) and law-preserving (*rechtserhaltend*) violence, where violence, in German *Gewalt*, is not without relation to the legitimate force that exercises it; between mythical and divine violence, and between power (*Macht*) and justice (*Gerechtigkeit*).[1] The first distinction clearly deconstructs itself in Benjamin's own text, and the latter two are precisely the object of a deconstructive reading, that is to say, one that attempts to expose the aporias of unconditional exigencies in order to favour a delicate negotiation or transaction between them.[2] Derrida shows how divine violence in particular is a little too close to the worst. It is not that one may close off the possibility of the impossible, including the worst—certainly not.[3] Yet, one does not need to embrace the worst as such to suggest new forms of thinking the political, the legal, and to dwell in the tradition of a radical enlightenment to come.[4]

For the purposes of the emergence of democracy in Derrida's work, it is the first distinction that matters the most. For Derrida identifies in Benjamin here a nostalgia for origins and purity, which is incompatible with the co-belonging of purity and impurity, manifestation and non-manifestation. In this regard at least, Derrida acknowledges that Benjamin's text provides for the deconstruction of itself. This could not be clearer than in the treatment of the powers of the police. For Benjamin already affirms the police's spectral role. They exercise executive, law-preserving violence, for they pursue legal pre-established ends. Yet, they pursue these ends within wide limits, 'its power is formless, like its nowhere-tangible, all pervasive, ghostly presence [*gespenstische Erscheinung*] in the life of civilized states.'[5] Derrida does not oppose this proposition; his problem lies elsewhere, in the status of this ruin of legality. Is this an originary ruin, anterior in fact to the modern State? Or is it a strong degeneration, akin to a lack of vitality? What Derrida appears to single out in Benjamin is his, somewhat ironical I would say, praise for monarchy:

> It cannot finally be denied [or discarded, verkennen] that in absolute monarchy, where they [the police] represent the power of a ruler in which legislative and executive supremacy are united, their spirit is *less devastating* [*weniger verheerend*, my emphasis] than in democracies, where their existence, elevated by no such relation, bears witness to the greatest conceivable [*denkbar*] degeneration of violence.[6]

Benjamin is certainly not advocating the return of monarchy. Note the expression above, not actually cited by Derrida: 'it cannot finally be denied.' He is not even affirming that, but raising the question of a certain absolutist decency or honesty that 'cannot be denied.' That does not mean that this decency is unavailable to democracy amidst a different type of relation to its indecency. In fact, in many ways, as we shall shortly see, this is precisely Derrida's project; to thread a fine line between honesty and lie.[7] After such a reference to monarchy, Benjamin immediately raises the question of Parliaments, and of how once they have lost touch with the violence that constituted them the 'institution falls into decay [*so verfällt es*].'[8] The praise for monarchy turns into what it really is, a critique of parliamentary democracy and its compromises and negotiations. The problem with these compromises, says Benjamin, lies not in their non-violence, but rather in their disdain of open violence. Compromises, as contracts, belong to a structure of violence.[9] Whatever goodwill there may be in reaching them, they are pervaded by the violent structure of the law that they give rise to.

Indisputably the language of vitality and decay, the praise of uncompromising 'decrees' may indeed give rise to serious reservations, and some of Benjamin's legitimate concerns may today be much better expressed by a different vocabulary, one that has been put forward by Derrida himself. The Benjaminian heritage, though, is not unimportant. Assessing the following extract, much closer to Derrida's contemporary thematic, one may find essentially a reformulation of Benjamin's critique of violence:

> The consequences or implications are twofold:
>
> 1. Democracy would be a degeneration of law [*droit*], of the violence, the authority and the power of law.
>
> 2. There is not yet any democracy worthy of its name. Democracy remains to come: to engender or to regenerate.[10]

Certainly, Derrida does not embrace this entirely (even though in *Rogues* he cites this passage to situate his use of the expression 'democracy to come'). Law here is also the law of a decreeing might, the unconditional authority for whom the suspension of executive and legislative powers is originary and honest, one that is paradoxically and concomitantly determinate and involves a system that affirms and preserves itself in the world through clear-cut decisions (as we shall see in the next chapter, Derrida develops his very understanding of law in his other essay of 'Force of law,' in a way that law's calculating demeanour becomes predominant, for a moment at least).

In addition, Derrida cannot, by definition, defend any 'regeneration' of democracy; it remains to come in a more originary fashion, because 'foundation is a promise.'[11] A foundation cannot finally found anything, unless in the precarious mode of calling upon the assistance of that which is still to come. In that way only, in an already spectralized mode, there will have been a foundation; and a promise and the 'to come' will have happened in the 'here and now.'[12] The distinction between law-making and law-preserving violence is here clearly destabilized. In the promising foundation, one notices that 'Positing is already iterability, a call for self-preserving repetition. Preservation in its turn refounds, so that it can preserve what it claims to found.'[13]

At bottom Derrida is embracing the degeneration that Benjamin allegedly rejects. Admittedly, degeneration is too strong a term, Derrida provides us with this magnificent passage, explored in legal theory by Johan Van der Walt:[14]

> Ruin is not a negative thing. First it is obviously not a thing. One could write, maybe with or following Benjamin, maybe against Benjamin, a short treatise on the love of ruins. What else is there to love, anyway?

One cannot love a monument, a work of architecture, an institution as such except in an experience itself precarious in its fragility: it has not always been there, it will not always be there, it is finite. And for this very reason one loves it as mortal, through its birth and its death, through one's own birth and death [à travers sa naissance et sa mort], through the ghost or the silhouette of its ruin, one's own ruin [sa ruine]—which it already is, therefore, or already prefigures. How can one love otherwise than in this finitude? Where else would the right to love, even the love of law, come from [d'où viendrait autrement le droit d'aimer, voire l'amour du droit]?[15]

In Derridean terms, this love of ruins is the condition under which one has to think these issues of the life and death of law. This passage is illustrative of the extent of Derrida's devotion to that 'degeneration' *of* law. One loves law, and here law to its full, not the calculating law, as we will see in the first part of Derrida's seminal essay 'Force of Law,' but law itself as a space of differential contamination between the conditional and the unconditional, the universal and the singular, the manifest and the non-manifest—the spectre of law.[16] It is precisely here that the *force* of law (in restlessness thus) and democracy meet. They become almost indistinguishable.

In this context, it is worth noting the ineluctable law to which Derrida has devoted himself ceaselessly, the law of homonymy, the value of random coincidences, in a sense a deep etymology, one that takes place virally, without genealogy and without origin. It is in this register that one may begin to understand Derrida's writing. Here Agamben seems to have come across something important.[17] The French term '*force*' entertains a certain relation to two other French terms: '*fors*' and '*for*'—the first somewhat archaic of course, but young enough to have attracted Derrida's attention.[18] '*Fors*' means 'outside' or 'except for.' By contrast, '*for*' means inside oneself, in consciousness or within an interior forum. This adds another element to Derrida's dwelling at the aporias of law, in an inside–outside movement, in a process of constitution and deconstitution. This process is ineluctable, it has always already been, and here is the law [*loi*], that is, law in a general sense but, as we have seen, this general sense has an impact on the juridical sense of law.

I do not of course endorse Agamben's claim that 'force of law' refers necessarily to a decree with force of law, but not as law itself.[19] Force of law poses the question of the 'force'-outside-inside of every law. In a way, force of law already debunks the division that Derrida will somewhat artificially set up between law and justice. In this sense law, and more specifically modern law (as opposed to monarchic law in Benjamin), are essentially 'constitutional'; that is, requiring a constant process of constitution and deconstitution, determinateness and ruin. This is, however, not to exempt Derrida from the explicit claims that law [*droit*] is the element of calculation. Fitzpatrick has provided a cogent critique of that notion that still stands. For in his work, law is aptly characterized as already both determinate and responsive.[20] Yet, such a crucial critique stands mainly on the 'strategic' level, as we shall see better next chapter. For Derrida law is not, in any practical way, the realm of calculation. Indeed, what he attempts is exactly to convey and to require a more heightened sense of the mutual and concrete contamination of 'law' and 'justice.'

The question that a force of law raises is not a critique of law, not even in the name of justice. If the practice of law already involves constitution and deconstitution, the calculable and the incalculable, then what Derrida does is to raise awareness and sensibility of/to this very 'constitutionality.' In this light, what Derrida did in 'Force of Law' was in a way a democratic practice. If democracy is to insist on the dividing lines, to expose the law, the practice of 'force of law' is a democratic one. Democracy here would have a clearly epistemic value, as in one of the richest democratic traditions.[21] Its value is to help social actors come to terms with their differing lines of sociability and their different moral, sensorial, and epistemic experiences.

However, the term 'force' is important not only in revealing an esoteric agenda in Derrida's text. 'Force' is constitutive of the very strategy of Derrida's work (and here the very distinction between 'strategy' and 'substance' trembles). It must be understood within the limitations of this epistemic perspective, however valuable it may be. Forces touch upon, agonize, and instil suffering. Derrida is not simply willing to expose it purely in the epistemic sense (learning, consciousness, or knowledgeable sense; falling short of intervening in that which is exposed anyway).[22] He is performing, rather, its exposure through the taste of the pain and joy of the force of his writing, and launching the chain reaction of the autobiographical machine. In addition, one needs to understand better how this exposure happens. We shall do that in the next couple of sections.

2.2 Democratic Licence

Democracy belongs to the tradition of the exposure of the force of law (or of the constitutionality of law), that is also to say, the careful enjoyment of a differential, intense, and non-architectural experience of law. In his thought of democracy, Derrida attempts to take into account a certain lawlessness, predicated on a certain tradition of freedom, or licence of the people (in other words to give emphasis and intensify deconstitution). Yet, this cannot entirely debunk the law, even in a maximum of licence; there is still an irreducible bond, and a fragile law. The constitution remains, even if only as the very firmness of the call or postulation for deconstitution. Democracy operates as the spacing in which a plurality of forces clash (not necessarily in antagonism) in the apportioning of what is right; that is, the right and changing divide that orientates sociability, that which creates (and eventually destroys) 'common sense.'

The interest in democracy, the passion for democracy cuts deep into Derrida's writing. In fact, democracy for Derrida even follows the contours of writing. The relationship between democracy and the law is tantamount to the relationship between writing and speech. In 'Plato's Pharmacy,' a text published in 1972, one encounters much of what would be later discussed extensively.[23] More than thirty years later, in *Rogues*, Derrida takes on Plato's view of democracy in the *Republic* (see Derrida's references to the standard citation method of the *Republic* in brackets). Let us pause to check what Derrida wrote about this still in 1972:

> At the disposal of each and of all, available on the sidewalks, isn't writing thus essentially democratic? One could compare the trial of writing with the trial of democracy outlined in the *Republic*. In a democratic society, there is no concern for competence: responsibilities are given to anyone at all. Magistracies are decided by lots (557a). Equality is equally dispensed to equal and unequal alike (558c). Excess [*démesure*], anarchy; the democratic man with no concern for hierarchy ... [Derrida then moves on to speak about the democratic individual or democratic 'type' that Plato derides]. This errant democrat, wandering like a desire or like a signifier freed from logos, this individual who is not even perverse in a regular way, who is ready to do anything, to lend himself to anyone, who gives himself to all pleasures, to all activities—eventually even to politics or philosophy ... this adventurer, like the one in the Phaedrus [Plato's diminishing of writing] simulates everything at random and is really nothing. Swept off by every stream, he belongs to the masses; he has no essence, no truth, no patronym [*patronyme*], *no constitution of his own* [my emphasis]. Moreover, democracy is no more a true constitution than the democrat has a character of his own [*caractère propre*].[24]

Plato gives Derrida the perfect cue. This attack on democratic life, the life of the democratic person, is not unusual in philosophy. To use Derrida's words, albeit much more recently, 'democratism in philosophy is something rather rare.'[25] To such a quote one could also relate Derrida's protestation against the 'great rationalisms' (and Plato figured in the series) of philosophy and political philosophy to the extent that they were 'rationalisms of the state, if not state rationalisms.'[26] In Derrida's code, the State is the sign for the One, the undivided and un-deconstituted sovereign, but in a constant process of warding off madly its very deconstitution. The philosopher of the polis cannot accept the one who has 'no constitution of his own' or 'character' as a citizen, nor a 'constitution' (democracy) that cannot even be called truly a constitution. What Derrida does, as we see below, is that, as with Benjamin, he seizes Plato's rejection to think, embrace, and rearticulate that which (for reasons of economy) I call deconstitution.

His project in *Rogues* is almost entirely predicated on this democratic character without character, the rogue, whose condition of rogue is not, though, easily distinguishable from that of those who govern. That is, the official constitution has in itself a roguishness; it is roguish often in order to preserve itself, but also as we have seen, to found itself, for there is no law prior to it. Another way of saying this is that there is 'something rotten in law,' law announces its own ruins, or a constitution always imports a deconstitution.[27] Yet, there are different ways one can relate or choose to relate, or respond, to this process. I argue now that, for Derrida, it is a question of how to be open and sensitive to deconstitution (how to perceive it in the first place), and how to enjoy it accordingly. This is a subtle form of enjoyment, not that of a self turning onto itself incessantly,[28] but a more subtle and troubled curving towards the exposed enjoyment of that which makes 'people' (those prone to be 'roguish') apart.[29] One should, though, delve deeper into *Rogues*, before coming to that conclusion.

Derrida takes on Plato and Aristotle to discern crucially between two forms of freedom: *eleutheris* and *exhousia*.[30] The former is the most usual term for freedom or liberty, the latter would be translated more readily as licence. These are the two Greek terms associated with freedom and used by both Plato and Aristotle to describe the life of democracy and the democrat. About the first Derrida speaks sparingly. Yet, he does imply, through several passages by Aristotle, that this is a freedom of common participation, common belonging in the matters of the community. Such a participation would be unsustainable without something that granted non-participation. *Exousia* itself has a role to play here in allowing for that which unties one from the suffocation of community.

Yet, such a common belonging is not entirely absent from the other term, *exousia*, licence, this entirely restless freedom. First, because Plato, speaking about *exousia* (as Aristotle on *eleutheris*), always recurs to concepts widely held, that which is said generally. Secondly, one finds a certain symmetry in *exousia*. In this account, there is a widely held practice of licence that pervades the entirety of democratic 'constitution.'

Licence, though, includes by definition that which overflows any commonality. Licence and the licentious are thus both included and excluded from the *polis* (but it will be relevant to pursue later how exactly the inclusion–exclusion takes place).

It is crucial for Derrida to show how Plato, especially, associated both freedom and licence with democracy, and how these two terms lend themselves to a more profound and generalized logic of a certain force of law:

> Before even determining demo-cracy on the basis of the minimal though enigmatic meaning of its two guiding concepts and the syntax that relates them, the people and power, demos and kratos—or kratein (which also means 'to prevail,' 'to bring off,' 'to be the strongest,' 'to govern,' 'to have the force of law' ...)—it is on the basis of freedom that we will have conceived the concept of democracy. This will be true throughout the entire history of this concept, from Plato's Greece onward.[31]

A little later, Derrida reflects on Aristotle's notion that this freedom requires no one to be governed by other men, or at least only 'governed in turns' (1317b–15).[32] This general freedom (both *eleutheris* and *exousia*) is equated with a restless movement of taking turns, alternating, varying, and deferring, in a circle that envelops people and power: 'a freedom without which there would be neither people nor power, neither community nor force of law.'[33] This freedom allows room not only for this uncontrollable plurality in the history of freedom itself, but also for what is crucial for the 'concept' of democracy:

> This freedom in the concept is all the more striking inasmuch as it takes into account, as the empty opening of a *future of the very concept* [*avenir du concept*] and thus of the language of democracy, an *essential historicity of democracy*, of the concept and the lexicon of democracy (the only name of a regime, or quasi regime, open to its own historical transformation, to taking up its intrinsic plasticity and its interminable self-criticizability ...).
>
> It can *thus* [my emphasis] be pledged [*on pourra ainsi alléguer*] that the syntagm 'democracy to come' belongs to at least one of the lines of thought coming out of the Platonic tradition. This cannot always be said without a bit of duplicity, if not some polemical bad faith, but it also cannot be said without some verisimilitude. After all, to speak of democracy to come might consist in being content to explore, in a perfectly analytical, descriptive, constative, politically neutral fashion, the content of a concept that has been inherited and thus claimed and taken up since at least the time of Plato's Greece.[34]

Yet, this 'thus' that Derrida uses conceals what comes after, that is, another necessity of authorization for this very information that democracy to come can be traced back to Plato. Derrida can say that democracy to come is within the Platonic tradition for another subsequent reason. It is part of that tradition not only because the concept and the practices of freedom are opened from within (as suggested in the quote above), but also because Plato explicitly denies democracy the status of a constitution (*politeia*).[35] Thus, Derrida comes back to the passages of Plato in the *Republic* that he had cited in *Dissemination*. With that corporeity and restlessness of the rogue, without character, licence itself is brought to the fore again. It is this openness to licence and licentiousness that 'authorizes' Jacques Derrida, himself a self-styled rogue, to authorize himself to use democracy 'to come.'[36] Let us return the stage to Plato for a minute:

> 'In the first place, the members of the community are autonomous [*eleutheroi*] aren't they? The community [polis] is informed by independence and freedom of speech [*paresias*], and everyone has the right [*exousia*] to do as he chooses, doesn't he? ...'
>
> 'I should think, then, that there'd be a wider variety of types of people in this society [*politeia*] than in any other. ...'
>
> 'It's probably the most gorgeous [*kaliste*] political system [*politeion*] there is,' I continued. 'Its beauty comes from the fact that it is adorned with every species of human trait, as a cloak might be adorned with every species of flower. And I suppose,' I added, 'that plenty of people would find it highly attractive, just as women and children are attracted by the sight of colourful variety.'
>
> 'It's a good place to look for a constitution [*politeion*], Adeimantus, as well,' I said.
>
> 'Why?'
>
> 'Because it's so open that it contains every type of political system [*politeion*] there is. For anyone wanting to construct a community, as we were a short while ago, a visit to a democratically governed community is essential, to help him choose the kind he likes. It's a sort of general store for political systems [*pantopolion aphikomeno politeion*]: you can visit it, make your choice, and then found your community.'[37]

It is worth noticing that Plato associated each constitution with a type (today regarded as psychological types), so that 'there are bound to be as many types [*tropon*, hence also character] of human being as there are of political system [*politeion*].'[38] Derrida in contrast is not and cannot be so assured about many constitutions (in the sense of *politeion*). For his reality is that of democracy as a general horizon of legitimation. This is a horizon according to which democracy is not so extensively pervaded by the plurality of constitutions and, more radically, the absence of constitutions. On the contrary, democracy has, with settled institutions and practices, a whole map of who can speak and who cannot, who can enter and who cannot, well delimited borders and so forth. So, following a well-established strategy of deconstruction, Derrida emphasizes a term in a series that is subordinate or concealed; showing how it (in this case licence) is not in fact so marginal. The 'type' of democracy (to signify both the structuring of institutions and individual demeanours) cannot thrive without that which is insusceptible to 'type,' or at least, for a while, a non-type, and that is licence, whose most dramatic figure is roguishness.

Derrida places himself within a tradition that, albeit negatively with Plato, attributes to democracy the capacity to accommodate, without arresting, this very licence or excess

> democracy, the passage to democracy, *democratization*, will always have been associated with license, with taking too many liberties [*trop-de-liberté*], with the dissoluteness of the libertine, with liberalism, indeed perversion and delinquency, with malfeasance, with failing to live according to the law, with the notion that 'everything is allowed,' that 'anything goes.'[39]

The rogue, the licentious, is the very matter of democracy, not only because it shows the full extent of the *cratos* within the etymology of democracy, but also on the side of the people, the *demos*: 'the *demos* is thus never very far away when one speaks of a voyou. Nor is democracy far from *voyoucracy*.'[40] Here we see the contours of the debate in *Politics of Friendship*, the asocial [*insociable*] rogue is indissociable from a regime of sociability, democracy. The universalizing force of democracy has to live with the singularizing force of the rogue. Democracy is precisely this spacing of negotiation of different forces that ascribes to itself laws, always drawing porous and irresolute laws (certainly these laws can also crystallize, and what is worse, the very brilliant beauty of this irresolute process may obfuscate one to the limitations of democracy).

Derrida repeatedly seeks to take advantage of that which already 'takes place' (instead of rejecting democracy for the sake of an oppositional dialectics).[41] Amongst that which already 'takes place,' Derrida elects the subaltern element, the rogue, the licentious, the intimate, the invisible, the non-manifest, engaging with their force. For in what may appear weak, and indeed may be weaker, Derrida also perceives forces.[42] It is a weak force, not because it lacks in intensity, but because it is placed under a hierarchy in a system of subaltern differentiation (which does not mean simple exclusion, it is inclusion and exclusion at the same time leading to hierarchy).[43] Derrida thus adheres to the 'rogue' in democracy, and sees the force of roguery on the 'margins,' but also what is most daunting in the 'centre' of the democratic constitution. In fact, one could well argue that roguishness is in fact another name for sovereignty. Its intensity and force is the force of the sovereign, the sovereign (divine and/or beast), the singular and indivisible uncompromising affirmation of oneself.

In emphasizing the role of roguishness, Derrida is not attempting to suppress it, to suppress sovereignty for instance. With his allegiance to democracy in conditions of roguishness, Derrida seeks to expose that which already is, and to expose precisely that which in the tradition of democracy pertains to a radical exposure. Democracy exposes the indivisible 'moment' of sovereignty without destroying it (I shall problematize the relationship between indivisibility and sovereignty in chapter four). Democracy is here the very work of exposing the dividing lines between margin and centre, inside and outside, law and lawlessness, which lie at the bottom of juridical restlessness itself. In exposing them, democracy allows for a role to be played by the weak, who are also the promise of strength. A careful reading of Derrida will attest to that.[44]

2.3 Forces: Sovereign, Democratic, Deconstructive

Let us now take advantage of the issues raised to inquire more deeply into the force that underpins both democracy and sovereignty; and, surprisingly or not, deconstruction itself. I shall in this way further clarify, but also complicate when necessary, Derrida's postulation of democracy to come. For that I must dwell for a moment on the distinction between sovereignty and democracy (sovereignty can be seen here as an image of the unity and indivisibility of law, resisting democracy). One cannot, I argue, distinguish between sovereignty and democracy in the way Derrida proposes. It is much simpler and salutary to consider the actual political experiences of self-determination, affirmation of oneself today, as sovereign democracies.

Sovereignty and Democracy

For Derrida, indivisibility is the crucial characteristic of sovereignty, in contrast to democracy, which is announced by the 'more than one.'[45]

Derrida expands on sovereignty throughout the whole of *Rogues*, and of course throughout his entire work. What is relevant here is to realize this contrast between sovereignty and democracy in order to understand the subtle enjoyment of democracy that Derrida proposes in his practice of writing. In relation to 'God,' the 'Sovereign,' and the 'Rogue,' Derrida speaks many times about the turning to oneself, the enjoyment of this circle, which is so intense and absolute that it exceeds sense itself, and time, and all that could divide itself.[46] The work of exception can only be understood in this light: 'it is also the concentration into a single point of indivisible singularity (God, the monarch, the people, the state or the nation-state) of absolute force and the absolute exception.'[47] In short, it is 'indivisible and thus unshareable.'[48]

This distinction, however, is highly problematic, even on the level of principles. If one distinguishes sovereignty from democracy on the basis of indivisibility, would that mean that sovereignty lacks sharing out [*partage*], that democracy lacks a moment of indivisibility? And what would democracy be without a moment of indivisibility, when 'time' and 'sense' are overflowed? It would be mere calculation, or at least, the radical, albeit always ultimately unsuccessful renunciation of indivisibility. The best way forward is not to oppose democracy and sovereignty, but to think more incisively about the nature of sovereign democracies, the actual universal today; or democracy simply put with this sovereign element.[49] If one does that, one may start thinking on the possibilities and impossibilities for societal transformations, for better and for worse (and the chance of that paradox of paradox, so daunting, that Derrida referred to in *The Other Heading*).[50]

To play Derrida against Derrida, one may conceive of at least three forms of *in-divisibility*, in a certain way they all coexist in sovereign democracies. First, there is one in which in-divisibility, or as I shall discuss, the 'to come' itself, is underexposed. Secondly there is another in which it is exploited, abused. Here there is already more exposure, the abuse takes place through the mobilization of exposure in a certain way. Yet, this abuse of in-divisibility is not exposed enough. It often denies the access to, and the possibility of enjoying, the equality of enjoyment and suffering of that indivisibility. Thirdly, there is relationally a type of overexposure that takes place only as a more generalized insistence on the process that led to the second moment. The tasks of today are, first, to warrant against the return to underexposure and, secondly, to strive for overexposure, which is also, in a certain way, a more truthful exposure. For overexposure is more radically faithful to the fragile possibility of enjoying the experience of what I call here in-divisibility and shall call later 'to come.'

To continue the explication of Derrida's analytical distinction, democracy is not simply, of course, sovereignty's opposite. Derrida here was very careful not to say that. He speaks in fact of a 'dominant discourse on democracy,' according to which 'democracy supposes this freedom as power, faculty, or ability to act.'[51] To simplify this, one can recall, as I have, that current democracies are essentially sovereign democracies.[52] To be sure, Derrida emphasizes other aspects of the democratic experience, those aspects that he adheres to, including a certain unconditionality, which is hardly discernible from sovereignty. He does not aim to debunk this 'sovereign' element of democracy; what he aims is to avoid its abuse, and that will be the theme of the next section.

Yet, on the question of democracy, it is absolutely crucial to emphasize the aspect that sovereignty is supposed to lack; that which the democratic experience calls forth, the experience that I referred to earlier as the contemporary contour of a logic of universalization. Democracy calls forth the question of the number: 'the question of the number, the question of the multitude or of the masses—and thus of democracy.'[53] Moreover, as I suggested previously, the importance of democracy must be articulated as that of a spacing that brings together, in a tensional relation, the name and the number, the singular and the universal.

There may be a question to be raised as to whether sovereignty is indeed all so clearly that indivisibility, or even the principle of affirmation of that indivisibility. It must also be in relation to something else, it cannot be exclusively itself; if there were not a relation with an outside it would not be able to sustain itself as itself. Derrida suggests that 'sovereignty is round; it is a rounding off.'[54] This may give the impression that sovereignty is simply a mad reversal to oneself. If it is not one without relation (for that, we take, would be unsustainable), at least it would threaten all relation. Yet 'it is a rounding off [*arrondissement*]' means also, and more idiomatically, 'it [sovereignty] is an administrative division [*arrondissement*].'[55] The term *arrondissement* means currently this: any administrative division, and in particular a sub-mayoral division of major French cities. Such a noun immediately refers to the 'rogues' (with all the symbolism of this) who are left outside the walls of the *arrondissement*, outside the initial walling-up of the city of Paris (here a metaphor for all experiences of exclusion that create 'rogues,' but whose enforcers are themselves roguish).[56] By establishing a division, sovereignty organizes a type of relationality, in this case by means of exclusion. Another form of relationality that sovereignty establishes is by the *roué*—wheeled person.[57] The latter relates to the very extortive practices which those who happen to be inside the wall of the metaphorical medieval city end up suffering. The effects of sovereignty are felt inside and outside its division; it establishes, without necessarily a centre, two forms of control: exclusion and exploitation. In the structure of sovereignty there is both exclusion and exploitation.

One now has to think whether sovereign democracies may in any way contain elements of the dislocation of this structure. As I have argued, the term democracy signifies for Derrida the exposure to the ruins of law (or the exposure of modern law as such); to the restless malleability of the dividing lines of sociability. Sovereign democracy is the social formation in which exposure to the dividing lines is not incompatible with conditions of exploitation and exclusion. That is, exposure itself occurs in a mode compatible with exclusion and exploitation. Cognitively, that means cynicism; bodily, that means insensibility. The deconstitution of law, the restlessness of a lack of assured borders and positions, is as such exploited, so that exclusion and material exploitation may occur (which entails a key reconstitution). But so that exploitation may occur, one has to assume that this deconstitution has a force.

Sovereignty and democracy should neither be distinguished through the attribute of indivisibility, nor through the notion of relationality, or lack of relationality. There may be another mode of differentiating the conflicting experiences that take place within democracies (sovereign ones). How though is democracy intrinsic to Derrida's style, and how may an element of force still be of value in understanding the relationship between deconstruction and democracy?

Force of Deconstruction

The issue of force may still help in clarifying how exactly Derrida can claim that all these exigencies of sociability are compatible within democracies, which we have established have something of sovereignty (note that sociability is a term I use to signify the interdependence of binary machines such as visibility–invisibility, conditional–unconditional, divisibility–indivisibility). What brings these exigencies together, what allows Derrida to treat two incommensurable exigencies in a spacing of encounters and negotiations, is differential force; that is, force that does not necessarily fold back on itself (it is made in difference), force as differentiation and deferral, intensity and tension, pervasive, but also in a certain sense egalitarian, for it equates for a moment everything that it encounters with a quantity. One must not disregard Derrida's subtle materialism; subtle and troubled, for it has to reckon with that which, uncompromising in its terms, is irreducible to quantification. Yet, it does so, treating 'impurely' what is pure, not to disable purity, but to allow it to organize itself differently:

> Every time one speaks of what is meta-discursive, nondiscursive (but not meta-textual, you understand, in the sense I give to these words text, mark, trace, etc.)—what we have been doing the entire time with the word *negotiation*, in other words—one is speaking of force ... when I name force I am thinking of a differentiality.[58]

As for democracy, when Derrida places it as the background of several oppositional and non-oppositional tensions (singular–universal, visible–invisible, powerful–weak, but also margin–centre, distant–near, low–high in a hierarchy), both in *Politics of Friendship* and in *Rogues*, he is basically saying that democracy is the precarious exposure to the laws of these tensions; in a sense the very law of these tensions. It allows for the accommodation of several moves in countless directions. Derrida deals with these divides as both 'legitimate' and 'illegitimate.' They are legitimate for they are part of the social code. All discourse can be encoded and taught, caught by knowledge, not only scientific but also practical. It is the very practice of technique to encode, simplify, and 'handle' the world. But such divides are also illegitimate to the extent that their actual contours are, if not arbitrary, susceptible to challenges of authority, reason, and sensitivity.

This is the fundamental perception of Derrida's thought, what Sloterdijk aptly calls 'semiological materialism,' here 'applied' to legal-political-ethical discourses.[59] This is the perception that all discourse (including non-linguistic ones, and perhaps all information) is based on a coding of differentiation and iterability (some of which, male–female, white–black, centre–margin, are deeply entrenched and cause acute suffering to those who experience them). It follows a possible description of the scales, the degrees of intensity involved, the flow of forces, and causal relationships.

Yet, Derrida knew that this descriptive practice, albeit accurate and part of an important exercise, will do nothing to undo those structures, codes, and legalities. In order to succeed in that, one would have to repeat, expose, and practise the same philosophical-metaphysical--technical method that brought them about; for, in emphasizing an aporia, Derrida requires something to happen—a decision, an event. He succeeds precisely because no way out is given, no *euphoria* is allowed. In the sustained suspension of his aporias, Derrida multiplies ad infinitum and reactivates the forces that lay dormant in oppositions and distinctions themselves; performing all the time, more than merely describing or prescribing solutions. To prescribe, for Derrida, always runs the risk of simply giving way to a calculation. He proceeds (and note the role of 'force' and 'strengths' here):

through a certain *strategic* arrangement which, within the field of metaphysical opposition, uses the strengths of the field to turn its own stratagems against it, producing a force of dislocation that spreads itself throughout the entire system, fissuring it in every direction and thoroughly *de-limiting* it.[60]

Yet, in de-limiting the force field of signification, Derrida often offers new vocabularies that will name and, in a sense, sustain the newly arisen arrangement; and because they are unheard of, fresh, strange, and awkward, these terms should help avoid the reproduction of the old hierarchical arrangements. Gasché has extensively treated this theme, calling these terms infrastructures, later more widely known as quasi-transcendentals or undecidables.[61] To name but a few, one can refer to arche-writing and arche-trace, *différance*, supplementarity, double bind, hymen, *restance*, desistance, and more recently *aimance*, spectrality, and, in *Rogues*, 'the reasonable.' Derrida has broadly accepted Gasché's particular diagnosis, albeit problematizing the term infrastructure itself.[62]

Perhaps astonishingly, Derrida took democracy itself as an 'infra-structural' term, or an undecidable (a current undecidable; that is, it is not brought about by textual deconstruction; and as I shall later argue, this is precisely what is necessary in addressing law). In *Rogues*, democracy is brought to the close vicinity of *différance*: 'democracy is what it is only in the difference by which it defers itself and differs from itself.'[63] Even more clearly, democracy is in the exact background of the tension between law and justice: 'democracy seeking its place only at the unlocatable border between law and justice, that is also between the political and the ultrapolitical.'[64] Does this mean that democracy cannot be deconstructed, that the deconstructive theorist is bound to pay allegiance to democracy?

A 'characteristic' yes and no is necessary. Democracy to come is not to be confounded either with actual democratic institutions or with the ideals that inform these actual institutions. Sovereignty informs every aspect of 'the dominant discourse on democracy.'[65] Yet, democracy raises the questions and the calls of the number, of who, of what, and of the line that divide a polity. It radicalizes the possibility of dividing affirmation of possibility (sovereignty), and the chance of, perhaps, sharing sovereignty more equally. Democracy, as we have seen in *The Other Heading* dwells at the divide between the visible and the invisible; in *Right to Philosophy*, in the autonomous and the heteronymous; in *Politics of Friendship*, on the restless line between the name and the number, singular and universal. In 'Force of Law,' democracy appears between the one and the ruin, and in some problematic ways between law and justice. In *Rogues* we see that form of dwelling on the line between law and justice and, in fact, a rehearsal of all the other instances. Derrida gives no other name to democracy, for ultimately deconstruction and democracy inhabit the same terrain.

Here there is a discursive strategy that I would like to retain and to which I will later return. The complexity of Derrida's allegiance to democracy is such that it allows him to account for it in a much more concrete and effective way. There is quite a drastic contrast between this take on democracy and the distinction performed between law and justice in part one of 'Force of Law,' and indeed other instances of Derrida's writing (in part the contrast between 'to come' and future), such as the distinction between conditionality and unconditionality, or calculability and incalculability. The institution of democracy is perceived in its complexity. Not even sovereignty is placed in stark contrast to democracy, given the etymological and semantic vicariousness of the term.

It is in this light that it becomes clear that Derrida requires democracy, that there is 'no (pace of) [*pas*] deconstruction without democracy, no (pace of) [*pas*] democracy without deconstruction.'[66] It is also in this light that indeed all philosophical enterprise and all philosophical colloquium is 'linked to the *form* of democracy.'[67] These felicitous indications, however, also show a reserve with regard to democracy, and announce Derrida's allegiance to a 'democracy to come.' For, as I have indicated by including the French original word 'pas,' Derrida is not only referring to the interdependence between democracy and deconstruction. The sentence could equally be translated and read as 'pace (or step) of deconstruction without democracy, pace (step) of democracy without deconstruction.' Equally, Derrida's emphasis on the *form* of democracy conveys that, since the 1960s at least, democracy has been deemed crucial for deconstruction. Yet more than that, it conveys that philosophy could all too well be accommodated by democracy without *troubling* anything (Derrida uses the term *gêner*, which should be a feature of deconstruction in its quasi-revolutionary demeanour).[68] In this direction, deconstruction requires philosophy's engagement with the force of democracy as well.[69] That would be an engagement that precludes nothing and welcomes everything: nothing is primarily dismissed from democracy, even though a question will always be raised as to the place of the line:

> The whole question of 'demo*cracy*' might be configured around this 'transcendental force' [Nancy's notion of freedom as the force of things, as the force of every this and that 'is there,' by virtue of its very spatiality[70]]: how far is democracy to be extended, the *people* of

demo*cracy*, and the 'each 'one' of democracy? To the dead, to animals, to trees, to rocks?[71]

This question is not simply that of the empty space of power. Admittedly, democracy as such, as we know it, organizes itself around a certain empty space of power. And yet this very empty space, from within Derrida's thinking, is still *to come*. This means two things: if there is a true empty space it ought to be significant enough not to close off the possibility of an entire democratic or post-democratic rearrangement (a relevant question would still be: empty in what way?); also, the empty space is still *to come* expresses how the power of the One is not so easily circumvented by the form of democracy. The One, the monarchic principle, the future (as a cunning substitute for the One) survive in a much more diffuse and generalized way. A type of subjectivity shared by all (and Derrida is quite suspicious of this sharing) is at stake. That is a type of appropriating form of subjectivity, and appropriation-prone institutions thrive in spite, and even in conjunction with, all the emptying of power. Derrida's democracy appeals from within to a 'to come' that happens, is happening, but is yet subordinate and exploited.

The postulation that democracy to come offers is one towards discerning the threads of a force that does not turn over itself indefinitely. It resists accumulating incessantly, harvesting for the active and 'possible' sake of itself. It must enjoy itself, but also its law; that is, not the law of the One, but another law, that which limits, delimits, and rearranges itself, beyond the grip of the One and the grip of itself—the law of its deconstitution (more radically, its constitutionality, which includes deconstitution and constitution; the constitution of the firm postulation itself, the constitution of deconstitution). It must expose itself to its own injustices and the suffering that it exacts; expose itself in fact to the exposure that already is, this cynical and insensible form of exposure. With the discourse of democracy to come one still promises, but the promise now must be to scrutinize and sensibilize exposure itself (as we shall see, in Derrida's writing, in Derrida's own practice of exposure, one can see democracy to come in practice, in its frail autobiographic self-exposure).

A common reference to 'force' makes democracy and deconstruction closely linked. Democracy is described even as a type of negotiation intrinsic to the type of negotiation that takes place in the deconstructive operation. Moreover, there is a deconstructive operation, impure, almost machine-like at times, in its acute sense as to the void that deconstructs any discursive code from within (though later we shall see how many problems there are in the passage from the exposure of forces, the forces in play in the deconstitution of law, on the one hand, and the strategic discourse that deconstruction adopts to that effect, on the other). Yet, I have shown how Derrida is prepared to let go of democracy, if need be, in spite of that connection. No term should be treated here as irreducible and irreplaceable. I claim that the exigency of exposure to the deconstitution of law is often violated (by its denegation or its abuse) in the current 'dominant discourse on democracy.'[72]

2.4 Inviting the Exposure of Dominant Discourses

I have argued that Derrida's approach to sovereignty can be further integrated into Derrida's discourse on democracy to the extent that 'a dominant discourse of democracy' effectively requires the legal-political feature that Derrida attributes to sovereignty: indivisibility. Derrida's approach to democracy, in that it articulates the aporias of sociability, must include divisibility and indivisibility. I have also suggested that the intense and indivisible force that appears in both sovereignty and democracy has something of democracy in common with deconstruction itself.

Yet, with respect to current discourses of democratic legitimation the dominant focus is entirely different. Democracy is generally perceived as a given, and not as an inclination in constant need of justification and reformulation. More than a given, democracy is said to face certain paradoxes or contradictions, which almost irremediably invite some form of ingenious solution. Derrida is certainly not attempting to resolve the 'paradoxes' of democracy, but his writing can contribute to assessing whether such paradoxes are correctly framed as paradoxes. One can understand better, therefore, what is wrong with current models of democracy, and why Derrida wishes to depart from them. In this light, one can confirm the existence of a postulation to constitutional exposure, in Derrida's insistence on democracy's exposure.

With regard to dominant discourses, the putative paradox between fundamental rights and popular sovereignty (more recently recast through the paradox between liberty and security) is instructive.[73] My interest here is not to critique such discourses directly. A Derridean reading of these elements of the contemporary democratic discourse, in being aware of their insertion in systems of legitimation, highlights the relevance of his concerns and the contribution of his postulation.

Autonomy and Autoimmunity

According to my reading of Derrida's approach to democracy, the paradox between fundamental rights and popular sovereignty can only be sustained in a very superficial way. In fact, only a few authors maintain that fundamental rights and popular sovereignty constitute a robust or true paradox. Most eminently, Chantal Mouffe has claimed that

> while it is indeed the case that individual rights and democratic self-government are constitutive of liberal democracy—whose novelty resides precisely in the articulation of these two traditions—there exists between these two 'grammars' a tension that cannot be eliminated.[74]

Mouffe is aware that dwelling at the border of tensions, and experiencing or acknowledging such tensions is beneficial to democracy. Yet, this tension fails to acknowledge that the relationship between rights and people is not only constitutive of liberal democracy, but conceals a profound alliance, one that pertains to the affirmation of autonomy and determination concealed in 'rights' and 'people.'

The authors who have put forward the necessity of resolving the contradictions of the different democratic traditions do acknowledge a bond between human rights and popular sovereignty (mainly Rawls and Habermas, but I use Habermas as a model here).[75] Habermas in particular discovers an alliance through the notion of autonomy that underpins both modern constructs of individual rights and popular sovereignty. The issue at stake is not a tension between the individual and 'the people,' but between private autonomy and public autonomy (in which case the latter is exercised by individuals in communication in the public sphere and not by the metaphysical entity of 'the people').[76] Indeed he strives to reconcile this latter dichotomy, dismissing almost entirely the question of a symbolic or material collective bond (except by means of ethical narratives of belonging expressed by individuals and part of the formation of public opinion in the public sphere).[77] What Habermas fails entirely to point out is the problematic nature of the notion of autonomy itself, especially in relation to heteronomy.[78]

Habermas assumes that it is desirable to exercise freedom and autonomy in both the private sphere (as opposed to arbitrary interventions of the State or other individuals) and the public sphere (through participation in neutral procedures of decision-making that arrive at norms that can claim at least the possibility of rational acceptance by its addressees).[79] To be sure, Habermas cannot ultimately avoid the attribution of power to a collectivity, since his notion of public autonomy is also based on idealizations about the communicative powers that grant the possibility of effective democratic procedures, and the quality of debate in the public sphere. So, his reliance on language, and its grounding in non-specialized and fundamental human interactions (his use of Husserl's concept of the life-world)[80] betrays a non-problematized question of community.[81] But in any case, autonomy as such (exercised according to Habermas by individuals in both the private and the public sphere) is pursued as a goal. As such, Habermas attempts to reconstruct the models of legitimation based on autonomy and which have been, in his reading, the foundation of the modern democratic tradition.

For Derrida, conversely, autonomy cannot be embraced in this unproblematic way. To begin with, the very movement of the *autos* is fundamentally troubled; the movement of the self, that returns to itself, to protect itself, and immunize itself against others, against the control or interference of others. Here I approach the vicinity of Derrida's notion of autoimmunity. For Derrida, at work in individual life and political community, autoimmunity is not at all the mere work of immunity and exclusion of otherness, but the very sapping of immunity at work in the *autos*. In *Rogues*, Derrida explains that such an autoimmunity is not reducible simply to self-destruction, or a form of suicide: 'autoimmunity ... threatens always to rob suicide itself of its meaning and supposed integrity.'[82] The safety of autonomy's possibility of self-closure is here put in question, and the *autos* already appears not to be so clearly self-contained or delimited, requiring at least something that overflows itself.

However, in spite of several occurrences throughout *Rogues*, the notion of autoimmunity is not clearly explained in that work.[83] One has to go back to where autoimmunity appears in the first instance, to 'Faith and Knowledge,' in order to understand the contours of the term.[84] Without recourse to this other text, autoimmunity could have meant simply that the excessive sense of personal or communal protection leads to the destruction of the conditions of exercise of an autonomy, or the very reason for autonomy and an *autos*. Yet, in 'Faith and Knowledge,' it becomes clear that the ruin of the *autos* is anterior to any excess belonging to the autos. An excess as the affirmation of the incommensurable to life or autos itself must be conceivable. Something beyond (or antecedent to) itself is necessary, and the *autos* is constitutively linked to otherness. This otherness refers to both an 'other' of the self/autos, and hence necessary to the self, at the service of the self, but also to an 'other' which cannot be entirely reducible to the self, threatening it radically.[85]

Derrida explains the difficult notion of autoimmunity in relatively simple terms. He starts by positing a true tension in the notion of life [*vie*] itself: that between 'absolute respect' for life (epitomized in the commandment 'Thou shalt not kill') and the 'sacrificial vocation' of life.[86] Then he explains it by formulating the principle according to which 'life has *absolute* value only if it is worth *more than* life,'[87] where the first life can be understood as a singular life experience and the second as life in general. He continues to clarify that 'respect for life concerns thus, in the discourses of religion as such, the single "human life", so long as it bears testimony, in some way, to the divine transcendence of what is worth more than that life.'[88] And if one takes into account the indications provided in *Rogues*, autoimmunity goes even beyond the self of suicide (the life that is worth more than life must be one that overflows the pursuit of individual glory and pride that often leads to death).[89] Or, in other words, the self that is in play in any action that results in self-destruction must be here a constitutively unfinished self, one which announces its death or im-possibility since its inception.

This structure is not only applicable to individual life (not least because this individual life's condition of affirmation lies outside itself), but also to a community as a whole. In fact, the term autoimmunity is born auto-co-immunity. A community, the charge, work, or task (*munus*) of being together (of constituting a collective body) is pervaded by that which transcends itself—the gap of an impossibility or the excess of an affirmation—something which since its inception announces its own death, and its own mourning.[90] But this is in no way a negative condition. On the contrary, for Derrida,

> this self-contesting attestation keeps the autoimmune community alive, which is to say, open to something other and more than itself: the other, the to-come [*avenir*], death, freedom, the coming or the love of the other, the space and the time of a spectralizing messianicity beyond all messianisms.[91]

Thus, not being closed onto itself, not being pure *autos* is a condition for its subsistence.[92] But what happens when major representations of democracy describe it as the realization or pursuit of autonomy?

Such theoretical representations include, surreptitiously or not, a robust version of autonomy in normative models of democracy. They have, in this way, an impact on its practice, refraining from favouring the enjoyment of an exposure to heteronomy that is always in play. In the conceptualization of the relationship between law and democracy, one can often notice this refraining from or even exploitation of exposure towards the continuation of situations that entail hierarchy and suffering. But in order to answer the question of the effects of those representations of democracy, it is important to heed Derrida's own performativity. How has Derrida described his own practice? Has it actually moved away from autonomy, and the *autos*, and how and why?

Democratic Autoimmunity

Derrida states that '"democracy to come" can hesitate endlessly, oscillate indecidably and forever, between two possibilities.'[93] These possibilities, he explains, are the constative and the performative aspects of 'democracy to come.'[94] On the one hand, Derrida describes democracy as a democracy that includes the 'to come,' a democracy in which the 'perhaps' happens and has already happened, of undecidability. It is a patient process that invites a passive messianicity: 'a non performative exposure to what comes, to what can always not come or has already come.'[95] On the other hand, Derrida invites and calls for the practice of precisely such a democracy, more actively and engagingly attempting to 'win conviction by suggesting support or adherence.'[96] And in fact there is exposure also here; the exposure of the claimers themselves (the exposure of the dividing lines between them) who put forward their positions and allow the possibility of being critiqued.

Derrida's approach to democracy comes thus to an excess of exposure. It not only puts forward the exposure of the ruins of law in democracy, but it also calls upon an insistence upon exposure. And this distinction is not simply between the constative and the performative. The constative is not a simple and totally neutral constative, to the extent that Derrida's 'description' is radically unsatisfied with dominant discourses, and strongly endeavours to disclose unwarranted assumptions and reductionist models of democracy. Here democracy is

> aporetic in its structure (force without force, incalculable singularity and calculable equality, commensurability and incommensurability, heteronomy and autonomy, indivisible sovereignty and divisible or shared sovereignty, an empty name, a despairing messianicity or a messianicity in despair, and so on).[97]

The performative that insists and calls upon embracing these aporias, in turn, is not a pure performative, entirely effective and adequate for its context. Derrida's call, if not absolutely unheard of (there have been other discourses to which it is broadly affiliated), still troubles and challenges the dominant democratic discourse.[98] Derrida's discourse postulates a radical exposure of the lines of sociability (those mobilized by modern law) even at the border of the intelligibility of his own writing, beyond the clarity of the pre-established borders of learned discourse (here between activity *and* passivity, performance *and* constatation).

But a question remains as to how this discourse and the inclination that I have argued to be located there to exposure could respond to the discourses of autonomy? And how could they respond in the language of historical redescription which is current (allegedly or not) in political philosophy?⁹⁹ In many ways, I have shown Derrida's response to reductive versions of political theory in his fine analysis of the contours of friendship, this 'private' or 'intimate' matter that pervades the drive towards the constitution of a polity or a people. Later, I shall also demonstrate how Derrida complicates and enriches our understanding of the fundamental concepts of law and sovereignty. Yet, with respect to democracy, and somewhat differently from law and sovereignty, Derrida embraces, with all due reservations, the name itself—democracy. He comes to *claim* that it is necessary to

> take into account the absolute and intrinsic historicity of the only system that welcomes in itself, in its very concept, that expression of autoimmunity called the right to self-critique and perfectibility. Democracy is the only system, the only constitutional paradigm, in which, in principle, one has or assumes the right to criticize everything publicly, including the idea of democracy, its concept, its history, its name. Including the idea of constitutional paradigm and the absolute authority of law. It is thus the only paradigm that is universalizable whence its chance and its fragility.¹⁰⁰

One can clearly see that in Derrida's allegiance to democracy, the notion of right becomes pivotal. The possibility of democratic autoimmunity, the possibility of institutionalizing democratic deconstitution is predicated on the self-critique that rights allow. There is for sure a fundamental difficulty here, namely rights' proximity to sovereignty, the sovereignty of the people. And that difficulty should indeed underpin the critical rereading of dominant discourses of democracy, but is not without a positive element:

> The Declaration of Human Rights is not, however, opposed to, and so does not limit, the sovereignty of the nation-state in the way a principle of nonsovereignty would oppose a principle of sovereignty. No, it is one sovereignty set against another. Human rights pose and presuppose the human being [*l'homme*—literally, man] (who is equal, free, self-determined) as sovereign. The Declaration of Human Rights declares another sovereignty; it thus reveals the autoimmunity of sovereignty in general.¹⁰¹

So, one should not celebrate too much the end of sovereignty in the name of human rights. They also involve an image of 'man,' the free individual, in control of its will and its body. Yet, there is also something salutary in rights in their display of the question of 'the autoimmunity of sovereignty in general.'¹⁰² But if I agree with Derrida that rights do pose the problem of divisibility, and indent the security of sovereign indivisibility, I do not see how 'human rights' (Derrida refers to the post-World War II experience) actually reveal 'the autoimmunity of sovereignty in general.' That 'revelation' (better, *exposure*) would have to involve a degree of effacement of the *autos* itself, as I have shown in relation to autoimmunity. Rights' discourse raises the question of intensity and division, but these elements, as much as the notion of 'people,' have been conceptualized as pure markers of indivisibility. That is profoundly problematic, and even Derrida does not live up to the complexity of his performance in addressing them.

The dominant discourses of democracy fail to take into account the dimension of democracy that Derrida calls autoimmunity—also indissociable from the general discourse of democracy to come. The inclusion of the 'to come,' though, attests to an appeal to trust in the experience of autoimmunity, or the actual democratic experience of the 'to come.' Moreover, in Derrida's allegiance to autoimmune democracy, and in his careful departure from sovereignty, the notion of rights becomes crucial.

∽

I have argued that 'democracy,' for Derrida, already indicates the exposure to the constitutionality of law (or the exposure to modern law itself in its mobilization of fundamental dichotomies that orientate sociability, with an emphasis on deconstitution). I have shown that Derrida does not reject that which Benjamin seemed to reject, that is, the 'corruption' of modern law.[103] I have also illustrated how the 'people' of democracy come to the fore as 'roguish' and excluded from the enjoyment of power. Yet, I have indicated how the autopositioning of power involves suffering and exploitation. Derrida strives ceaselessly against the agony of settled distinctions (see how these are part of the formation of 'common sense' in ch. 2) that warrant all those hierarchic binary machines. The latter inhabit even the most democratic political practice and cause the exploitation of the forces of the traces that compose the people: the exploitation of democracy.

It is most important to appreciate the insight that democracy is, already for Derrida, a rearrangement of the binary codes of sociability, that is, a current undecidable where the several sense-making forces and codes can be reactivated and negotiated. Democracy is tantamount to the differential force itself through which ruin is exposed. The call to or the postulation of democracy is that firm affirmation of ruins, of deconstitution. In that very description, though, there is something that trembles. Especially in the difficulty of differentiating sovereignty and democracy, it comes to light that democracy's rearrangement is perhaps insufficient. Albeit necessary, democracy is in fact compatible with 'sovereignty.' More than that, it can be compatible with extortion or exploitation and exclusion.[104]

In Derrida's attempt to bring to light that which is already by definition exposed, of the matter of exposure, what he promotes, wittingly or unwittingly is the exposure of exposure, that is, the exposure of one's participation (cynical and/or insensitive) in the 'common' roguishness of the city, State, nation, or community. The exposure of the exposure is most clearly articulated with the expression 'democracy to come.' There, a democracy that is already exposure and the restless move of differential forces has to come to the fruition of its 'constitutional' dimension.

The remainder of this book is dedicated to contributing to, and intensifying, Derrida's discourse, and to the conundrums of modern law and the 'to come' as crucial elements of democracy 'to come.' Through them I seek to intensify Derrida's postulation of democracy and to craft a certain postulation for democracy to come. In law, I find that Derrida's starting point, although understandable given his general strategy, is not the most conducive to radical exposure, and hence ultimately insufficient to furthering democracy to come (my contribution here is on the level of Derrida's strategy), and I put forward the early contours of a thought of the constitutionality of law that seeks to take full account of the modern democratization drive so as to conduct a radical democratization of law. In the 'to come' I find a phrase that, like democracy, is complex, involving differentiation and force, and should not be starkly opposed to sovereignty. Again, Derrida's starting point may not be as conducive to the exposure of sovereignty, which could further benefit Derrida's approach to democracy itself (again Derrida's strategy is not as conducive to overexposure as one would expect in this instance). I postulate that both 'law' and 'to come' could be better explored, particularly in their inclination to ward off exploitation, and calling upon enjoying and playing on the space between social distinctions.

— 3 —

LAW

My reading of the experience of democracy and the discourse of democracy to come has to face an important challenge. It comes from another dimension of Derrida's work: his approach to law. Theoretical-political representations of law are often oblivious of the process of democratization and politicization of law that is inherent in a modern democracy (within the interpretation that I have proposed so far democracy should be understood on the border lines of sociability, in which the people and its powers are always in question), but this is not at all necessarily a consequence of legal practice or legal-theoretical discourse itself.[1] The key problem here is that Derrida's main references on law are these modern representations, particularly Kant's.[2] Because of this starting point Derrida downplays the exposed character of law itself, an exposed condition which requires yet another exposure.

He thus fails to realize that an experience of exposure is characteristic not only of democracy but of law itself (democracy's hyperbole being its opening to expose itself constitutively to law's exposures). Symptomatically, Derrida's take on law, in the exercise of destabilizing oppositional hierarchies, tends to overlook the extent to which destabilization, flexibility, and incalculability have already been integrated into currently existing configurations of subjectivity; in particular into a knowledge of obliqueness (obliqueness here stands for terms such as destabilization, flexibility, and incalculability).[3] The problem here is strategic: why not take advantage of the exposure that is already in play? For the problem with law (as previously with democracy) is not quite its fixity, but the fixity of exploitation and exclusion in the process of organizing itself and its own restlessness.

In spite of such a strategic problem, I shall argue that a deeper look into Derrida's work on law can wield an approach to law that is compatible with the discourse of exposure that we have examined so far (that is, exposure not only to the impossibility of exposure and commonality, but also exposure of the complacency with this impossibility. This latter exposure is inherent in any self-exposure). I thus argue that there is a chance of an overexposure of law within Derrida's treatment of what he considers the mainstream of legal philosophy, the philosophy of Kant.[4] This overexposure depends fundamentally on the interpretation of Derrida's use of 'justice' and 'force.'

Moreover, I arrange Derrida's texts in order to propose an intensification of his legal discourse, one that may be deemed strategic (from within Derrida's understanding of the term). The problem here is that Derrida, in deconstructing the dominant representations of law, uses as a starting point the very representations that he attempts to undermine. In this way, justice is ab initio excluded from law, only to be included later by means of a process of contamination. I argue that this is detrimental in this particular case because of the current epistemological condition of legal thought.

Having established how Derrida addresses democracy in its own terms as already a practice of exposure, I shall now argue that this is precisely needed in relation to modern law itself (and for our purposes modern law is precisely the law of democracy, that is a system that is key for the subsistence of democracy, and democracy is marked by dwelling at the exposure of its laws of sociability; and hence any exposure of democracy is incomplete without the exposure of its laws). Democracy is already a way of organizing the power and lack of power, that is a constitutional exposure, in its exposure of the limits of exposure itself. This dynamic is precisely what is needed in relation to law: experimenting with discourses on law, which articulate exposure of exposure in law itself.

The problems in Derrida's reading of law that I address here are in many ways replicated with regard to the 'to come,' particularly in its problematic opposition to sovereignty. This chapter shall thus contribute to a reinterpretation of Derrida's postulation towards constitutional exposure, in which undoubtedly the strategic question is at stake, as well as an understanding of the predicaments of Derrida's law that will lead to a new take on the problems of the 'to come.' One can find here how a legal theory of exposure requires the exposure of sovereignty and futurity. That is, their treatment belongs to a 'theory' of law; for in sovereignty and futurity exposure as such, the exposed constitutionality of law is sanitized, domesticated in an experience that should not fail to resemble what I have called underexposure.

In Derrida's French, the main term of reference for the English term *law* is the French term *droit*. This term appears systematically in the two main texts that address legal institutions directly, the foundations of law, and the relationship between law and philosophy. The two texts concerned are 'Force of Law' and *Du Droit à la philosophie*.[5] I argue that both of them must be read in light of Derrida's postulation of constitutional exposure. I initially address some of the basic contours of Derrida's approach to the relationship between law and justice, and I identify the key role of the law of the law, which in Derrida's work is more complex than in Kant, for it includes conditions of possibility and conditions of impossibility of the law (see ch. 3.1). I later investigate this basic framework with emphasis on the question of justice, showing that Derrida is indeed not endorsing a strict definition of law, but rather articulating the opportunities of the juridical relevance of the law of the law (see ch. 3.2). Finally, I argue that there is a strategic predicament in Derrida's writing, in relation to the choice of the terms that frame a hierarchical opposition in the legal field, and indissociable to his starting point identified earlier (see ch. 3.3). Another strategy is also tentatively pursued so as to indicate other avenues for a democratic understanding of law open to the force of exposure to the dividing/sharing lines of sociability; following the threads of key thinkers of law such as Michel Villey and Johan Van der Walt, and a key thinker on law, Jean-Luc Nancy. In sum, Derrida's work on law can be intensified as a 'constitutional exposure' that may pave the way for what I have called an overexposure, which leads to what will be called here an expositivist view of legal theory.

3.1 Derrida's Law

With depth of analysis, it is possible to read Derrida on law in a way that is compatible with the democratic experience that we have addressed so far. In other words, it is possible to read Derrida on law with the background of the experience of constitution–deconstitution of law characteristic of democracy. In any event, I shall follow the thread of the thematic of modern law in Derrida's work. My attempt at this point is to understand the mechanism, the basic structure of Derrida's claims about the articulations between rational calculations and urgent justice. Let us pursue what he means by 'justice' itself in relation to the place it occupies vis-à-vis calculation.

For Derrida, in the legal realm of rule application, calculation demands symmetry, and foreseeability. At the same time, a right decision has to be singular, irreducible to a common measure, and hence incalculable. Law is thus heterogeneous to justice, whose appeal is urgent, incalculable, and irreducible to rules. Yet there is also a key contamination between these two domains: calculation and the incalculable, law and justice. How exactly can these two heterogeneous domains (law and justice) be also dependent on each other? Derrida claims that law announces and requires an element of the affirmation of justice, and every measure that aspires to justice also demands to be actualized and to enjoy the protection of the law. In everyday practice they are also intertwined.

However, Derrida's enterprise is predicated on the risk he seems to perceive that the unforeseeable and urgent elements of legal practice can be suppressed, or at least severely hampered by the growing role of 'administrative-machines' or programmatic decisions.[6] His aporetic description of the juridical field also avoids a seamless narrative which would neither acknowledge its own limitations, nor the limitation of knowledge itself.[7] Yet, the starting point of law as calculation is very problematic, in fact reductive of law's complexity. In addition, such a calculation, in Kant's tradition, is equated with strictness and symmetry. Again, many problems may follow.

Attention must be drawn to the parallel character of titles in each of these texts: the first part of 'Force of Law' is called '*Du droit à la justice*.'[8] This can mean both 'from law to justice' and 'on the right to justice.' The same goes for the title of the book *Du droit à la philosophie*, which can mean both 'from law to philosophy' and 'on the right to philosophy.' On the one hand, if the first reading is chosen, one can interpret Derrida as invoking the distinction between law and justice, and law and philosophy. He would be pursuing the goal of reaching closer to justice and philosophy, and in a sense, deconstruction as a philosophical enterprise, which again must be read in conjunction with justice (the now famous 'deconstruction is justice').[9] On the other hand, if the second reading is chosen, one can interpret Derrida to be calling upon law in order to reach for justice and philosophy. There is something in law (and particularly in 'right') that is necessary for both justice and philosophy. Derrida does not quite clarify which meaning he uses; and in this undecidability, he keeps between these two readings. Now it is crucial to understand what Derrida wishes to depart from and mobilize in his 'juridical' work.

Early in 'Force of Law' Derrida states that one should not speak *directly* about justice (this is part of Derrida's 'defence' of deconstruction for not having addressed the theme of justice before).[10] He stresses 'directly' to denote the law, in a reference to its being somehow strict. If justice and law are heterogeneous, speaking *directly* about justice would mean imposing on justice both legal parlance and thinking, and to inhibit or undermine justice. One must be reminded here of the proximity between the French term *droit* and Latin *directum* (straight, direct).[11] Justice, in turn, is equated with the oblique. According to Derrida, one can neither thematize nor 'objectivize' justice (that is directly, in a straightforward way) without 'betraying' it.[12]

Even earlier in the text, Derrida associated law [*droit*] with force, and 'enforceability' with exteriority. Following Kant, Derrida argues that 'there is no law without applicability, or *"enforceability"* of law without force.'[13] This is not to be read in a trivial or commonsensical way. Here one enters the realm of the 'essence of law,' the element that characterizes the legal system as distinguishable from morality and ethics. Moreover, Derrida aptly brings together such enforceability with Kant's notion of exteriority (Kant in turn drew heavily on earlier thinkers, in a line of influences that dates back at least to Hobbes).[14] Enforcement can only be effective (and enforceability credible) if it restrains itself to what it can tackle and control. That is why the internal forum (moral consciousness) must be ultimately excluded from the scrutiny of the state (unless to the extent that it enlightens the nature of a conduct; so unless internality is part of a show or theatricality of the public, such as in criminal law).[15] It is the external world and external actions and reactions that can be geometrically measured. Derrida is very attentive to Kant's geometric view of law. In 'Force of Law' he refers and cites §E of the 'Introduction to the metaphysics of right' (*Recht*).[16] In *Du droit à la philosophie* he gives even greater weight to this passage. I shall return to Derrida, but let us briefly pursue Kant's view.

In Kant's text, 'Strict law [*Recht*] can be represented as the possibility of a fully reciprocal use of coercion that is consistent with everyone's freedom in accordance with universal laws [*Gesetzen*].'[17] Subjective rights and obligations are not to be deemed separate or isolated. Coercion should be mutual and made consistent with a symmetric exercise of freedom. This notion is derived from Kant's supreme principle of law (*Recht*): 'Every action which by itself or by its maxim enables the freedom of each individual's will to co-exist with the freedom of everyone else in accordance with a universal law is right.'[18] On this basis, he can derive a maxim according to which one's external actions must 'be such that the free application of your will can co-exist with the freedom of everyone in accordance with a universal law.'[19] The corollary is that restrictions to freedom can be justified only if they work towards establishing or re-establishing a status of strict symmetry in freedom, in other words, towards the universal law of freedom.[20] All these formulations are ultimately legal specifications of a moral principle clearly defined in the *Groundwork of the Metaphysics of Morals*, the categorical imperative: 'act only in accordance with that maxim through which you can at the same time will that it become a universal law.'[21]

Yet, in Kant's passage that Derrida highlights in 'Force of Law' (and in §E as a whole) law's *strict* definition is not derived from morality.

In spite of being founded on morality, law's strict definition must do away with its origin, morality itself. The categorical imperative and the principle of law can serve as criteria for assessing the quality of law, but they are not to be called upon in the regular practice of law. An action or omission of a given agent will be legal irrespective of whether such an agent undertakes to act or not to act for the sake of, or because of, a duty (moral persons must be judged in that way). What matters legally is whether such an agent acts or not according to duty (so there is no place for morality, for law's foundation, in Kant's terms, in his own strict definition of law). Of course, there is here a very problematic homology between law and morality, and in fact a derivation of the content of law from morality. In 'Force of Law' and *Du droit à la philosophie*, Derrida emphasizes that the strict definition of law is not tantamount to its foundation or justification. The crucial quote from Kant, in this respect, is that

> this law [a strict notion of law, *Recht*] is certainly *based on* each individual's awareness of his obligations within the law; but if it is to remain pure, it may not and cannot appeal to this awareness as a motive which might determine the will to act in accordance with it [my emphasis].[22]

We will have to take a longer detour to understand exactly the huge significance of this reference for Derrida.

Such a concern with Kant's relation to law's foundation appears in both 'Force of Law' and *Du droit à la philosophie*, but it is only extensively treated in the latter.[23] Even if only in a somewhat elusive fashion, in that text Derrida explores the adjectival meaning of right and its etymology (from Latin *rectus*, literally straight) and Kant's analogously geometric and physical notion of a strict law. In the writings of Derrida on legal institutions, §E of Kant's 'Introduction to the metaphysics of right' is almost ubiquitous, if not as a direct reference, at least as a background reference.[24] For Kant in that paragraph, law is equated to a symmetric diagram of individual parts each having the same freedom and force. The action of one leads to the reaction of another (here the analogy is with Newton's third law of motion). Equality of freedom and of force is an axiom here.

Yet, one may attack, by actions or omissions, freedom itself. And that is precisely the only moment at which freedom can be restricted by the State, the guardian of that legal symmetry.[25] One does not *conform* to the principle of right in lying, neglecting, injuring, breaking one's word, and hence in externalizing a failure to *embrace* the categorical imperative (which could have been breached, but not enforced, had the relevant actions been externally conformed to duty). If one does not conform to the principle of right, one may be compelled to do so by he whose freedom has been curtailed (and the State will adjudicate and enforce such a claim, and the State itself will initiate action if such a curtailment of freedom can be felt by all, such as in the classical understanding of the nature of the criminal offence). Coercion is deemed to be symmetrically strict, as opposed to being oblique.

In Kant's work, strictness (and 'right') is understood in two ways. First, as the shortest line between two points (as opposed to curvature) and, secondly, as the line that constitutes two adjacent right angles over a given base, as opposed to oblique lines, such as those that constitute acute or obtuse angles. In Kant's understanding of law, there is neither space for curvature nor for obliqueness (see, for instance, his denegation of equity, necessity and ambiguity in legal discourse).[26] What he does here is to make the classical understanding of justice apply in a 'universal' manner within the modern apparatus of the State, endowed with force, and indeed taking for granted, as Rousseau, that the modern State ought always to enact legislation that is universally applicable.[27] The classical notion of justice 'to give each his own' is applied in an architectural and 'universal' manner (and pseudo-universalist, *heavily* constrained by the State).[28]

Derrida in turn sustains that strictness is only possible because references to what constitutes the diagram of forces *as such* are excluded (one could well say that it is the violence of the *as such*, the fictionalization between morals and law in this case).[29] The foundation (a moment of non-symmetry and incommensurability) is excluded. It is constitutive but suppressed (and we will see that Derrida departs heavily from Kant in seeing such a foundation in terms more related to force than to morality or to morality itself as force).[30] In order to function smoothly this diagram must allow no differential force, no intensity.[31] Whatever intensity (represented in Kant's system here by morality and internality) is excluded from the functioning of the system. One must be able to ascribe exactly what is the relationship of one to another, of creditor and debtor, criminal and victim, tort and liability. Everything relevant for the legal system must be either already external and exposed or, at least, exposable:

> It is a pure domain of visibility or of theatricality without folding [French *pli*—more on theatricality in the next major section of the chapter]. Even when a certain interiority is convoked ... it is always supposed to be entirely exposable—in a discourse of expressive gestures ... But exteriority is not enough to *found* law [*le droit*].[32]

Moreover, for Derrida, Kant's 'legal' discourse reveals the precariousness of his exposition, his presentation, at the very moment in which it attempts to legitimize itself (and this theatrical presentation of law is epitomized in the discourse of rights, which I will address with Nancy later).[33] In attempting to delimit itself, to constitute itself, it also exposes itself, albeit unwittingly, to the accidental nature of its case, in its pleading for a constitution or a ground.[34] Deciding, assessing, delimiting its own role, the proper role of reason, without renouncing its superiority amongst the mental faculties, is what Kant brings 'reason' to perform.[35] The role of reason, and more specifically in its practical interest, is fundamentally architectural. It stands above all experience (characteristically non-categorical and non-necessary) and above 'lower' faculties (albeit in occasional relations of 'accord,' within judgement in particular).[36] Such lower faculties are the 'passive' pure sensibility (time and space), and the active faculties of imagination and understanding.[37] What Derrida attempts is precisely an exposure of this putatively crystalline conceptual cathedral in which law will have a determinate place.[38]

In Derrida's appreciation, Kant's exposition revolves around an apparatus of multiple binaries, a flourishing rhetoric of differentiations, oppositions, and analogies. Derrida calls it his 'rhetorical-conceptual armature' and his 'discursive machinery.'[39] The very discourse that attempts to be apodictic and differentiated from aesthetic manifestations is itself pervaded with taste, and fiction.[40] It is, in a sense, a creative discourse, apt to employ such mathematic and/or intuitive distinctions between strictness and curvature, strictness and obliqueness, between externality and internality, foundation and non-foundation, which allow room for the distinction between law and non-law. If both morality and law are very well explored in Kant, it is precisely the moment of differentiation and foundation of law that is 'missing' (but one could possibly expand the problem to the foundation of morality itself).[41] Why is moral conscience banished from legality? Why should there be, or why should one need, a strict concept of law? And more radically, more than a question as to the absence of grounds, one could enquire into the very distinction between grounds and non-grounds, the irruptive and creative exception and the norms and normality of law.

For Derrida, following Nancy closely in this regard, Kant's critical discursive machinery is in a very specific sense 'properly juridical.' It raises ceaselessly the question of law, of right in relation to practices and 'facts.' It raises the question of their conditions of possibility. It is philosophy that performs such a task, and not for the sake of actual practices (the practice of law for instance); for they should work irrespective of their grounding or ultimate justification. Philosophical reason needs to *figure* itself.[42] It is necessary for the sake of itself, because it has been lost (dogmatism) or because it has never constituted itself properly. But according to Derrida, in commenting on Nancy, such a founding reason, in an apparent paradox, is only 'properly juridical' if it is excluded from the strictly juridical (that is from the functioning of law itself, from the symmetry that is ascribed to law):

> Juridicism consists here in the limitless extension of the (non strict) form of the question *quid juris* ...[43]
>
> By virtue of this doubling [*quid juris*—what of law—is a doubling inflicted upon all practices associated with law: foundation, explanation, interpretation] the hegemony of the juridical consists precisely in the erasing or even re-treat [*re-trait*] of the 'properly juridical.' Or yet, if the *properly juridical* is absolutely wanted under these conditions, it is on condition that it should no longer be *strictly* juridical.[44]

If we understand this discursive conundrum, Derrida's take on law will be much clearer. On the one hand, 'properly juridical' refers to the pursuit of grounds characteristic of legal practice, or more radically the exposure of these grounds to their abyss. The excess that Kant extends to philosophy—an excess that he makes philosophy appropriate for itself—is an excess 'of' legal discourse as such (and which in turn he wishes to exclude from law, for the sake of the order of philosophy, the higher law of philosophy). This is the excess of appealing to ever higher grounds, and in that restless process—for want of grounds—fictionalizing the ground; 'believing' in the ground, in the constitution, in the ground of grounds, in a higher law. At the extremes of legal discourse, since grounds cannot be simply 'found' and are rather created or fictionalized (in a fragile sense 'founded' or *forged*), the very distinction between foundation and non-foundation is disrupted.[45] The 'properly' juridical (a term Derrida only uses in reference to Nancy), if pursued earnestly, will unveil the deconstitution of law, or more properly, the undecidability between constitution and deconstitution.

On the other hand, in Derrida's (and Nancy's) reading of Kant, the 'strictly juridical' is a function of the containment (or re-treat) of the 'properly juridical' into the well delimited institution of philosophy, in the strict separation between the constituting question of grounds (pertaining to philosophy) and the constituted question of grounds (pertaining to legal practice). In other words, 'the juridical' is betrayed and sanitized within philosophy itself, and away from practical discourses. Philosophy performs the important function of sanitizing and schematizing (from the privilege of its hierarchical place) the world around it; by sanitizing the practical world from access to its own 'grounds,' and creating the distinction between ground and non-ground.[46] The excess of the juridical is thus tamed, or at least contained: 'the hegemony of the juridical [the dominance of the Kantian strictly juridical] consists precisely in the effacement or better in the re-treat [*re-trait*] of the *properly* juridical.'[47]

Law, in this respect, presents us with an extraordinary paradox. At least according to certain traditions—that of the history of judgement, and Roman legal history—legal practice originates and resonates the excess of the 'properly juridical.'[48] But it becomes itself sanitized by the leading (and pedagogic) role of philosophy. That is the case when philosophy takes for itself the role of the juridical. Derrida perceives Kant to have had an influence on the history and institutions of philosophy, but also to be representative of a certain historical moment. Kant's philosophy must be connected with the development of the modern State and its centrality in modern life. The centrality of the State, and almost literally the professorial Chair of State that Kant occupied, allowed for the socio-historical conditions of philosophy's new and forceful jurisdictional role.[49] And how does Derrida perceive himself with regard to Kant's philosophy and its role? What is he, Derrida, doing when *addressing* Kant? I have referred already to the machinery of oppositions that Kant deploys. Once again here lies the crux of the matter:

> As for the 'internal' difficulties of this machinery, when it has the most difficulty maintaining the purity of its oppositions ... they have also become canonical. Such difficulties not only do not hinder the process of propagation of the canon, but endow it with a surplus-value of potency, authority and longevity... .
>
> Deconstruction, which produces itself first of all as deconstruction of these oppositions, therefore immediately concerns, just as much and just as radically, the institutional structures founded on such oppositions.[50]

When Derrida employs 'deconstruction,' he does not destroy or discredit the 'critical' discourse. What Derrida does is to 'follow' Kant's discourse closely.[51] And by doing that, he *exposes* the power of title, its privilege of philosophy and law. He exposes philosophy's power to its grounds, and even to the very fragility of the distinction between ground and non-ground. In philosophy's practice, Derrida finds a concealment of itself behind the exposed symmetry of the practical world, and above all, of law; but deconstruction is also prepared to take responsibility for what it owes to these constructions/structures built upon Kantian oppositions. As Derrida claims, philosophy can be perceived to attach itself to the privilege that it exposes in its self-founding role.[52]

But what Derrida really aims at, with and beyond Kant, becomes much clearer precisely when he tackles law itself in his own terms.

There one can find both the disruption of Kantian structures and a radical fidelity, an intensification of the Kantian transcendental approach (which asks questions on conditions of possibility and which for Derrida were also conditions of impossibility).[53]

3.2 Beyond Strict Law

In 'Force of Law,' one clearly notices the same concern for the 're-treat' of the 'properly juridical,' the excess of grounds. Such a concern must not be confused with a critique of ideology. Derrida did not simply try to show what was hidden in current ideological discourses, as if a hidden power (economic or otherwise) could be always in the background, performing a type of concealed control over whatever can become manifest. He refers to that 'critique of ideology' in relation to the possible interpretations of the works of Montaigne and Pascal. Instead of classifying them as mere cynics or conventionalists (conscious of the contingency and power-related grounds of all legitimating discourses), Derrida finds in them a treatment of the 'mystical foundation of authority' (where in fact 'ground' would have been a more accurate translation of *fondement*). That is, in Montaigne and Pascal's work, there would be in play not a hidden or concealed ground, but the radical lack of ground itself as a violent 'ground':

> The very emergence of justice and law, the instituting, founding and justifying moment of law implies a performative force, that is to say always an interpretative force and a call to faith [*croyance*]: not in the sense this time that law would be in the service of force, its docile instrument, servile and thus exterior to the dominant power, but rather in the sense of law that would maintain a more internal, more complex relation to what one calls force, power or violence. ... The operation that amounts to founding, inaugurating, justifying law, to making law, would consist of a coup de force, of a performative and therefore interpretative violence that in itself is neither just nor unjust.[54]

This very moment of foundation attempts to erase the traces of its own violence by attributing legitimacy to itself (and often a higher authority to itself), and hence, by violently positing the distinction between the founded (its order) and the non-founded, absolute power (itself). As such, this 'grounding' violence attempts to warrant against the risk of being questioned as ultimate ground by attributing further 'unfounded' higher grounds to its order.[55] But it only masks, or delays the 'mystical' limit of its own power and authority (it brings about not a 'mask' of something else, but its own power of deception, its own masks, its own doubling and ruining figuration):

> They [origin, founding, and positing of law] are neither legal nor illegal in their founding moment. They exceed the opposition between founded and unfounded, or between any foundationalism or antifoundationalism. Even if the success of performatives that found a law (for example, and this is more than an example, of a state as guarantor of a law) presupposes earlier conditions and conventions (for example, in the national and international arena), the same 'mystical' limit will re-emerge at the supposed origin of their dominant interpretation.[56]

This issue is essential for understanding Derrida. There is no ultimate assurance of legitimacy, even in the cunning procedure of attributing one's authority (a revolution's) to a previous historical moment, idea, or hierarchical instance. The 'mystical limit' cannot simply be evaded. It is 'constitutive' of institutions and legal systems insofar as every (legitimating) discourse has a limit that is constitutive. There cannot be a discourse or even language without an outside. This does not to mean there is always physical violence in acts of foundation. Rather, it is to say that discourse itself has an inescapable dimension of force that is either material, symbolic, or semantic.[57] The founding act of law, the constitutive act, cannot exhaust itself in an apodictic discourse. Not only does it recur to an outside of itself, but that outside is itself pervaded by its limit. There is here a fabulous retroactivity of legitimation, but, most importantly, the 'mystical' dimension of authority must not be conflated with that process; for what matters is not 'a process,' but the moment which no process can explain in full.[58]

Instead of just a fabulously retroactive process, here one is faced with the force of law as a groundless ground. That is, as a groundless force that constitutes itself as law. The term 'foundation,' also used by Derrida as we see above, but used misleadingly in the translation of the title of the work ('the mystical foundation of authority,' a quote by Montaigne that Derrida reproduces) suggests indeed this historical quest.[59] Yet, 'the mystical' is not located in the remote past; that 'foundation' or 'ground' is rather a monument to its pervasive effects, here and now. The 'ground' of law, albeit often concealed by its own effective violence is in *forceful* play right now.

In Derrida's view, following Kant, this ground has been denied entry into the concept of law, or as he puts it, into 'the essence of law,' even though it is always in play. This 'essence' appears in 'Force of Law' to signify the law in the Kantian and 'strict' sense. This (strict) 'essence of law' expurgates legal practice from the 'properly juridical' (in Nancy's terminology that, to recall, Derrida follows in *Du droit à la philosophie*), from the work of restless 'grounding' (or constituting).

That is, Derrida identifies an attempt to ban the risk of finding out that the distinctions between ground and non-ground, constituting and non-constituting, constitution and deconstitution are not natural or settled. In the Kantian sense, the passage from morality to law is in play in every moral agent's mind, but excluded from the external symmetry necessary to make the system enforceable. Internality would lead to an insurmountable *complication*.[60] Derrida's work on law must be read in that light, in its quality and problems.

Thus, when Derrida says that 'law is the element of calculation' (to oppose it to, but also connect with, the incalculable that justice epitomizes), one must read it against the backdrop of Kant's transcendental critique. Certainly, Derrida also adds much to Kant's notions of strictness on the one hand, and curvature and obliqueness on the other. In Derrida's articulation of law and justice, law is the element of calculation, strictness, and universality; here he follows Kant closely. Yet, justice plays a much more intense role than that of morality in Kant's work. Derrida radicalizes the oblique, the ground that is excluded from the 'essence of law,' so that everything that destabilizes the stable, the ordered (titles and classifications for instance), can be included.[61] In any event, a certain homology between Kant and Derrida on law can be found. I will come back to that radicalization, but for the moment let us pursue that homology.

Even after having established his distinction between law and justice, and comparing deconstruction to justice (and of course after the initial reference to the 'essence of law,' and to Derrida's own work on Kant) Derrida comes back to Kant.[62] He comes back to Kant's renowned distinction between acting in conformity with duty (*pflichtssmässig*) and acting because of duty, or out of duty (*aus Pflicht*); on the one hand, the calculable and conditional exteriority of law, on the other, the incalculable and unconditional interiority of morality. To be sure, justice in Derrida is itself a more radical and pervasive version of incalculability mainly because it is not at all based on subjective free will (*Wille*), that is, a monological use of reason.[63] This justice rather could pertain to an intensity that overcomes or derails decision-making certainty and subjectivity itself.[64]

Most importantly, in contradistinction to Kant, Derrida attempts to complicate the relationship between calculable law (on the order of non-grounds) and incalculable justice (on the order of grounds). His purpose is certainly not to do away entirely with 'the mystical ground of authority [*le fondement mystique de l'autorité*],' but to restage 'it' in a different way. Derrida deems that authority and law cannot be ultimately based on their own 'terms' (namely, structure, procedures, or expectations). Law cannot encompass its own outside, and yet it depends on something that goes beyond itself. In Kant, as I have argued, such a 'mystical ground' is expunged from the concept of law and from his view of legal practice and legal consciousness.

Derrida, on the contrary, does not propose a sharp practical distinction between law and justice. Law requires justice; it requires that which goes beyond any of its determinable 'terms' (and that in a very 'constitutive' manner, it is an internal exigency of law, and not an external requirement juxtaposed or grafted onto law). Justice, moreover, requires law; it requires that which makes itself effective, that which actualizes its incalculable and unclassifiable claim. Law and justice are intertwined.[65] Kant's attempt to sanitize law from its grounds, and such grounds from law, fails dramatically.

The very element upon which Kant aims to define and circumscribe law (force) is, in Derrida's language, another name for that which, *beyond calculability*, pervades law.[66] Force is *differential* and speaks to that which cannot be readily measured and calculated.[67] Indeed, force need not be only actual coercion, as Kant took it.[68] In Derrida's work, force refers also to 'symbolic' power and the violence that language itself conceals.[69] Instead of being a monument to the discernibleness of law from morality, or from justice, 'force' in 'Force of Law' becomes the very restlessness movement that derails all settled distinctions, all safe oppositions in the realm of law, be they Kantian or otherwise.[70]

The *truth* of Derrida's 'Force of Law' appears here. If all law is *forceful* (in a purely etymological sense and bearing in mind the above paragraph), if law is intertwined with justice ('justice inasmuch as law, justice as law'), what after all is the point of emphasizing justice, or stating that 'deconstruction is justice'?[71] The question becomes even more problematic if one considers Derrida's subsequent explanation that, on the one hand, the deconstructibility of law makes deconstruction possible, and that, on the other hand, the indeconstructibility of justice makes deconstruction possible.[72] In this simple opposition nothing seems to be added; one seems to remain purely within the realm of existing distinctions (as in the equivalences between law and calculation, and justice and the incalculable). Yet, as we shall now see, what I omitted in this opposition is absolutely essential.

Derrida claims that law's deconstructibility makes deconstruction possible, but only 'for example' (countless examples could be given: institutions, texts, practices, modes of subjectivity, etc.).[73] With regard to the undeconstructibility of justice, though, Derrida does not add any caveat: 'the undeconstructibility of justice makes deconstruction possible.'[74] Moreover, in relation to undeconstructible justice, Derrida says that it is 'inseparable from' (or, in another possible translation, 'indistinguishable from': *se confond avec*) deconstruction.[75] Even though there is a necessary relation between deconstruction and deconstructibility, it is undeconstructible justice that is indistinguishable from deconstruction. Derrida's enterprise (deconstruction) seems to attempt to locate a form of justice that is minutely extricated not only from law, but from 'justice as law.'[76] Derrida seems thus to carefully favour the undeconstructible over the deconstructible.

However, this preference must be very cautiously appreciated. Were Derrida to push head-on for justice and incalculability he would risk falling back into the errors of 'anti'-metaphysicians, the errors of inverting metaphysical oppositions.[77] On the contrary, Derrida strives to suspend these oppositions and rearrange or reorient them. What remains is not in my judgement a pure preference for the incalculable. That is, Derrida intensifies the incalculable within an already existing set of relations between calculation and the incalculable. In fact he would not be able to intensify 'it,' were it not the case that it, the incalculable, already existed albeit in 'impure' form. Relationally, though, one may conclude that Derrida pushes not for the incalculable as opposed to the calculable, but as I have contended, on the *exposure* of the incalculable, that is, on a qualified incalculable. This is an incalculable that is not appropriated in a system, horizon, or subject: an incalculable that is insubordinate to systems of appropriation and exploitation.

What arises out of my reading of Derrida is not justice, but the justice of *justice*, a more intensified thought of justice (where justice should be read as involving also an element of force, the linguistic-formal element of its own enunciation and given history—etymology—and, more importantly here, a case of paronomasia between justice and justness-adjustment-restriction). As I have maintained earlier in relation to democracy, Derrida does not simply dwell endlessly on aporias. He makes a distinction (albeit implicit) between dwelling on them and not dwelling on them.

On the one hand, there is an order of suffering and exploitation in which the calculable and incalculable are combined by means of the former's exploitation of the latter. On the other hand, there is chance of another move to suspend the terms under which calculable and incalculable are brought together. The justice to which Derrida appeals is an altogether different justice (even though 'altogether different' should be read relationally, that is, in its proposed difference in relation to the juncture of 'law' and 'justice,' in which some form of calculation prevails over some form of incalculability). Derrida's aporias, thus, are elected as a key site of political-juridical-ethical practice and thinking, one that undertakes to disarm the mechanisms that set hierarchical oppositions together.[78]

Moreover, Derrida's identification of justice and deconstruction conceals a rigorous meaning within Derrida's work. There is certainly nothing greatly innovative here, unless in making it explicit.[79] I mean that the very relationship between facts and norms, history and historicity, (historical) revelation and (supra-historical) revelability, order (or structure) and chaos, have all been at the heart of deconstruction.[80] And more importantly the approach that Derrida favours clearly radicalizes the transcendental tradition (Kantian and Husserlian) that has informed his philosophical background. It is not by chance that he used expressions such as ultra-transcendental and ultra-structure.[81] He clearly suspends existing structures, transcendental foundations, valid norms, and claims to revelability by asking transcendental questions, by asking the question what is the law of the law?[82] Let us see:

> Attentiveness to the 'fact' of language in which a juridical thought lets itself to be transcribed, in which a juridicalness [*juridicité*] would like to be completely [*de pen part*] transparent is a return to factuality [*facticité*] as the de jure character of the de jure itself [simply: *comme droit du droit*]. It is a reduction of the reduction and opens the way to an infinite discursiveness.[83]

Thus, without doing away with transcendental practice and metaphysical oppositions, Derrida reinscribes the questions of history and facticity as experiences of radical exposure to im-possibility itself (incidentally one notices how the question of law, and the 'juridical' discourse internal to 'philosophy' appears very early in Derrida's work).

The problem that I am confronting here, however, is that it is no longer sufficient to appeal to the limit that disrupts an apodictic discourse, be it legal, democratic, or otherwise. With regard to democracy, Derrida certainly tackles that democratic transparency (enlightened and self-satisfied), but also a more difficult question of 'light': democracy's autoimmune exposure to its own incompleteness, and more than that, to its own 'roguishness' or corruption—today, here and now. As for law, it is also possible to redescribe Derrida's work to show, as I have been doing, that there is also a more radical exposure in play. Yet, there are serious strategic issues that undermine Derrida's approach to law, and more specifically to modern law, democratic law, the law exposed in the practice of democracy.

There is thus a significant difference between these two approaches, namely, to democracy to come and to justice. With regard to democracy, Derrida's starting point is the tradition of exposure, it is democracy as such as a tradition of exposure, which comports in itself the *to come*, but whose *to come* can and must be intensified in light of so many limitations to democracy as currently experienced. This intensification is not being proposed by contrasting it to democracy, but by reinventing yet new distinctions and rearrangements of oppositions. Such rearrangements expose democracy more radically to 'its' 'to come,' particularly beyond the self-satisfaction of exposure, including contentment with the impossibility of full democratic exposure, that is, self-foundation and self-legitimation. If there is dissimulation, it is always our dissimulation, our indulgence in a fiction that 'we' involved in the democratic process can reinvent (and not at all suppress).[84]

With regard to law, Derrida's starting point, or, more accurately, Derrida's main reference point is a tradition that still dissimulates the groundless ground of law from juridical practices and discourses (certainly not for being unaware or unrelated to that groundless ground, but for receding before the abyss, and finding refuge in the fortresses of subjectivity and rationality: underexposure rather than non-exposure). As just seen, the Kantian tradition precludes the oblique, the complicated, and the unruly ground of law (morality) from entering the fully external/exposed legal world. By definition, in affirming self-foundation and self-legitimation, the modern democratic tradition has exposed itself to its own impossibility; it was nurtured by 'constitutional exposure,' and even in a mode of overexposure.

Conversely, the modern legal tradition, and most prominently Kant, could operate within a broadly subordinate field and transfer questions of legitimacy through an overloaded doctrine of separation of powers.[85] The latter isolates questions of grounds within a particular social sphere—the political—which itself is also ruled, or at least informed, by laws. In this way, democracy would be profoundly undermined and rendered meaningless if law did not go through the experience of exposure and the chance of overexposure as well. The problem is not that it does not, but how to dwell in there instead of harking back to underexposures.

I have articulated Derrida's understanding of law and justice in relation to his opposition to Kant's concept of law. Derrida is not satisfied with the Kantian rhetorical machinery that posits a law well extricated and delimited from other domains of communication and interaction. Derrida strives to make justice (parallel to Kant's interiority) happen, at least as a referent, in legal practice and legal decision-making. But by claiming the coming of justice, Derrida also dwells at the point where the strict separation between law and justice is exposed, and ex-posed, disseminated in their mutual contamination (in their differential exposure). Derrida, thus, is not only attempting to praise and expose justice (the incalculable and ground of law) against the law (the calculable, the founded, whose grounds must be found outside itself). He is also engaging in the more radical work of emphasizing justice over a space in which justice already occurs (albeit in a way compatible with the prevalence of calculation, constitution, systems of exploitation, and exclusion).

He puts forward a justice of justice, and not simply the law of the law (justice), for such a higher ground of law can still be contained by the very distinction between law and justice. The exposure of the differential contamination between law and justice should debunk—or open the space for such a move—any complacency with both 'law' and 'justice' as they are. Derrida's implicit move is beyond a 'strictness' that is never simply 'strict'; that is, beyond an already existing articulation between 'law' and 'justice,' which would be implemented by virtue of an opposition. With *justice* Derrida strives for a form of legal overexposure (here exposure reaches a moment of excess in which the experience of exposure, the experience of exposure to the 'mystical ground of law,' is generalized and experienced beyond current power formations and complex structures of exclusion and exploitation).

In the next section, I will further pursue the possibilities and impossibilities of constitutional exposure; facing a still adamant underexposure that pertains not quite to simple concealment of 'the mystical ground of law,' but to its knowledgeable and subjective containment. Is Derrida's strategy adequate to fight this containment of 'constitutional exposure,' (constitutional exposure may yield either under- or overexposure), and to actually depart from the experiences of exploitation and suffering that the 'law–justice' distinction condones? Does Derrida not borrow too much from Kant, and hence concede too much to a model that is eminently underexposed? Is the discourse of exposure furthered by taking the Kantian model of law as modern law's main paradigm?

3.3 Strategic Predicament

In spite of Derrida's apt identification of a law of law in the 'mystical ground of authority,' and in a way in justice itself, it is necessary to assess the possibilities and impossibilities of yet another push in the drive to exposure. Derrida has enquired of a law of law, but the conditions of possibility and impossibility of that law have not been addressed; that would amount to a further 'transcendental' question. Moreover, demand for such questioning is also strategic. I shall argue that contemporary discourses and practices of law and democracy have exploded or at least challenged the troubling effect of Derrida's 'constitutional exposure,' in other words, the exposure of the law of the law. For that purpose, I shall address the work a modern-classical jurisprudential author, Michel Villey, in showing a forgetfulness of philosophy in Kant. Villey's work also raises the question of the modernity of law, which is essential to addressing Derrida's legal predicament.

An ultra-transcendental investigation on Derrida's law of law should yield a double bind of exposure. On one hand there is underexposure, a retreat of exposure at the height of exposure to the abyss of grounds. On the other hand, there is overexposure as an insistence on dwelling on the abyss, on the limit of grounds, on their im-possibility. The former is compatible if not complicit with hierarchies and exploitations of the experience of the exposure to the abyss of grounds and the otherness that is constitutive of it. The latter is not compatible with hierarchies and exploitations of such experiences, for it maintains the chance of a general and equal enjoyment of the exposure to the groundless. As previously seen, I side decisively with the latter. Here I argue that Derrida's approach to law, because of current legal transformations, is problematic, and that it does not correspond to the cogency of his approach to democracy.

There is one predicament in Derrida's legal theory.[86] That is its point of departure, 'law is not justice,' 'law is the element of calculation.'[87] Is there not an element of justice that must figure as part of the 'concept' of law (not as a mere terminological-scholastic dispute, but as a description of legal practice)? Or better, is there not an element of justice that should belong to the understanding of law as a social institution and a set of discourses and spaces? There are, though, several approaches convenient for addressing this predicament: one that may be described as a modern reconstruction of a pre-modern world view, and another that should be described as the problem of the radicalization of modernity.

In that first approach one could claim that Derrida's Kantian starting point indulges in 'forgetfulness of philosophy of law' (forgetfulness of the case by case task of judging what is good or equitable law).[88] This is the approach of the legal historian and philosopher Michel Villey. I do not exactly espouse Villey's view, which is broadly based on a pre-modern approach, or more properly on a modern appeal to a reconstructed pre-modern world view (a reconstruction of Aristotle's law, Roman law, and of the Thomist approach to law).[89] If Villey's approach may be applicable to Kant, it is not quite applicable to Derrida. But it raises problems that Derrida's engagement with justice does not resolve.

For Villey, Kant's philosophy crowns a forgetfulness that was characteristic of the school of Natural Law.[90] In its positioning of law on the grounds of abstract principles, such a school took away what is most dear to lawyers: judgement on the right condition of sharing. Since some form of sharing is always happening, and since it is always in question in a legal case, the 'lawyer' becomes the artisan of sharing.[91] Villey is correct to affirm that Kant's strictness was never able to explain legal reasoning. A few years later another classicist came to offer invaluable proof of that, namely Chaïm Perelman.[92] The deconstruction of Kant's 'strict' approach to law does have a role inasmuch as that stricture has also located itself in the doctrine of the separation of powers, on the one hand, and, on the other, has paved the way for an antihumanistic reduction of the scope of legal practice.

Yet, in Villey's work, in order to succeed in its 'light and open art,' jurists should proceed in an essentially descriptive and observational fashion.[93] Legal practice (*jurisprudence*) consists in 'the understanding [*connaissance*] of human things.'[94] The entirety of his approach seems predicated not so much on what may look like a fundamental distinction between description and prescription, but in fact on the belonging of jurists in a polity, their acute sense of certainty,[95] the sense of a 'sharing' that in spite of concrete conflicts was already defined in the research of a concrete form of 'life.'[96] In spite of the failure of this 'return' to the ancients, it added another layer of complexity to the modern legal system, and should not be disregarded.[97]

There is in this light at least another take on the predicament of Derrida's legal strategies, pertaining at once to a historical and epistemic question, and that is whether Derrida's point of departure does not disregard the fulfilment of modernity (post-modernity, hypermodernity, late, or liquid modernity, depending on theoretical subtleties and affiliation).[98] A similar point is whether, in current social and theoretical conditions there is not a certain trivialization of justice-based discourses (discourses of legal flexibility, obliqueness, and rhetoric).[99] The modern (or post-modern) awareness, if not cynicism, is by default debilitating, including the awareness of what Derrida was putatively trying to disclose, namely the blind spot of the Kantian model of law: justice. It is not that law is deemed to be just, but that justice is trivialized; that is, legal actors know that justice ought to be mobilized, and it is, at least in theory or in rhetoric, but its effects in bringing about any change are null. Justice can become trivial, legal actors become cynical. If Derrida were read as attempting to bring about exposure, the exposure of a hidden 'justice,' then our reading would have to face an insurmountable difficulty (exactly at this juncture my two discursive layers—interpretation and intensification—meet).

Yet, in my appreciation, Derrida does not strive to expose hidden 'realities.'[100] He rather attempts to expose the conundrums of exposure itself. In other words, he tries to reactivate the ground of law that is neither legal nor illegal, and the force, source, or unconditionality that makes law and justice. If democracy is brought to the fore, one may say that one has thus a clear and ultimate ground, namely the people as ultimate foundation, transparent and exposed to itself. To be sure, though, a 'transcendental' question may be asked yet again and 'the people' of democracy will offer good reasons to justify their allegiance to their own powers. A law will be called upon yet again, and the structure of the 'mystical foundation of authority' will be reclaimed.

This apparently mysterious expression, 'mystical foundation,' or mystical ground, means simply this: a force (problematically called a performative by Derrida) that by definition cannot be referred to the order of any law. This force's manifestation depends on nothing apart from itself. It simply manifests itself. Yet, historically, this 'manifestation' will involve certain conditions, circumstances, explanations, and hence the question will once again be referred to an anterior act. This 'fabulous retroactivity' cannot, though, explain fully and finally the creation of a new order.[101] Even in recourse to a higher principle, the ground of authority has to ask one's trust or belief in its representativeness, in its embodiment of a given higher principle.

One cannot escape entirely from this mystical ground. The moment of foundation or the ground call forth both law (a higher law) and that which overflows all law, an eventful act of faith. This very structure of the act of foundation is in turn transposed to the realm of more quotidian legal applications and decisions. And that is achieved through the distinction between law and justice (such a transposition, rather then that distinction, makes good sense in the history of legal theory).[102] Law dwells within the realm of calculation (following ever higher norms). Justice dwells within the realm of the incalculable; it calls upon a decision that will never be satisfied with given legal options.

Yet the question that I have been asking and that here becomes crucial is whether there is anything special about the claim of democracy as a ground. As I have argued, one should not be so enchanted by the democratic powers of exposure. Democracy to come certainly requires a call to what is still unheard-of in the task of exposure that already takes place in democracies. However, as I have argued, democracy to come is not simply a Derridean argument; it is already happening. Democracy blurs or begins to blur the lines, and the laws, between the public and the private, the visible and the invisible, the citizen and the foreigner. And the legal system is not unaffected by the democratic experience. I have already referred to many examples of reinterpretations of the role of law throughout the twentieth century. Even Derrida is aware of recent transformations within law, but these do not seem to have an impact on his take on the Kantian scheme.

Derrida is aware of legal transformations, for instance, in his identification of the shift from a language of 'rights of' (*droits de*) to 'rights to' (*droits à*).[103] 'Rights of' pertains to the more settled civil and political rights that can be safeguarded by the 'simple' inaction of the State. This is the area of negative freedom: the right not to be unlawfully arrested, taxed, seized, etc., the right not to be tortured, enslaved, molested, and so on. 'Rights to' are already inscribed in the 'possibility' of 'rights of,' but are certainly more pronounced in a time of social, economic, cultural, and environmental rights, requiring positive action of the State and other powerful actors.[104] Democracy indisputably plays a role in this shift.

Moreover, as I have argued, Derrida does not pursue a strict separation between law and justice. In every corner of his writing he also shows how calculation is necessary, how 'justice' and 'law' depend on each other.[105] Derrida does not simply seek to expose justice, but to engage and 'locate' justice, the unconditional and the mystical foundation within the sphere of modern law (including through the aporias of making decisions). And by juxtaposing calculation and the incalculable, he strove to make them coexist without reconciliation in the medium of a 'differential contamination.' But he could well call the latter a law (*loi*) in the sense of an experience of differed and differing relations.[106] Indeed he went far beyond strict distinctions in his own performance as writer, a performance that goes even beyond performance (beyond the expectations of audience-readership).[107]

However, one can still argue that the Kantian starting point is not helpful in the task of radical exposure, and that Derrida fails here in his own strategic game, particularly in a time when all Kantian distinctions seem to have been blurred already; when, in spite of all that tradition, the complexity of law seems to be exposing and acknowledging its own predicaments, and even its own unpredictability (albeit in a mode of control, but here is the problem, one of taking advantage of the unpredictable in favour of exclusions and exploitation).[108]

Democracy and indeed even deconstruction, as enjoying the right to democracy, have been fundamental in the process of transforming law.[109] Yet this task is far from complete. Too many obstacles and forms of stabilization and hierarchization of law and democracy remain. It has been my contention that it is necessary to continue along the process of democratization and intensification of democracy and its process of exposure to, of, and within law (law here broadly conceived, including orientating distinctions and the modern legal system).

In spite of Derrida's luminous approach to democracy, his initial and strategic approach to law is only helpful to the extent that the Kantian scheme still required some deconstruction; and in fact does not take into account, unless in passing, the deep impact of democracy on law, as a legal system. The more accessible layer of his writing assumes law in general as if it were always necessarily the Kantian law and hence fails to realize the (post)modernity and 'democraticity' of law. That is, if Kant is the architect of the modern legal ideal construct, such a construct has been since then—and since Kant's work itself—in flagrant ruins, and especially since the legal transformations of the early twentieth century (for which the judicialization of politics, the politicization and pragmatism of courts, the rise of the powers of the executive, the de-generalization of the legal form and the commodification of legal discourse are key elements).

Certainly, Derrida's approach to law is more salutary precisely where the grounds of law are indeed well established, when the fundamental force of law's foundation and/or the continuous exercise of legal force are properly concealed or at least well justified within an acceptable narrative or discourse (better still, as I argued previously, underexposed). The work of unsettling the borders and distinctions between law and morality, law and justice, public and private, national and international (and so many other organizing distinctions which Derrida aims to expose), makes sense when such distinctions are well 'in place.' What happens when they are not, or when they are no longer 'in place'? Does Derrida's task of unsettling such distinctions until finding their ultimate grounds (until finding the groundless, the abyss of grounds) coincide with their most eloquent effacement? Is Derrida part of this final push of modernity towards its self-effectuation? Or is Derrida correct in insisting on this unsettling task precisely because the modern project of self-foundation and break with the past cannot by definition be fully realized ('realize' as 'causing to happen' and as 'becoming aware')?

With qualifications, I tend to respond all these questions affirmatively. Certainly Derrida's work is not simply a result of its historical time, but it cannot be extricated from it either. Indeed, Derrida's move towards a complex exposure, a constitutional exposure as we have seen in earlier chapters cannot be extricated from its modernist drive. It does not disqualify and in fact adds to discourses of emancipation and liberation. However, Derrida tends to emphasize the limitation of the modern project of self-foundation and, above all, self-legitimation (at least on a symbolic level, on the level of accepted justifications). Derrida thus discloses the limitation of modernity. Despite all the advances and clarity, and exposure of our institutions, there would still be an unaccountable mystical ground of law.

Yet, my argument is that contemporary discourses and practices of law and democracy undermined the troubling effect of Derrida's 'constitutional exposure,' in other words, the exposure of the law of the law; in particular the type of democratic discourse that Derrida himself engages in, that he engages in not only with 'democracy to come,' but with deconstruction itself as occurring within a democratic context.

We are already living in a time of exposure. The contemporary time is one in which 'the secret' is increasingly no longer a novelty. That is to say, exposure no longer challenges, troubles, or changes anything, at least not as much as in Kantian, pre-democratic, pre-deconstructive times; and that is why a constitutional exposure is so relevant, a more radical exposure of the suffering that the current controlled exposure engenders. To some extent, society has been living with uncertainty (and it is often a painful experience, especially for those who feel excluded, marginalized, or exploited), learning to dwell on the limits of sociability, with democracy, in a word—but in a way that is compatible with new hierarchies and forms of social exploitation. In this regard, there are mechanisms that sustain the hierarchical system despite the unruly structure of democracy, despite the institutionalization of restlessness through democracy and the exposure of the groundless creativity of the people.

3.4 From Acknowledgment to Exposure

In order to consider the quality of exposure and to approach a jurispudence of constitutional exposure (expositivism), or a truly democratic jurisprudence, I shall bring to the fore the insightful works of Johan Van der Walt in legal theory and Jean-Luc Nancy in the discourse of rights. I seek to bring Van der Walt's jurisprudence to its limit in deconstructing the underexposure found in its theory of legal acknowledgment, but not without retaining its gesture towards common exposure. And with Nancy's discourse on rights, I suggest an example of the theatricality of law, as a playful moment of law, to be enjoyed in exposure.

Van der Walt attempts to deal with legal incompleteness and the experience of violence felt irrespective of whether legal or governmental decisions have been deemed legitimate or illegitimate. Considering judges or institutional bodies always have to take decisions that to some extent harm plurality itself, for being always particular, and do not have access to an unproblematic notion of the public good,[110] Van der Walt asks himself what is the measure of an acceptable and ultimately democratic (post-apartheid) jurisdiction. He formulates thus the way in which some of his interlocutors put the question:

> Does deconstruction's general reference to the violence of all linguistic economies not deprive us of a criterion for distinguishing between violence in the strict sense, that is, violence that is normatively speaking unacceptable, and other forms of harm that do not call for normative condemnation and intervention?[111]

Even though the framing is broader here, from this starting point he ultimately sets out to distinguish between legitimate and illegitimate violence, bringing about what I call the 'acknowledgment thesis.'

With regard to an analysis of the role of Dworkin's Herculean judge (with whom 'any ambiguity in the law can be expelled so as to find the right and single answer to every legal question'),[112] he formulates a cogent response to that problem:

> The Dworkinian understanding of law turns on a vertical imposition of the one and only applicable ruling in the case, from below or above, that is, on the basis of underlying or overarching normative principles. This vertical imposition of the ruling in the case does not allow for horizontal depth of space in which two or more valid claims to justice can continue to co-exist *alongside* one another, despite the fact that the ruling must *set aside*, at least for now, one of the competing claims to justice. The normative understanding of the law does not tolerate this kind of legal ambiguity. Its vertical imposition of the correct ruling in the case simply dismisses one of the competing claims to justice as mistaken. Everything turns here on the distinction of *setting aside* and *dismissing*. The dismissal of a claim to justice expels that claim from the ongoing process of the law. It allows it no place in the future of the legal system. The inevitable setting aside of a claim to justice, on the other hand, keeps that claim in play. It thus keeps in play a plurality of voices in the ongoing process of the law. This is what the understanding of law as sacrifice sets out to do. It seeks to turn the law on its side. It seeks to horizontalize the verticality of the normative understanding of law. It does so by stressing the need to acknowledge and explain the sacrifices required in the ongoing process of the law. The acknowledgment of sacrifice is, after all, a concession that the one from whom sacrifice is demanded is not wrong. The acknowledgment of sacrifice is also a concession that justice cannot be done under the circumstances. [113]

This passage goes a long way in demonstrating what I mean by the necessity of a further *exposure*. First, I share Van der Walt's deconstruction of the vertical imposition of the normative type (here another instance of a Kantian architecture in the shape of an ideal model and an ideal procedure at work in jurisdictional settings, even though I suspect there is a vertical instance at stake in this Post-Apartheid legal theory as well). I also share the purpose of distinguishing between setting aside and dismissing, in so far as the latter implies a degree of disrespect or disdain to a legal claim (which by definition should be granted respect). Secondly, however, one can wonder about the 'one only' correct ruling, when Van der Walt has rightly made explicit, in a subsequent passage, a fundamental point: 'the fact that the judge can only select one answer at a time.'[114] That is, irrespective of one's take on legal pluralism and legal cognitivism, the key is how to make and how to treat a decision that, if it is honest with itself, if it is truthful to itself, should strive intensely but finitely (or provisionally) at producing the best answer to the given legal problem. One could also speak of the antagonistic framework of the question here, which does not take into account various ways through which a legal decision is *shared or negotiated*.

If I could I would also discuss the use of the term sacrifice, which is here rendered coterminus with law itself, and thus erasing the possible tension entailed by the title *Law* and *Sacrifice* (my emphasis). Van der Walt quite aptly presents the theory of sacrifice and its location at the border of the sacred and the profane, and of language itself. In my view, even if all *facere* (making, doing), and 'human-animal' action were sacrificial (but I can imagine with Nancy a time without sacrifice), this would not allow for calling any law or any legal decision sacrificial any more than it would allow for calling any human activity sacrificial, like fishing, bathing, eating or brushing your teeth.[115] Nothing in any case excludes that *certain* decisions, as those that Van der Walt presents, could be considered to reproduce the sacrificial operation.

The situation of exception is also contemplated. It is brought about by a sovereign act, and partly Van der Walt follows Agamben here (and in this passage it works in the background) as a situation in which sacrifice is still at work, albeit in a way that is suspended and unacknowledged, and rendering the anomic feast somehow tantamount to the apartheid regime. But a view I share with many other theorists is that there is no exception without law, and not without exposure, for exposure is always in play, be it in a form of exclusion, exploitation or indeed acknowledgment (I would even risk this Clausewitzian formulation: regardless of the effectiveness of its suspension, the juridical order remains in the exception 'as law by other means').[116] But sacrifice is not the crucial point—I will refer to violence instead—as everything turns on acknowledgment.

The distinction between acknowledging and not acknowledging 'sacrifice' becomes the key, and in the passage above it gets translated into the distinction between *setting aside* and *dismissing* a claim. But the problem centres on the *position* and the closure *of* acknowledgment. It is revealing that in this passage the one who acknowledges does so from a position of 'concession.' It is the position of authority, kept in that way, conceding but *reserving* itself and its higher status. Moreover, it is also acknowledgment itself, which contains etymologically and pragmatically the self-closure of knowledge that is misleading, so far as it also furthers and certainly does not undermine the *authority* of the State.

Make no mistake, the exposure that I put forward closely follows

Van der Walt's 'acknowledgment thesis.' However, it aims to bring it to its most radical fruition. Clearly the purpose of acknowledging decisional violence is to set aside a claim, letting it remain within the realm of legal-political discourse, 'right now,' without recourse to a futural change in the law or improvement in jurisdictional methodology (even though the reference to future in the passage above may be misleading as to the general purpose of his work). I share this concern. Acknowledging, though, even more than a concession, has a role very similar to a confession, and it betrays in fact the original meaning of the verb 'to acknow.'

So, after we have confessed we have committed an offence, we are ready to obtain forgiveness. Knowing our predicament is a first step to controlling our anxiety and repressing our desire to respond, respond to an injustice, respond to the restlessness of the im-possible people. Substituting exposure for acknowledgment bears witness to more than a terminological difference. It is the difference between integrating a claim into the legal system (acknowledgment) and cultivating a space between the system and those for whom the system has failed (radical exposure). *Setting aside* here makes apart without the settlement of a knowledge of place and position, and rather requires an exposure that invokes a horizontal respect without hierarchy *on the back of the law*.

In my view 'acknowledging violence' runs a serious risk of hierarchizing the relevant claimant and her claim. As it were, it includes her when she should not be included (it sets apart but reintegrates her into an economy of knowledge, and possibly state knowledge). And including her, at least for that terrifying moment, is unthinkable and unworthy, in a way that inclusion means undermining her own capacity to keep pushing and struggling for *her universal* view of justice (always paradoxically singular-universal) to become applicable to herself (concrete). When one *acknowledges* the polity's violence, the lost party becomes a particular detail in the self-realization of the grand destiny of such a polity and it allows no space for a different universality to be shaped.

If, in contrast, the decision-maker were to seek the correct but allegedly fallible and concrete decision, with due diligence, be it in a demi-God fashion (like Hercules), or a humanist renaissance fashion, and indeed the more open and transparent the decision-making process the better, the exposure would appear of itself. For the void of groudlessness does not stem only from violence as such, but from the void of fallibility (in a way, finitude) itself, which is anterior to violence (or anterior to the definition of violence and nonviolence). Democratic legal practitioners should *expose* and *be exposed* not only to the legal system's indeterminacy but also its provisionality, its fallibility, its creative democratic groundlessness.

Here legal actors are called to let be that which exposes itself in the closure of a legal decision. They should justify a decision but not 'over-justify' it. They ought to leave a space open for legality's fallible finitude to show itself. A decision ought to be justified at the limits of the justification of the universality or the justice claimed by the constitution itself. That means to let the paradox of paradox happen: let the clash happen between the universalization of the given constitutional setting (always the universalization of a singular force) and the universalization of the new claim (also a singular force), which should be played out in ways that are *not* under the control of a given legal order, and hence open to come and unsettle given hierarchies, exclusions, and mechanisms of exploitation. Thus, this exposure each time differently and continuously depends on the exposure to the ground-making groundlessness, which involves the inevitability of violence. Indeed, not only of the individual decision but of the whole constitutional *scene* (for there is always the possibility that ascribing the problem of injustice to the isolated norm or decision could preserve absolutely the constitutional order itself). This is not a regulative ideal or hope that in future the claim will be integrated. Rather, it means allegiance to the democratic openness of a society that ceaselessly raises the exposure of its own dwelling at the borders of inclusion and exclusion, liberation and exploitation. It also means making public the justifications given, the pursuit for a right decision, and eventually calling for a change in the law,[117] and contributing to the quality, changeability, and responsiveness of the democratic debate.[118] This would be the answer to the problem of 'legitimacy' of state violence ('sacrifice' in Van der Walt's terms, or its capacity to claim justice successfully): a constitutional exposure. If this 'constitutional exposure' fails to fail; if it has no openness to 'failing better' (or, in Derrida's terms, to perfectibility); if this exposure is radically contained, but never destroyed, by various forms of exploitation; then this experience will not be worthy of the name democracy, such as during South African apartheid or the Brazilian dictatorship (military rule between 1964 and 1985).[119]

Furthermore, in the thought of constitutional exposure, in democratic law, legal actors are called to be responsive and to heed the theatricality of law. After all, every legal uttering (every *juris-diction*), be it a claim, an opinion or a decision is also an address to, a salutation to the other. This care for the other, this courtesy, ought to be maintained by all parties. And this is so that exposure as overexposure, a common exposure to equality can happen.

As previously seen, the sustained exercise of a certain divisibility is crucial for democracy; found in a way through the intensity of the affirmation of justice in general, but also through the intensity of affirmation of justice that the form of rights instigates. There can be no democracy if not through a process that Derrida called autoimmune, in which democracy is threatened by that which in itself threatens not only its subsistence, but the very notion of a self, of an identity, of a turn to itself. One of the elements for the sustainability of this process is the notion of rights. They have, though, in themselves a structure that can replicate the underexposure of identity and constitutiveness in play in certain images and concepts of law and in the sovereignty of 'the people.' Allow me to take a detour through Villey and Nancy (excursus I) and through Brazilian constitutional history in order to lead back to Van der Walt (excursus II).

Excursus I: Composing Rights

I refer to Nancy to rethink right in a more divisible sense, exposed to its own autoimmunity, to what deconstitutes itself. It is in an old text of his that I find such treatment of rights, 'Lapsus Judicii,' which addresses the lapsus (the slip, accident or case) of judgement. This text influenced Jacques Derrida himself, in his discussions of Kant and the juridical law. The essence of law, Nancy states, is its accident, its case, the fall and failure to reach the fullness of the foreseen law of statute or precedent. That accident happens in the vicarious saying of law: 'right says, it does not operate. It does not "produce" ever anything other than itself—or anything other than the fiction of its identity in the permanent mobility of its case-law.'[120] I could reaffirm the initial expression 'right says,' with 'right claims' in order to emphasize the intensity of the legal claimant as we shall shortly discuss, but here Nancy refers to the etymology of jurisdiction (the saying of who is right, who is entitled to what). The incisiveness of such a claim/saying does not bend to any given power (jurisdiction has its own timing and spacing, it cannot be fully foreseen or circumscribed), but gets bent only to itself, to its own creation, its creation in tandem with legal and political action. Such is also what Nancy calls 'the right of what is by right without right.'[121]

The problem of modern law, though, is that 'right' has become a 'part' of the legal structure. Law as a whole has furnished a model for the State, but without the above vicarious reference to what saps law and rights from within. Thus reducing or controlling the 'case' as the difficult 'structure' (and not derived directly from the State) of the legal experience. Let us check more closely this reference to a 'without right':

> One knows well that law [*droit*] does not cease to furnish the model and ideology of the bourgeois State. But it did so with one condition, that is

hypostasizing juris-diction, making it an Essence and a Sense—at the cost of forgetting or repressing its 'essential' lapsus. It is hardly surprising, then, that the State engenders a sometimes open, always latent revolt over the right to say—the ultimate demand of the right to say the right of what is by right without right.[122]

Modern law abandons its lapsus, its accidentality, which is also that which constitutes itself. It abandons a certain inoperativeness constitutive of law: 'the juridical act, hardly an operation.'[123] 'Right' is, thus, not inscribed in a programme or coherent totality, and its enunciation is pervaded by the uncertainty of every new case in a precarious relation between claimants, the judge, the generality of the law and the novelty of the concrete case. His main reference to law and the accidentality of law and rights rests in Roman Law:

> By right, the law should be the universal code whose definition even implies the annulment or the reabsorption of all accidentality. The case should be foreseen. In fact (but this fact is constitutive of law—it is the fact of jurisdiction) right must be assigned and legitimated case by case.[124]

Roman legal formulae are referred to implicitly as the means through which a strictness of determination may be imposed as pervasive forms of legal practice (they are the ancestors of universal rules). And yet these formulae have to be enunciated by legal actors who make their figures (as persons, etymologically involving masks) felt by the legal structure precisely by engaging in those formulae. In spite of their existence as formulae, they can only become effective and concrete law if they are taken upon, repeated.[125] Here, even before any error, or explicit innovation, the case, the incident, the factual 'falling' of a person (and the making of a person) within the formulaic net is already a type of accident that belongs to the essence of law.[126] But more than that, the rigorous formulae are not immune to transformations, and Nancy refers to the relevant use of legal fictions in Roman Law, which effectively, by means of variable repetitions introduce slight changes in the formulae which mean significant changes in the law.[127] And in the use of fiction within the theatricality of the law (persons in their spoken and written 'parts'), 'rights' cannot create an entirely new space or world for themselves; at issue, rather, is an assignation of the 'right' sharing amongst the parties involved in relation to an existing wider world.

While Michel Villey wrote—in relation to how Kant represented the moment of modern philosophy's forgetfulness of law—of the juridical (shared) as opposed to the legal (imposed); for Nancy, what takes place here is the forgetfulness of accidentality in the imposition and definition of law by the State (and State philosophy), and the somewhat naïf, if not hypocritical, assumption of judgement by a discourse of philosophy blinded or simply aloof to the problems of its own accidentality. Nancy's work complements Villey's earlier indictment of Kant.

But the issue of rights, and the transformation of right from an assignation of what is due to each party within a legal-political-ethical world, into modernly subjective fixed freedoms and faculties (social and civil rights) or State-societal programmes (social rights) can only be well understood in addressing Villey himself. The whole language of forgetfulness of accidentality, the notion of rights as sharing in contrast to modern rights as fixed impositions, and legal fictions as fictions with the world (and opposed to poetry, *Dichtung*), and the theatrical metaphor are all reminiscent of the great French legal philosopher of the 20th century and they all appear in Nancy's text, which indeed refers to Villey on the characterization of legal 'subjects' in Rome.

For Villey, the classical experience of law is the fine observation of reality (discerning carefully what is 'proper' to each one within a given polity), and benefiting from that observation, the careful discernment of 'the good and equitable sharing'[128] in each singular conflict of interests. The law is never created *ab nihilo* (in fact, the concept of law [*loi*] is derived from a much later theological confusion); it is rather a flexible experience whose end is justice. Justice in turn is defined through Aristotle ('particular justice'), Cicero, and the writings of Roman jurisconsults as a matter of the right sharing: 'the office of the judge—more generally the jurist—tends to sharing—the best possible—of goods, debts, charges, and honours amongst citizens (especially amongst claimants).'[129]

Villey emphasizes, thus, the practical aspect of law, as opposed to any attempt at deductive coherence; and indeed, what is crucial here, its horizontality (whether historically accurate or not, the judge here is an equal to the parties). At issue, in any instantiation of legal practice, is the pursuit of justice, defined as above. But it is a 'justice' pursued and created out of experience, guided by practical experience:

> Born of experience, always submitted to the control of experience, Roman Law does not present itself as a finished edifice—as a logical ordering of implacable and fixed rules, a 'science,' in the strict sense, or a 'normative order.' [Roman Law] is a research, a life.[130]

For Villey, as I have already pointed out, the main task of legal actors and of the jurist is to find out the right sharing of goods, things, or honours. For Nancy also, there is a sharing at stake in the jurist's relation to the world. He puts forward a marked contrast between poetic fiction and juridical fiction (the Roman legal fiction is also a theme explored by Villey). Nancy affirms that in poetic fiction, 'the poet [*Dichtung*] composes a world: by definition, the casual or accidental "structure" is excluded'—here poetry 'produces itself the unlimited field of its production.'[131] Moreover, it says something about its actors (who could not even be properly called actors for they do not undertake a shaping or *figuration*): 'poiesis/poetry presupposes the sovereign autonomy of its subject.'[132] But the proper actorness of the juridical world sets another tone (or paints another picture of the matter)—these actors *compose* something 'with the world.'[133]

With regard to juridical fiction, Nancy notices a crucial fictionalization of the legal actor himself as actor, exposed to the game of the law. Such actor loses its 'substance' in its enunciation, in its playfulness as actor of a 'theatre' in which 'he,' the actor, can only be understood, and understands himself only as a mask, a *person*. He first states that it is a 'subject,' but one who 'is worth less as substance than as capacity [*puissance*] for "action and claim [*prétension*]" ... less through its presence than through the contours of the area which defines its figure and its identity: the outline of the *persona*'[134] (and its theatricality is clear here: 'this capacity itself is artificial and theatrical'[135]). But later he claims that the legal person 'is the reverse of the subject.'[136] What matters here is that 'law proceeds always by delimitation, localization (what he refers to as an area), that is, by dislocation. What arrives/happens [*arrive*] to the subject is dislocation—the limit of its own figure.' And this limit, this incompleteness, fragility and accidentality open up the possibility of sharing.

Finally, we come here to the crucial question of the relationship between the thoughts of Nancy and Villey with regard to sharing. I have already referred how crucial sharing is for Villey's view of law: 'the concept of law presupposes a plurality of persons amongst whom takes place a sharing of exterior things.'[137] But Nancy's notion of sharing is much more complex; it includes the sharing of an 'areality' (a contour, a spacing, or space-making, but also fiction and non-reality) that troubles itself and exposes the separation between fiction and supposed reality (the drive towards substance, autonomy, freedom of a subject). Legal persons thus share their own troubled dislocations. They share themselves in exposure to a void which cannot be ultimately rendered present to itself.[138]

Yet, it is undeniable that Nancy, with the reference to '*composition*' and sharing cannot avoid referring to the law of the city (in a broad sense of the laws of sociability) to something that already is. Otherwise his distinction between 'composing a world,' and 'composing with a world' would not hold.[139] In these references to all the uncertainty and flexibility of Roman juridical practice, there must be a reference to the spiritual unity of Rome itself as an idea full of meaning and symbolism. And he is very open at one point in a footnote, the only point in the whole text in which he uses the expression sharing [*partage*] in relation to the Roman juridical experience. Here he tries to show how Rome differs from totalitarianism, but his admiration for Rome shows something crucial:

> Rome has tried—within the enclosure of its limes [Latin for limits, but also track or traces] to constitute the juridical unity of an internal network of limits, borders, and differences. Ultimately [*à la limite*]... it would be necessary to say that law sanctions or signs differential sharing/divisions [*partages*], whereas the State reabsorbs them, having transformed procedure into process (organic and historical).[140]

This passage is crucial because the juridical order that Villey and a certain Nancy admire (the juridical order that figures as the originary scene of modern law) is well situated, beyond its flexibilities and uncertainties, within the unity that is proper to itself, the unit of the Roman city. Certainly, this type of juridical order permits a healthy distinction between State and society, but this is not necessarily a reason for emulation (after all, the model of law here is one that involves a significant, for modern ears, 'private' element, a private or independent justice). In principle, what Nancy refers to in the passage above is not at all uninteresting, but the sharing and distinctions which that order lets thrive are not the limits and borders that invite more differentiation, a sharing of accidentality of differentiations.

Without at all espousing Villey's nostalgia, it is important to realize the difficulties of utilizing the Roman model. As Villey has argued, the work of the Roman jurist is essentially one of observation and description. His role is not at all to be involved in discussing the good laws (the task of political actors), but to 'research' into what currently is law. Drawing also from Aristotle (to whom he attributes the first realization of the role of law in discerning the good sharing), Villey believes that the task of the judge should revolve around divisions 'previously established.'[141] Moreover, these previously established distinctions can be really well established, constituted (and underexposed) as such before the law.

The most dramatic case of this underexposure, of this lack of exposure to the precariousness or accidentality of law is the sharp distinction between 'public' and 'private.' The issue here is that the world of the household (including relations between slaves and slave owners, pater familias and children and wives) is fundamentally settled as irrelevant to the law, and hence to the differing and flexible world of legal persons, fictions and figurations: 'over his little rural dominium, over all things of which he is owner the *pater familias* possesses a complete and exclusive mastery.'[142]

In this light, assessing what the law stands for and deciding on the basis of previously existing divisions means to legally entrench given hierarchical scenes. In the works of Derrida and Nancy, legal decision-making and legal discourse as a whole must attend to a different impetus and, in a way, a different strategy. The form of sharing here must include a reflection upon what cannot entirely be shared. The exposure of legal actorness must not long for the originary moment of the enjoyment of legality as enjoyment of the clear distinctions between the political and the legal. As we can see, actorness in Villey—as in many other instances of legal theory—is predicated on an epistemic isolation of the law from other social domains, and, within the law, an application of a form of sharing that is decided elsewhere. With Nancy, though, despite the same admiration for Roman legality, what shines forth is the exposure of the legal actor irrespective of his mask in the dehiscence of his diction: a *composition* happens.

It is precisely this epistemic isolation of law that the thesis of acknowledgment reproduces, albeit in the process of attempting to supercede it. There life itself gets appropriated by the verticality of the one who knows the law and applies, magnanimously, to the one who does not. The law-giver is unscathed. And it is precisely an insistence on the exposure and 'composition' of those who bear rights and share them in claiming together-against each other, beyond the contours of settled distinctions, where the opportunity lies for what I would call an expositivism.

Excursus II: Right Carnival of Democracy

Be that as it may, what remains is the figure of the exposed legal actor, artificial and theatrical, who, to rejoin Van der Walt and be faithful to his injunction to contemplate the horizontality of citizens, perhaps should also change habits and expose themselves to the plurality of voices and social spaces. A true judicial responsiveness should not fail to open space for the claimant who brings to the court of law all the world that she bears. On the side of the State, democracy requires that there be space, listening, and response to that. It requires legal actors, despite their professional duties, who may also relate on a one to one level with each other *as if there were no State or hierarchy above them*. This legal aesthetic expositivism should be a jurisprudence of democracy informed not only by a democratic paradigm or episteme, but also by an acute democratic sensitivity: a democratic *understanding* of the law (where understanding introduces a sense within legal knowledge itself and debunks its standing, deconstituting such a standing from within: under-standing).

This type of 'carnivalization,' albeit improbable or surreal *happens*. It is thinkable and it arose in Brazil at a key juncture of the democratization process. In 1985, Luis Alberto Warat published his notorious *Legal Science and Its Two Husbands* book, which contained a strong, albeit aphoristic, condemnation of legal science and education in Brazil. Its concern was a liberation of legal thinking from repression and self-repression that impeded a more convenient and properly democratic orientation:

> The first decisive trait of a carnivalized discursive practice goes through its self-positioning as a semiological democratic order ... in a carnivalized signifying process there are no safe grounds for defining the place for one and the other. We are before an open version, a democratic version of the world.[143]

Yet, Warat's view of canivalization is mainly epistemic, despite opening up epistemology: 'carnivalization as an epistemological place would be only and always the place where the sign of the new can be detected. It would always be the arrival point of the new that comes.'[144] So there is little about a carnivalized view of the courtroom, of litigation or even legal interpretation. There is a hint, however, as to how such an approach could be brought into relation with the systemic position of law and the ethics and the politics of the courtroom:

> Democracy traditionally bound to law—in the strict limits of the liberal view of the world—is presented as the historical realization of the Democratic State, which should secure itself as such through the instituting mechanisms of the 'rule of law' [*Estado de Direito*]. This expression means principally the necessity to make law-enforcement, the application of law into the cornerstone of democracy. In this way, in the juridical-liberal conception of democracy, political order is reduced to the legal administration of the State's power. Conversely, the carnivalized version of democracy will open itself to the space of creation of the law. Whereas the juridical-liberal conception of democracy shows instituted rights, carnivalization invents, or better, shows the possibility of inventing them permanently.[145]

In the dawn of a new democratic beginning in Brazil (1985 is the first year under civilian rule after 20 years of military dictatorship), Warat calls for the carnivalization of democracy through law, as a practice of legal creation that knows no settled boundaries, and the carnivalization of law through a novel conception of rights dwelling on its own singular reinvention. Irrespective of the fate of Warat's thought in Brazilian legal academia, this mode of thinking had a concrete bearing on what has been characterised as the judicialization of politics in Brazil. Warat's approach must also be studied in the context of the emergence there of 'alternative law jurisprudence,' the association 'judges for democracy'[146] and the lively social movements that around that time took a rather radical view of the possibilities of the law in the new democratic context.[147]

Yet, this line-blurring, albeit important, can hardly be transformative if the indistinction in hand is not radical enough to the point of challenging deep-seated structures of thought and knowledge that account for an exclusionary and exploitative social system. As we shall see in the next chapter there are certain structures of sovereignty and futurity still in play, often in subjectivity, in statehood and even in social movements that hinder the fuller exposure that is at issue here. Politics has already been judicialized, law has already been politicized. But that is insufficient to challenge prevalent hierarchies. In-distinction, decisionlessness, or characterlessness are key realizations but do not go far enough without a true democratization of social spheres, in the sense of a sensitivity to the common productivity of exposure that can happen either in a mode of exploitation or in a mode of true fuller exposure or overexposure.[148] In other words, despite appealing for democracy, the truth of that period and the one we live in today, in which the Supremo Tribunal Federal has become ever more active (with lower courts and individual magistrates following suit), is rather a form of indistinction between law and politics, and with it, between law and various conceptions of justice.[149]

This contemporary condition renders any attempt at distinguishing law and justice untenable and un-strategic from the outset. Moreover, getting to the point of knowing and acknowledging this system's failures is to stop short of avowing its deconstructibility, perfectibility, substantial innovation, and joyful fruition. It is an allure of sovereignty that is still in play under the form of subjective knowledge and hierarchical apartness. The claim of rights and its common sharing (and sharing of division), though, hint at how a legal-democratic avenue (claimant-centred and not judge-centred) can be put forward so as to challenge current combinations of rules-justice and to expose in the courtroom the fruition of a binary horizontal relationship between actors facing the experience of systemic injustices. In other words, one ought to bring to its ultimate consequence the horizontality of which Van der Walt speaks; it can only derive from a *sense* of equality in the experience of claimants and as such it is *politically* universally applicable: to all and to state actors themselves, implying fidelity to democratic decision-making processes and a radically republican and egalitarian approach to judicial proceedings.

In these excursus I have shown how constitutional exposure may be described in a way that avoids the conundrums of acknowledgment and the settled sharing characteristic of Roman Law in Villey's appreciation. I have also put forward Nancy's right theatricality, supplemented by Warat's carnivalized view of democracy, so as to open a door to the gate of the law and let the call of people be heard (the people of rights): an exposure of democratic law, an exposure of exposure.

༄

So, to pursue a 'democracy to come,' from an emancipatory perspective, *comes* with a background that is already exposed, towards an overexposure. But Derrida, in particular, fails strategically when he treats justice initially as foreign to law: as democracy is always already the doing and undoing of exposure, so is law also always already the doing and undoing of justice. What is necessary is not justice in law, nor justice against the law, but a law *to come* with a new articulation of rules and justice, calculation and the incalculable, exposing the whole of the constitutional setting and the legal practitioners' exposure to exposure so as to challenging current ways of securing a society of exclusions and exploitations, without closing the system to the rules that will render it prone to its criticizability and fallibility.

Law in Derrida is not approached with the force of democracy in the background. It is law in Kant's architectonic construction, and hence opposable to justice, in which justice is still lurking in the background, the elusive ground of both decisions and law as a whole. This structure is problematic not only because it fails to take into account legal transformations, but also because it fails to account for the historical effects of democratization itself. Not democratization of the self-founding type, but democratization of the autoimmune 'type,' from which self-foundation cannot escape. With democracy to come what *comes* to the fore is not pure clarity, but the exposure of the absence of an absolute ground, and exposure of the plurality of fragile grounds. And this structure cannot fail to be transposed onto law as a legal system. Otherwise one risks at best undertaking a huge effort to achieve what we already have. At worst one risks merely fuelling more and more of the same: the consciousness of impossibility, the consciousness of the groundless, the 'acknowledgment thesis'; when this consciousness helps reconcile what was previously irreconcilable.[150] Certainly, deconstruction itself is key to the disarmament of this 'consciousness,' but this cannot signify that Derrida is immune from feeding into the structure of consciousness (here an element of underexposure).

My contention, rather, is that what Derrida calls law (and the fixed rules he implies in there) is already intertwined with justice. And this is neither good nor bad, but our epistemic condition. The mystical ground is no novelty anymore, and it is becoming trivial.[151] This situation may be seized upon and such an epistemic condition itself should be challenged as precisely what sustains the continuation of an open, fluid, and restless order of exploitations. I mean that there is still a task of exposure, that this 'epistemic condition' is precisely what contains the true restlessness of the democratic plurality of grounds or the constitution of democracy.

Constitution (or the constitution of deconstruction) itself requires a thought of law; but not law opposable to justice. Rather, law itself, as democracy, should be here an undecidable, thoroughly 'touched' by the experience of aporia. Democratic law should thus be ready to be enjoyed, played with, and eventually mobilized against the ways through which the experience of law's aporias is appropriated and fixed into complex mechanisms of social exploitation. Beyond the law of the law, Derrida himself begins to unfold the law of the law of the law, a law of exposure within a world of exposures (underexposures), an overexposure of the law. Here I call it 'a law' for it is a choice of fidelity to a certain firmness; a distinction indeed, but a novel one, capable (but also open to its failure) of reinventing a commitment to emancipation and to emancipations, and with a necessary distinction between underexposure—the truth of our time—and overexposure (in radical fidelity to the equality of experience of law's aporias). This novel exposure can only impact upon 'constitutional exposure' itself; that is, no longer upon exposure qua clarity, but exposure qua putatively pure fragility as well; even though, there should be always a preference for, and an emphasis on, the disarming, disrupting element of exposure, deconstitution, and justice.[152]

This overexposure (and the specific expositivism or democratic understanding of law is here part of this general effort) is an attempt to localize and generalize the enjoyment of the 'event of the impossible,'[153] an event that is most conspicuous in the contours of im-possibility in Derrida's own work, and conspicuous in Derrida's practice of writing that exposes himself, his own limits, and not only concedes but practices the impossibility of fully mastering the matter of exposure. In the next chapter and in my final conclusion, I pursue the still uncanny 'perhaps' of another strategy and another vocabulary for the deconstructive treatment of law and politics. It is a contribution to another form of postulating democracy to come. This is one that takes issue with the strategic predicament in Derrida's work, not only in relation to law, but also in relation to his distinction between two unconditional exigencies: that of sovereignty and that of the 'to come.'

In this chapter I have addressed Derrida's treatment of law. I have thus discussed law as a key element in Derrida's discourse of democracy 'to come,' understood as a discourse of 'constitutional exposure' and pointed to the avenue of a legal expositivism. I have argued that 'constitutional exposure' of law and with law means also exposure of exposure (as in democracy), and, more than that, that Derrida's work gives a prominent role to 'the law of the law' and justice, severely disrupting the conceptual economy of classical works on law, particularly Kant's. For that argument I have revisited Derrida's main texts on law.

However, I also claim that there are strategic problems in Derrida's treatment of law, one which refers to Derrida's own insufficient attention to the societal conditions of juridical law and to developments in legal theory. The question is a transcendental one, which he has always applied so well to other theories, but which would be beneficial in relation to deconstruction itself. I argued that it is necessary to use, in relation to law, the same strategy that Derrida used for democracy. In other words, this means the identification and intensification of a current practice of negotiation, of a current practice of exposure to incommensurate exigencies. Moreover, I have shown that legal theory ought to take full account of the democratic experience, to the point of challenging structural hierarchies that taint even discourses that take into account and include justice, indeterminacy, and obliqueness or even the *acknowledgment* of violence. I also provided an instance of a radical democratic experience of law, based on the divisibility and shareability of exposure in and to rights.

Here I have sought to intensify a desire that can be found in Derrida himself (albeit limited by the Kantian starting point) and in Nancy. This is a desire towards the general and equal enjoyment of the aporias of law in its theatricality—a careful enjoyment, thus, of the 'mystical ground of law,' of the law of the law, of exposure itself—towards constitutional exposure as overexposure. In the next chapter, I put forward an intensification of the enjoyment of the aporias of the 'to come' itself.

Democracy's commendable role is not, following Derrida, to finally legitimize a society, to make society reconciled with itself. As seen previously, democracy's main task should rather be to sustain irreconcilability: challenging the authority of its own grounds, exposing its own groundless violence. But the challenge that Derrida set for democracy faces the containment of certain structures of thought and practice that are at work in both democracy and law. These structures have the names of sovereignty and futurity.

— 4 —

'TO COME'

The constitutional discourse of exposure finds a crucial expression in the phrase 'to come,' which plays a fundamental role in Derrida's work, and not only in his late publications. Throughout this chapter, I continue the analysis of an element of 'democracy to come,' the 'to come' itself. Such an element confirms and further enriches the understanding of the phrase 'democracy to come' as importing a discourse of constitutional exposure. I will now expand and further develop it with the purpose of articulating a postulation of constitutional exposure apt to integrate explicitly the 'to come' with 'democracy,' and to further intensify 'democracy to come.' With this aim, I argue that Derrida's distinctions between 'to come,' on the one hand, and futurity and sovereignty on the other, are not the most conducive to a richer and less hierarchical enjoyment of the experience of democracy.

There are interesting indications of the use of the phrase 'to come' in works as early as *Writing and Difference*.[1] It also appears noticeably in *Of Grammatology*.[2] Moreover, Derrida's engagement with Blanchot, in the text 'Pas,' which I shall be examining, provides many interesting elements.[3] In addition, one may benefit from Derrida's reading of Kant and the Book of the Apocalypse in 'On a Newly Arisen Apocalyptic Tone in Philosophy,'[4] not to speak of the pieces we have seen earlier that further develop the 'to come' towards the philosopheme 'democracy to come.' In spite of all these references, it is important to focus here on just two crucial distinctions proposed by Derrida. These distinctions will structure my approach to the different instantiations of Derrida's 'to come.'

I shall refer first to the apparently straightforward distinction between the future and the 'to come' (see ch. 4.1). Then I shall refer to a second distinction between two types of unconditionality, or two types of incalculability, which can be for the time being equated to sovereignty, on the one hand, and unconditionality without power, on the other (see ch. 4.2). The latter is a difficult distinction, and it could easily fall back on the terms of the earlier one. Through this second distinction one can perceive what I call a difference within the 'to come' itself. Yet, the terms through which Derrida sets up this distinction are, in my view, insufficient. One must construe such a distinction within the magnitude of the 'to come' in another way. That is, one must differentiate, albeit fallibly, between different forms of articulating constitution and deconstitution, underexposure and overexposure (see ch. 4.3). Finally, I shall give further evidence of the possibility of reading sovereignty as an exploitative conformation of the 'to come'—exploited or tortured 'to come'—for which the analysis of the political consequences of fear is crucial (see ch. 4.4). In sum, I argue for the adoption of a more 'radical' version of the 'to come.' Moreover, I develop Derrida's insight about the abuse of power that exists in sovereignty towards a notion of the detrimental exploitation of the 'to come,' in contrast to the opportunity for a more sustainable and continuous way of engaging with the 'to come.'

This second distinction intensifies Derrida's postulation for democracy to come. We have already foreseen such an intensification in the discourse of constitutional exposure, but its intensity reaches another level with this radical appraisal of the 'to come' as facilitator of overexposure. This is a postulation to radical deconstruction, to the exposure of exposure, democracy of democracy, the 'to come' of the *to come*. This postulation bears the trace of an interpretative intervention in, and a contribution to, Derrida's work. My approach to overexposure fleshes out Derrida's 'performance,' as opposed to his merely stated meaning. Let us then start where an understanding is most urgent: the reductive nature of the future, in its constraining of the 'to come.'

4.1 Future and 'to Come'

In 'Force of law,' Derrida refers to an infinite 'idea of justice' (*idée de la justice*).[5] By referring to an 'idea of justice' in inverted commas, Derrida distances himself from this very attribution of an ideal character to justice. Yet, it is important to refer to it, for the Pascalian reference to justice is not in fact distinguishable from law (*droit*). Derrida claims that what Pascal tried to show in the passages discussed in 'Force of Law' was, in fact, that a system of administration of justice requires force, that is, Pascal would have used 'justice' instead of law.[6] This very use of justice as law has a meaning; indeed in the direction of ascribing moral authority to that which is, essentially, a matter of force.[7] Here, it is an 'idea of justice' (not justice itself) that can trouble the settled and institutionalized practices of law–justice, 'present justice.'[8] And what the 'coming' of this infinite 'idea' of justice does is that it shatters this present justice's presumption of certitude. According to Derrida, the affirmative character of this 'idea of justice' 'seems indestructible' and cannot be contained by any theoretical rationality.[9]

Before I explain the full and rich consequences of this rejection of both the knowledge of justice and its rational-theoretical character, let us briefly investigate the messianic (pertaining to the 'to come') nature of this 'idea.' One may legitimately enquire about the relevance of 'justice' to the 'to come.' Derrida makes this relationship indisputably extant by explaining the infinite dimension of this 'idea': 'infinite "idea of justice"; infinite because irreducible, irreducible because owed to the other—due to the other, before all contracts, because it has *come*, the *coming* of the other as always other singularity.'[10] This can be reinforced by what is said of the messianic itself. The 'idea of justice' is made distinct from 'whatever content of a messianic promise.'[11] That is not to say that this 'idea' does not contain a messianic element: 'for any messianic *form* [my emphasis] is never absent from a promise, whatever promise it is.'[12] With this in mind, one can be more aware of the weak messianic structure of this 'idea' of justice, and its relation to the fundamental notion of promise.

Yet as I have already noted, all these passages refer to an 'idea' in consistent inverted commas. Even when complicated in subsequent writings, Derrida's rejection of this 'idea' as a regulative idea is explicit (not only the Kantian architectural one but also the more naïf or trivial use as a counterfactual standard).

This 'idea' should not be contained by 'theoretical rationality'; it should not be theoretical and its urgency 'bars the horizon of knowledge.'[13] In fact, Derrida ceases to refer to 'it' as an idea, and starts to say simply 'justice.' The problem with a theoretical rationality, with regulative ideas, and with messianic contents is that they all belong to a *type* of horizon; type in the constraining sense that these instances always pretended to 'absolute privilege and irreducible singularity.'[14] This futural type of horizon involves waiting and the determinateness of a moment of waiting, a degree of submission to the power of horizons, even if one's position may in fact be restless or uncertain. That is, such a horizon can provide some putative certainty and insurance against the undecidable nature of all decisions (to include here not only the plurality of possibilities of decision, but also the incalculable affirmation that is by definition heterogeneous to any rule and any calculation).[15] Yet, the mastery of the horizon over the waiting is detrimental to the urgency of justice.

Given its urgency and debunking of the horizon of expectation, justice 'has a "to-come"' (*avenir*: its normal translation would be future indeed, but Derrida is playing with the idiom 'something/someone has a future, is promising, worth noticing,' but modifying it from *avenir* to *a-venir*, from future to 'to-come').[16] Moreover, Derrida states that 'to come' should not be confused with the future, even if, as we have seen in the French, this is not unambiguous. It is important to bear in mind that, in Derrida's discourse, the future would mean a 'modified form of the present.'[17] It would mean that the temporal dimension of the 'to come' is being used in a way that is not unforeseen and unheard of, equivalent to the future. In addition, the future also trumps the spatial and relational dimension of the 'to come,' the coming of the other, the standing before the other, whoever, or whatever comes: 'the future loses the openness, the coming of the other.'[18] So justice has a to-come; it is profoundly marked by a promise of that which is not present, and presented without the security of the present. It yet happens here and now, urgently; it *comes* and lets one/something *come*.[19]

Admittedly, the 'to come' also requires a determination, a calculation. Justice cannot dismiss the prosaic necessities of daily life. So that justice can happen, it requires primarily an unconditional and incalculable affirmation. But for justice (or better, law) to be sustained, it requires primarily calculation. Yet, there is a difference between calculation and the *typical* horizon of knowledge (*type* involves a drive to absolute determination). Without suppressing the 'to come,' such a horizon does conceal it. This horizon is the very veil under which the 'to come' is underexposed. (As I shall discuss, however, the way forward in view of this predicament is not always unveiling; in fact, the very game of veiling and unveiling may be problematic; and, in its intensification, this 'game' pertains to the modern predicament itself). And calculation involves a simpler determination, whose unconditional is justice itself and not the absolute type of attempted control over the future. So far the distinction between future and 'to come' may seem unproblematic; we shall shortly complicate it. The figures of the future may be more cunning; let us examine other experiences of Derrida's writing.

Futures

Another explicit distancing from future or ideals can be found in the treatment of the 'to come' in *Rogues*. In that work there are extensive references to democracy, which are invaluable. Yet, my concern here pertains more directly to Derrida's approach to the problems of ideals, horizons, and the future, which affect inter alia his take on democracy. He proposes three main reasons why the application of 'regulative ideas' is reductive.

First, Derrida is concerned that the ordinary use of regulative ideals tends to make practical action too constrained. The ideals that express a 'possible' and 'desirable' future as a measure for practical action are determined in advance in a grammar of possibilities (that of the 'I can'). That is, ideals are determined and fixed through the very process that defines possibilities. Here one has to make reference to the etymology of 'possibility' marked by the early Latin contamination between the verb *potere* (can), and the first person singular of the verb *essere* (being), that is *sum* (I am), which brings to the fore *possum* (I can). These roots are carried forward into the abstract noun 'possibility' (with equivalents in many languages), which imports, from its etymology, that which can become of the order of being of the 'I.' The grammar of possibility is precisely that intense becoming and inclusion into the living order of the 'I can.' It is the colonization of everything that there is into an order of control. A possibility that 'guides,' an ideal in the vulgar sense, can only mean the control of the infinite range of lines of movements, of 'coming' (or becoming) of time; the time of open and dangerous living (and dying) that is usually called 'present.'

The 'to come,' on the contrary, is *im-possible*. That is, the 'I' cannot control the coming of the other, and the lines of becoming 'of' itself through the other. The other that/who comes cannot be circumscribed by a horizon that authorizes its coming. *Im-possible* does not mean that which cannot happen, rather it imports that which may or may not happen, that which is not by definition inscribed into an order of control. Such a control settles the plurality of what exists, and withdraws it from that dense and sensitive urgency that a careful scrutiny of everyday life brings to light. According to Derrida:

> This urgency does not allow itself to be idealised, not more than the other inasmuch as other (the other is the site of a perception of difference that, as border between one and other, can only be idealised by means of inclusion and reduction into the order of control of 'the one'). This im-possible is hence not a (regulative) *idea*, or a (regulating) *ideal*. This is what is most undeniably *real*. And sensible. As the other.[20]

We learn, thus, how the coming of the other requires an im-possibility irreducible to horizons of power.

Secondly, Derrida insists that the responsibility for any decision cannot be reduced to following a rule (and for this, a more thorough account can be found in 'Force of Law').[21] That dense and sensible urgency of everyday life is forever disclosed in difficult situations of decision-making. The way through which the practice of the 'to come' must be informed involves a hesitation in decision-making; a decision should not be reduced by any assured knowledge. That hesitation is pervaded by undecidability, that is, pervaded by the extent to which a decision is irreducible to calculation and automatism. Derrida claims that an effective and responsible practical decision is not knowable in advance. It would be destroyed if such an advanced knowing were at all possible. This development closes the treatment of ordinary uses of ideals (for my treatment of law, see ch. 3).

Thirdly, Derrida addresses the more technical use of 'regulative ideas' in Kant. Derrida's treatment of Kant's regulative ideas is elusive at this point, even though further information can be found in the second part of *Rogues*.[22] Regulative ideas such as the world, the soul, and God are authorized by what Kant calls the regulative use of reason. Reason is in turn the highest faculty of the mind, capable of providing a unity to the representations and concepts of the 'lower' faculties (sensibility and understanding). For Kant, reason strives to attain ever higher levels of universality, and is by definition architectural. In Kant's critique of metaphysics a constitutive use of ideas such as God, world, and soul is precluded. A constitutive effect is attributed, for instance, to the pure forms of sensibility, time and space, which constitute the phenomenal world (that is, as it appears for us; the constitutive moment is experimental). Attributing a constitutive role to these regulative ideas (God, world, and soul) would jeopardize Kant's entire project of delimiting reason, that is to say, a self-limitation of reason. In any case, by virtue of precisely such limitations (reason cannot prove the existence of God, for example), an unconditional element is introduced—unavailable to proof—operating effectively, even though not avowed as such, on the dimension of reason's creative power.[23]

Derrida's concern is understandable. Admittedly, Derrida is enthralled by Kant's use of the unconditional: reason strives to achieve the unconditional, giving itself comfort and reassurance by finding a resting point. Derrida is also fascinated by Kant's use of the 'interest of reason': an interest in not contradicting itself, and interest in its architectonic structure.[24] However, this unconditionality seems at once too fragile and too strong. Too fragile for the unconditional elements that Kant seems to reach, God, the self, the world, have all been historically challenged. Derrida himself has striven to explain the deconstructibility of images of 'the self' and 'the world.' These unconditional ideas indeed may seem rather too facile to reach. Because they are too fragile, and prone to deconstruction, they have to *assert* themselves unconditionally. I shall argue later that this notion is at least problematic.

These ideas fit well into architectural designs and self-legitimation efforts. They impede the true unconditional move, without content, the pursuit of the unconditional itself, that is the pursuit itself, its very faith as unconditional, and a feature of reason (not of ration, proportion, calculability, but a feature of reason that constitutes that space of articulation of the calculable and the incalculable that Derrida calls 'the reasonable').[25] Here the difference between the 'to come' and ideals, in particular the Kantian regulative idea, becomes somewhat similar to another distinction, that between two forms of unconditionality, which I will address in the next section.

There is other 'evidence'—rather implicit than explicit—that Derrida distinguished the 'to come' from the future. It appears in *Of Grammatology*, hence involving an adherence to the language of the 'to come' at a very early stage of Derrida's trajectory. In the exergue to the 'book' (beware that Derrida problematizes the very notion of the book, and 'his' books),[26] Derrida characterizes his enterprise as

> the erring of a thought faithful and attentive to the world irreducibly to come [à *venir*] that announces itself in the present, beyond the closure of knowledge. The future [*avenir*] cannot be anticipated unless in the form of absolute danger. It is what breaks absolutely with the constituted normality and cannot be announced, *present* itself, unless under the genus of monstrosity.[27]

This encapsulates beautifully a great deal of what I have argued under this heading.

Yet, this 'coming' to which one is faithful and attentive seems to have always already happened.[28] One could ask, in this light, what is the purpose of this enterprise after all. The reference to the closure of knowledge offers us the clue. Later, towards the end of the first part of *Of Grammatology*, Derrida refers to the difficulties of articulating his new thinking about *writing* (to include the material trace, the imprint that leaves impressions and not a metaphysical, teleological, or systematic monument). This thinking or thought (*pensée*) must be seen as a bare minimum index for an epoch *to come* (as we have seen, this is to say that in its difference from what is constituted, it is already coming), the timing of *différance*.[29] It also means that even the minimum of coming is still something; and constitution, a choice, a position, albeit fragile, as argued before, is not entirely overcome.

This formulation of the relationship between 'thought' and 'to come' matters in combating a certain way through which the normality of knowledge is constituted, but not all constitution as such; and despite the emphasis on the erring of thought, the to come of a deconstruction. Derrida reinforces the elements in the life of knowledge that cannot be reduced to its 'normality,' elements too elusive and restless. They include passion, affection, sensibility, and above all that unlocatable sensibility to the other in its difference and deferral (neither the sensibility of an organ, nor the skin, nor the central nervous system, nor the individual, nor a memory, but all of them, inasmuch as affection-action happens).[30] It challenges the present, in its very *presentation* and sense of presentation, as that which the present cannot embrace.[31]

The enterprise that Derrida set out for himself and pursued ceaselessly was to discern the elements of the present that constitute it as normality from the elements of the present that open up themselves to the *to come* that is already taking 'place.' In other words, he aims to identify the different forms of 'coming,' especially those that deny or underexpose themselves (by attributing a fixed content, *strong messianism*), on the one hand, and those that expose themselves and experiment with their coming (often referred to as *weak messianism*), on the other.[32] He has always claimed that the distinction can never be assured.[33] But the very fact that Derrida insists on this ultimate lack of assurance betrays his similarly constant attempt to propose a fragile distinction. We have seen clearly an example of this effort to distinguish 'future' and 'to come.'

I have maintained that Derrida distinguishes between 'future' and 'to come.' This distinction is an index of a general distinction between a sense of the 'to come' that underexposes its very coming, through the closures of the architectures of knowledge and power, and another that affirms and revels in its coming. Yet, this apparently simple distinction displays some elements of a more complex distinction between unconditionalities themselves, in a sense within the very exposure to the joy of the 'to come.' For there may be a form of revelling in the 'to come' that subjects it to abuse, overwhelming it, sapping the conditions for its very enjoyment (that is, an abuse from within the realm of the 'to come,' not the simple future). I maintain that this more complex distinction is needed to redescribe the contrast that Derrida proposes between sovereignty and unconditionality (what he also calls two types of unconditionality: unconditionality with power and unconditionality without power).[34] That is so that sovereignty cannot be securely placed within the realm of the future at all. There is an important 'coming' element in sovereignty itself.

4.2. Two Unconditionalities

One must be careful here to distinguish the present concern from the earlier one. They are only delicately different. To be sure, in some ways, especially through the analysis of Kant's regulative idea, one can perceive the unconditional at work in some representations of ideas. If one were to conceive of other horizons, such as those of messianism, one could also perceive the impact of the unconditional in a way that is not without power or sovereignty. This is my concern here, the unconditional, and the risk that the unconditional may be appropriated and, as it were, abused; the unconditional at work for the sake of the exploitation of the 'to come.' Yet, there are more trivial and automatic 'applications' of the future and other horizons without any significant or perceived impact of the unconditional. These 'applications' take place from within a sovereign order, that is from within the concealment or denial of sovereignty itself, even though these borders between inside and outside the sovereign sign are very fragile (the experience of syllogistic rule application, for instance). A judge or a police officer cannot totally do away with the possibility of repetition giving rise to alterations, and this, in many ways, speaks for the possibility of justice, and of transformations in spite of dire legal-political conditions. Yet, their practices tend to conceal, unwittingly or not, the role of the unconditional (the 'to come' is underexposed, or the moment of constitution is putatively settled).

Rather, in this section, I speak of all those who do break away from the major framework of constituted normalities, those who experience and sustain a drive of unconditionality, who expose themselves to the 'to come' (through decisions that bring about change in the law, practices that challenge settled conventions, movements and discourses that disturb the good conscience, common sense and authority of previously established orders). Once having experienced it, wittingly or unwittingly, there are those who are faithful to the unconditional and those who are not. This distinction is also elastic, 'those' cannot be defined as persons or groups, but as situations and flows, series of continuities and discontinuities. Those who are faithful will by definition challenge inherited traditions and settled norms.

The major ethical-legal-political experience that expresses all these elements is that of sovereignty, an experience of the unconditional, of faithfulness but also of abuse, and misuse; hence suffering and ultimately lack of sustained enjoyment. For Derrida, there must be a distinction between practices that deny or conceal the 'unconditional,' and practices that embrace the 'unconditional.' Conversely, my attempt to intervene in Derrida's work involves discerning practices whose 'misuse' of the unconditional takes the shape of an exploitation, and in a sense of the containment of the unconditional (much more subtle than those practices that simply deny or 'conceal' the experience of the unconditional, which I would equate with 'ideals' and future).

This type of 'abusive' practice does not quite destroy or suppress conditions, but inscribes them into an apparatus of exploitation/exclusion (see above discussions on the wheel, the wall, and all the hierarchic binary machines of sociability).[35] Let us try and understand Derrida's approach to sovereignty (or unconditionality with power). Naturally, emphasis is given here to the latest characterizations of sovereignty in contradistinction with 'pure' unconditionality, since earlier elaborations would require a more nuanced and extensive reading to discern what exactly Derrida meant by sovereignty in any given instance.[36] We shall start therefore by focusing on *Voyous* (*Rogues*), 'The University without Condition,' and 'The Animal That Therefore I Am (More to Follow).'[37] Later, in subsequent sections, we shall arrive at Derrida's seminars of the years 2001–2 and 2002–3, 'La bête et le souverain' ('The Beast and the Sovereign'),[38] and also come back to some older texts, such as 'Pas.'[39]

One may wonder if Derrida really deems sovereignty an experience of the unconditional, or if sovereignty is not taken in itself as a blunt and automatic denegation of unconditionality, a force that simply reduces or conceals the scope of the 'to come.' I argue, however, that, for Derrida, sovereignty expresses an unconditional drive and cannot be easily dismissed. Derrida explicitly tried to distinguish between sovereignty and true unconditionality, precisely because sovereignty and unconditionality are 'very close.' Here Derrida does not offer many clues, but it is the beginning of the explicit treatment of this distinction:

> I would raise, I would distinguish, a thought of the unconditional, such as I have pursued here and there for a long time, and distinguish it from a thought of sovereignty. The two are very close, sovereignty and the unconditional. But there is an unconditional that is without power, while sovereignty ... remains a theological legacy. And thus, to this inherited theological fantasy of sovereignty, I would oppose an unconditionality without power. And it is there, in this 'without power,' that I expose myself to the event, to the arrival of an event for which no performative is ready.[40]

This passage attests to Derrida's concern with the proximity between sovereignty and unconditionality, but it does not quite clarify the distinction (he says that he proceeds too quickly in this text). As Derrida demonstrated a number of times, sovereign acts, the acts that created legal and constitutional orders, cannot be easily described as performative utterances. A manifestation of sovereignty, of supreme power, is not containable by the circumstances and conventions of a situation. It cannot at all be judged on the basis of any previous or higher order or principles; it hence overflows 'the performative.'[41] We will have to find further elements in other texts.

Even though without a direct reference to sovereignty, in 'The Animal That Therefore I Am (More to Follow)' Derrida grants unconditionality to a certain power, that is the power to name (this can be put in contrast with what we saw earlier that true unconditionality is one without power).[42] The theological reference to sovereignty is again present here. The rise of man's power to name the other creatures of God is placed in a time after the fall, after the original sin. This means a time of shamefulness and clothing, not one of the naked truth (hence, not a time of primary nakedness, when truth has to be revealed or unveiled). This shamefulness is also the index of a lack (lacking in human destitution, natural tools for defence, dwelling and heating). The lack grounds the pursuit of power; not a definite quality or property, but a bare human capacity to acquire qualities and property. Moreover, the lack is provisionally fulfilled with the power to name, a power that by the same token grounds a human infinite superiority over 'what is called animal life.' I maintain that this is very characteristically the ultimate unconditionality with power, where all theological attributes are present:

> From within the pit of ... an eminent lack, a quite different lack from that he assigns to the animal, man installs or claims in a single movement what is proper to him (the peculiarity of a man whose property is not to have anything exclusively his) and his superiority over what is called human life. This last superiority, infinite and par excellence, has as its property the fact of being at one and the same time *unconditional* and *sacrificial*.[43]

This infinite superiority is predicated on the 'human' lack, and hence on a pursuit of protection, goods, and survival. Yet, this superiority is also deemed to be sacrificial, in a somewhat under-explained passage. It can be understood though through Derrida's reference, with Benjamin, to the sadness of nature.[44] In Benjamin's inversion, nature is not sad or mournful because it is mute; rather its muteness derives from its sadness. This can be interpreted as man's own perception of nature as sad, and as nature's capacity to respond to being named. For Benjamin, the sadness of nature is due to naming: 'to be named—even when the namer [*Nennende*] is godlike and blissful—perhaps always remains an intimation [*Ahnung*] of mourning.' *Nennen* also means to call, and *Ahnung*, can also mean a premonition: what one notices here is that the call into the realm of the name is also a premonition/intimation of death.[45]

For Derrida, such mourning is due to the name's announcement of mortality. Being given a name means here to carry an attempt at survival ('the longevity of a name'), after death; and consequently one who is given a name always 'feels mortal.'[46] Here, man's unconditional pursuit of survival requires the 'sacrifice' of nature itself, sacrifice as the infliction upon nature of the possibility of death. What matters the most for my purposes, though, is the question of the name, and its relationship to a certain type of unconditionality, which is very clearly here a theological one, hence facing the same problem of 'sovereignty' as seen earlier.

In the above setting, the name is an index of a godlike, sovereign power (the preservation of God's power).[47] The name may be more than this though. The name, the proper name, is also given to 'man.' Moreover, as Derrida implies, the sadness of nature is not only 'of nature' as opposed to 'man,' but of anyone who is given a name. Hence, the taste of mortality is experienced by the named (the name indeed ignites a spectral structure of survival).[48] The name is here the index of an absolute dissymmetry, of an infinite debt.[49] This infinity imports not only a debt to him who gives one a name, bestowing on him the possibility of autonomy, freedom, and identity.[50] This infinity of the name instils in the named a debt to anyone who, by subsequent repetition of the name, at any time and every calling, reinforces sameness, a sphere of the proper.[51] The name is here the 'proper' at work, but ceaselessly haunted by an infinite relation (to the one who names and reiterates the name) that is irreducible to 'the proper.'

Precisely because there is such infinity, there is also an unknown element. One's proper name, and one's 'proper' in general—to which one may adhere so unconditionally—may not be so secure, and that is certainly one of the junctures of unconditionality. As Derrida maintains, since his first direct treatments of 'the proper name,' one should always raise the possibility that the proper name may in fact not be purely proper: the proper name displayed a certain divisibility; and this at the height of its power, in its very originary immediacy (here Derrida critiques Aristotle's theory of the metaphor, predicated on the originary character of the name).[52] Moreover, the name should neither be simply equated with subjectivity and identity.[53] In fact, the name always entertains the possibility of uncertainty, of a secret: 'It is never certain ... that there is only one of them [proper names], that it does not remain secret for some [people].'[54]

In this initial approach to Derrida's second distinction what one realizes is that the name shows that the two unconditionalities are more intimate than Derrida seems to acknowledge (rather than helping in producing a distinction between sovereignty and unconditionality, the name itself complicates this distinction). In fact questions around the name are so rich and diverse in the extension of Derrida's work that we could dwell a very long time here, and retake what was discussed in ch. 1. Yet, one needs to proceed with the clarification of the distinction between unconditionalities. It is certain that in *Rogues* and 'The University without Condition,' the distinction is put forward in clearer terms through recourse to the notion of sovereignty. I argue, however, that such a distinction is still unsustainable, at least on a concrete level. Let us attempt other avenues in order to think this distinction.

Sovereignty and Unconditionality

Close to the time of 'Performative Powerlessness,' in a conference (1998) and later a book in French (2001, *L'Université sans condition*), Derrida formulated his distinction between what he calls sovereignty and unconditionality. He formulates his hypothesis like this:

> *Perhaps* [my emphasis, but following Derrida's insistence on the term][55] my hypothesis would be this (it is extremely difficult, and almost improbable, inaccessible to a proof): a certain *unconditional* independence of thought, of deconstruction, of justice, of the Humanities, of the University, etc., should be dissociated from every phantasm of *indivisible sovereignty* and sovereign mastery.[56]

Derrida is again very careful here not to rush into a distinction. In fact he announces and enquires about his 'hypothesis' (in fact as he says earlier, this is not quite a hypothesis, 'not accessible to a proof,' more like a profession of faith), without quite determining it: 'how can one dissociate sovereignty and unconditionality, the power of an indivisible sovereignty and the powerlessness [*im-pouvoir*] of unconditionality.'[57] As one can see, the questions and announcements help in constituting the difficult distinction. There are clearly two sides here. On the one hand, one can identify an indivisible sovereignty, associated with the State, theological sovereignty, power, and mastery. On the other hand, partly by implication, there is a divisible unconditionality without power, associated with democracy, justice, the humanities, and the university.

The unconditional drive of the university is clear enough in that text, but a more precise distinction, and the side of sovereignty is wanting. In order to explain the role of the university, Derrida employs a very suggestive title: 'The University without Condition,' where 'without condition' does not refer simply to the university's incalculable and irreducible drive, beyond all conditionalities, towards an uncompromising freedom of thought, an absolute independence in its pursuit of truth.[58] That is so, indeed, as he often rehearses, but 'without condition' also means being without means, without resources, without power, vulnerable, risking appropriation and destruction at any time, 'an exposed citadel.'[59] Certainly this is a drive, a principle, and not the fact of university life.[60] Here the contrast with any notion of sovereignty, theological or otherwise is so dramatic that one may wonder whether an effort at distinction is at all necessary. In what way would the university then resemble sovereign power formations?

Earlier in the text, before formulating his final hypothesis clearly (see quotation above), Derrida refers to a sort of sovereignty, an 'exceptional kind of sovereignty.'[61] Further, and not without hesitation, in announcing his engagement, his subsequent treatment of the 'event, perhaps, to come,' Derrida calls this 'the proper sovereign essence of the university.'[62] Yet, in these passages Derrida is also referring to that which sets them apart, and does not suggest directly what the proximity means and entails. Unless, of course, the meaning of this proximity could be entirely derived from the semantic range of the term sovereignty. Indeed, on a semantic level, sovereignty cannot be extricated from a desire to independence, from a desire not to be under any other authority. In Derrida's text, the characterization of the university as in a pursuit of independence and freedom of thought seems the best way to characterize what makes the university and the humanities 'similar to' sovereignty (one could also point out that the image of the 'citadel' also involves a notion of power, as in a fortress, keeping within the vicinity of sovereignty but more fragile).

As the passage on the 'essence of the university' suggests, the question of the event and the affirmation of the event is crucial here. Yet, in what way can sovereign drives and movements really be distinguished from the event 'of' the university? Derrida claims that 'the force of the event is always stronger than the force of a performative.'[63] With this formulation he can say that the event (following an uncanny grammar of the disturbing effect of the 'perhaps' and the 'what if')[64] cannot be contained within a previous conventional setting. That is, the conventional and independent setting of the university is not self-contained; it treads a porous limit, a porous border which by definition is prone to the 'to come.' By implication, the sovereign, which is said to be indivisible, seems tied to conventions, its own borders and demarcations, and foreign to the event in this strong sense; the event that becomes stronger than conventions and performative programming.

The problem, however, is that sovereign manifestations, even in Derrida's own characterizations, are not so clearly distinguishable from the event in the strong sense. Derrida's notion of autoimmunity, applied to sovereignty in several texts, clearly shows that the sovereign is not immune to exposure, to the divisibility, to the 'to come' of the other. In fact, read carefully, this is what Derrida has always meant. A distinction between sovereignty and unconditionality is unsustainable for the simple fact, which Derrida actually recognizes, that sovereignty comprises an unconditional element. One notices that the only distinguishing characteristics of unconditional instances are 'divisibility' and passivity. But divisibility and passivity cannot prevail, for one would have to fall back onto the realm of calculability and the number. If one is stuck between these two realms or dimensions, then the only way forward is one of degree. Therefore, to make a distinction one would have to introduce a measure of degree, and that is exactly what Derrida does:

> As soon as there is sovereignty there is abuse of power and a rogue state. Abuse is the law of use; it is the law itself, the 'logic' of a sovereignty that can reign only by not sharing [*partage*]. More precisely, since it never succeeds in doing this except in a critical precarious, and unstable fashion, sovereignty can only *tend*, for a limited time, to reign without sharing [my emphasis].[65]

There is no doubt that sovereignty is abusive, as in the 'law of use' put forward here as that which the exercise of power and authority demand. A decision has to overflow the normative framework in which it is made, if it is a true decision, whether by a legislator, a judge, or a policeman. Moreover, the time frame mentioned above (*tending* towards indivisibility for a 'limited time frame') may be also attributed to the limited period of a situation of exception. Yet, if there is a formal suspension of rights, sharing as such is not necessarily suspended, whether it be symbolically or materially. What happens is that sharing is itself exploited for the sake of the sustainability of the exception (that is, there would not be an exception if a residual sharing did not keep the exception going as exception).

This degree that Derrida introduces is in any case highly problematic. I do not entirely deny its ultimate possibility, but it says little about actual power and resistance to situations of exception, where 'sharing' is still mobilized, whether it be the sharing of intelligence and information, the symbolic sharing of the affect of fear, and so many other forms of sociability that are compatible with oppression. The notion of a degree in the suspension of sharing is problematic for it overlooks the fact that it is the sovereign that most often mobilizes sharing, calculation, and conditions (in Derrida's vocabulary sharing is a code for universalization, the number, the more than one, the many). Derrida's invocation of a tendency towards the One, if not necessarily wrong, says very little about the contemporary forms of sovereign demeanour;[66] as if the sovereign could do anything 'today' without the techniques of calculation, the virtual technologies, the surveys, and all other modern controlling and normalizing mechanisms that take for granted the existence of the many; not to mention that aspect of sovereignty which is widely shared: subjective sovereignty—shared in a particular mode undoubtedly, the mode of production of subjectivity, but still divided and shared.[67]

Admittedly, one could equate the sovereign to the future, to ideas, to moments of underexposure, to a practice that already takes place under the aegis of a sovereign. This would challenge the very notion of sovereignty in its capacity to unsettle and remake a settled order. Yet, as I have suggested, even those moments do not involve a degree in relation to the extent of the experience of sharing. Calculability and incalculability, division and indivisibility, are always intertwined. There are, though, different ways through which one is exposed to these encodings.

The apparently simple futural moment is the most sophisticated form of underexposure, for its type of veiling is itself concealed in a project (towards the future) that seems liberating. The sovereign moment, however, already exposes more vividly the violence, the rupture, the breaking point, the deconstitution of law. Here there is a type of degree, between two levels of underexposure. So, these two moments are intertwined in the sense that both are still within the realm of underexposure, but also in the sense that there is an interplay between them. In order to challenge the suffering of this interplay, one needs to reach a degree of exposure incompatible with the interplay. One needs to reach the level of a true 'to come.'

I have argued that the distinction between sovereignty and unconditionality is hardly sustainable, especially if predicated on the matter of divisibility. That is so precisely because divisibility does appear in all instances of unconditionality. There is no pure unconditionality, and yet the restlessness of the 'to come,' of differences, of everything that is experienced, could not take place without a pure and uncompromising affirmation. There are other ways, however, through which one can locate oneself within the maze of experience; it is a matter of inclination, orientation, indeed the law itself and its unavoidability. I shall now attempt to tackle other ways to differentiate between sovereignty (in its exploitative exposure) and something else, which I prefer to call the 'to come' itself—the chance of an overexposure, of a more heightened experience of deconstruction, beyond the exploitative interplay of constitution and deconstruction.

4.3. Towards Another 'to Come'

It would be more convincing to think sovereignty in a way that does not *tend* toward the indivisible. I maintain that sovereignty is itself an articulation of the divisible and the indivisible, especially if, with Derrida, I agree that today sovereign democracies are predominant.

That is, sovereignty, or actual sovereignty, is not incompatible with the structure of differentiation and sharing of democracy (even in the most adamantly antidemocratic States, this structure of differentiation hardly fails to manifest itself). The distinction between sovereignty and unconditionality can be drawn quite simply: sovereignty is not only unconditional; it works with conditions (in the ambiguity of the term, that is with material means also). It is already pervaded by 'the number.'[68] How else could the sovereign move beyond itself, expand itself, justify itself, by means of a general law? This is exactly what Derrida tells us in *The Other Heading*, as we have seen: 'the self--affirmation of an identity always intends to respond to the call or to the designation of the universal.'[69] Thinking otherwise than that is also possible, but sovereignty would have to be equated with unconditionality, abstracted from any concrete practice. For concrete practices cannot be made a term in an aporia. They are themselves aporetic.[70]

Yet, one may be puzzled with this place of 'unconditionality' here. Let us take the figures of unconditionality, or of this pure form of sovereignty: the One, the father, the Monarch, the State, and the People. Are they not also conditional; can there ever be anything unconditional? There can be no absolute unconditionality in the sense of a destruction or suspension of sharing, but unconditionality can prevail; it prevails in sovereignty (and even to say this one needs to isolate the moment of unconditionality as that moment of the suspension of sharing). What matters in all these 'figures' is not that the unconditional *tends* to suppress conditions, and sharing, or the sharing of division (but certainly sovereignty, in important historical instances, which entertain a relation to its concept, has tended to absolute destruction, and may still do so). What matters is that, in these figures of putative unconditionality, an exploitative bipolarity between conditional and unconditional prevails (in a certain sense the sovereignty of this interplay prevails). With this notion, one is able to understand how, rather than suppressing sharing, such figures exploit sharing, and the forces of the many or the weak (who/which, as we have seen may be extraordinary and, albeit at one time ineffective, the strongest).[71]

One could concede that such an exploitation leads to a destruction of division and its sharing (as I indicated, I do not deny its ultimate possibility), but that is not simply the law of the sovereign. 'He' also *tends to* include, by all technical and virtual means available, more rather than fewer subjects. The result may be destruction, but 'he' *tends to* the forces of the many; to accumulate the forces of the many, which must be left as many in the calculation of the sovereign. This is not simply because 'he' requires forces that are multiple (the economic logic of decentralized loci of decision-making, or subjectivity, is evident here), but also because 'he' calculates, and calculation as such involves already the work of the many. In doing so 'he' deals with the number, the many, and includes himself into an economy of interdependence in which he is equated, at least materially, with the forces of the many. That is to say, ultimately, at the heart of sovereignty there is as much a tendency to the many as to the One—but how is one involved in this process, and what and who get involved? I shall maintain shortly that it is necessary to think with Derrida beyond Derrida.

This co-belonging of 'the many' and 'the one' is what needs to be acknowledged, and what Derrida clearly did in relation to Europe, and in more complicated ways in relation to friendship (see ch. 1), and even in equally complex ways in relation to democracy (see ch. 2). What Derrida fails to discern here, is what he had brilliantly diagnosed in *The Other Heading* (see ch. 1.2): that the true conflict does not take place between the singular and the universal, but between processes of universalization in which the conditional and the unconditional, the singular and the universal live together (in fact in *Rogues* too, he says that singularity and universality are not incompatible).[72] If this is true, accusing any entity of betraying either conditionality or unconditionality, calculability or incalculability does not yield many practical consequences. Here the true conflict does not lie between sovereignty and unconditionality, but between two articulations of unconditionality and conditionality, two ways of organizing the organization of the world, that is to say, two ways of arranging primary, and more or less inevitable bifurcations or simplifications. The problems around fraternity in *Politics of Friendship* also pointed in this direction (see ch. 1.3).

In this light, it is only the 'to come' that announces a new arrangement. The unconditional is stuck in a bipolar logic; the 'to come,' on the contrary, and as democracy (and also law in the way I have reinterpreted it), articulates a new arrangement of multiple drives. In spite of Derrida's often enigmatic rendering, there is in the 'to come' both conditionality and unconditionality, the number and the many, near and distance; and all these common-sense notions cease to make sense. This 'to come' is a term that indeed promotes a new arrangement of semantic and non-semantic forces. It is itself a marker of that general textuality that Gasché called an infrastructure.[73] This is one that comes about with the third moment of the strategy of deconstruction (the first exposes a dichotomy, the second opposes the subordinate element in a dichotomy, and the third rearranges it).

Given the simple fact that deconstruction moves strategically it requires a general picture of the social 'texture' that is itself marked by force, in its differential character. Furthermore, this differential character of force is explicated in terms of the restless movement of 'come':

> Force is excessive because it is different, different from itself, and double, both the force of a movement and a given force, force of a movement that one cannot describe but for its di-stancing [*é-loignement*] of come [*viens*].[74]

The extraordinary issue here is that 'force' is not entirely measurable. It is not a quantity, but pervaded by the 'to come.' As such, it evades philosophical classification, and conceptualization, but it does provide an image of tensions, pressures, gradations of intensity, proximity and distance. Derrida can often move strategically because he has this general force-text in the background. But that does not mean that this strategic element is instrumental for some obscure social goal. The social goal or the pre-strategic is precisely an allegiance, or faith, to the truth of forces (of living–dying), which includes what in them cannot be entirely explained or calculated, that is, the 'to come' of forces. So, if 'force' is a very important element in providing for the possibility of moving strategically at all, Derrida's work cannot be entirely reduced to the strategic moment.

In his text 'Pas,' with reference to Blanchot, Derrida dwells on all the aporias of 'come' (*viens*, second person singular), 'come' (*venez*, formal treatment second person singular and second person plural), and 'to come' (à-*venir*). He discusses 'come' as a word, a verb (in imperative form or not), a citation, a recitation, a return, a response—all as it appears in Blanchot's writing.[75] This 'come' (now around the word *venez*, which poses more clearly the distance and the call to proximity) affects being itself, the being of 'is': 'come (*venez*) speaks to the provocation of a pace [*pas*, also 'step' and 'not'] affecting without turning back the being of the "is".'[76] The proximity here of 'come' to *différance* is even more evident (recall also the proximity of democracy itself to *différance*).[77]

Yet, it is not only in that early writing of the labyrinths of the 'to come' that this restlessness and general rearrangement appears. Virtually all references to the 'to come' in Derrida's work involve not only the absolute novelty and disruption of a coming that is unforeseen and temporally complicated, but also the coming of an 'other' that poses the question of who, what, and number; both the autonomy or sovereignty of a singular time, and the 'heteronomy of the other.' We have seen, with regard to the future, how the 'to come' irrupts out of any settled horizon. Yet, the 'to come' appeals to another, relates to the impact of the number, the many, the impossibility of deciding who and what the 'other' is:

> The other to come (the messiah, the thinker of the dangerous 'perhaps,' the god, *who*ever would come in the form of the event—that is, in the form of the exception and the unique)—I have to let him free in his movement, out of reach of my will or desire, beyond my very intention.[78]

Albeit implicitly, the 'to come' is already occupying the space of that intense negotiation (the second moment of deconstruction's 'strategy') that Derrida himself puts forward in other instances. The 'to come' here requires the other as unique and exceptional, the exceptional moment (that in fact cannot be easily extricated from 'myself'; myself comes about in tension with the other that myself is and is not). Moreover, it requires the other simply as other—free, irrespective of my will or intention. Free so that it can be more than one, so that in a way 'I' can be more than one and relate to that which appears. What one finds here is a delicate relation, an im-possible one.[79] It is a relation that can only be glimpsed at with the distinctions of distance and proximity, power and powerlessness.

What does this relation import to the differentiation from sovereignty? Is not the sovereign also in relation, in relation to himself, appropriating himself, affirming himself by appropriating the forces and resources of others (also in a difficult relation of distance and proximity, power and powerlessness)? Exactly so. Very subtly, however, Derrida's 'relation' introduces a new postulation. Derrida's widely held insistence on the 'to come' is also a call for its exposure. Exposure understood in a way that is not devoid of epistemic value (cognitive learning, mental absorption), but which turns this episteme (the collective pattern of cognition) to sense, sensitivity and even a sort of enjoyment of this 'joyful eternal repetition of the come.'[80] Within the thinking of a 'yes, yes,' a double affirmation already announced in the iterability of every yes: writing 'to come' requires the fruition of the 'coming' that already is: 'an affirmation that does not say yes to a being, a subject or an object, the state or the determination of anything, but to what/who is to come, yet, yet.'[81] The 'to come' is, as sovereignty, a negotiation of many drives and exigencies. But the 'to come,' in its repetition, says yes to the coming itself, enjoys the coming itself.[82]

What sovereignty does is neither to abuse power (if power's law is that of abuse, it loses any significance to speak of the abuse of power), nor to suppress the other. Yet, there is a form of abuse in sovereignty, and that is precisely the 'abuse' (in the sense of an exploitative use) of the coming itself. Sovereign power 'abuses' by concentrating the enjoyment of the 'to come.' The restless movement, the flexibility, the virtuality, the number, the distance, etc., all of that is compatible with sovereignty. Yet there is something that the sovereign does that betrays the 'to come.' It concentrates the enjoyment of exposure—and in that concentration a minimum form of concealment subsists, or, better, a form of underexposure to sensitivity and compassion—to the other. The 'joyful eternal repetition of the come' ceases to be generally 'joyful' in any meaningful way and becomes marred by a general system of exploitation, extortion and extraction of forces.[83] A suffering sadness befalls the living, imposing ever more extensive, elaborate, and, in a sense, inclusive forms of suffering; all in the name of an overarching principle, revelation, ground, origin, constitution or decision.

One could aptly reply that there is always, and there always will be, suffering—always the ruin. There is, though, a chance of enjoying this ruin, and in fact the joy for life in all its impurity is the 'essence' of joy. That is why I prefer joy to love (unless, perhaps, the element of endurance in love is brought to bear). Indeed this joy is akin to a certain compassion, the compassion and equality of the sufferers, those who suffer love and joy, and love and enjoy in suffering. The equality of suffering is tantamount to the equality of joy. There is in both a certain equality of sense and exposure, exploited in sovereignty (equality in their very capacity to yield goods, products integrated to the expansive logic of sovereignty).[84] With regard to the 'unprecedented proportion of the subjection of the animal' in modern times, Derrida speaks of a system of exploitation of animals (which is in fact, in some respects at least, not so foreign to the human history of exploitation in general; of fellow humans, animals, and the environment as a whole).[85] This extract is particularly telling:

> The organization and exploitation of an artificial, infernal, virtually interminable survival, in conditions that previous generations would have judged monstruous, outside of every supposed norm of life proper to animals that are thus exterminated by means of their continued existence or even their overpopulation.[86]

Here one notices the themes of the calculability and multiplication of a sovereign activity that does not simply tend to the One, but also tends to the many. Differently from a more enduring or sustainable 'to come,' what sovereignty lacks is that shared 'sentiment of compassion.' Hence Derrida can speak of an unequal struggle in the last couple of centuries,

> an unequal struggle, a war being waged, the unequal forces of which could one day be reversed, between those who violate not only animal life but even and also this sentiment of compassion and, on the other hand those who appeal to an irrefutable testimony to this pity.[87]

One can almost hear this as an appeal to a 'coming' more truthful to the 'to come,' that dwells on the 'to come,' rejoices in the equal suffering of compassion, and the unequal distribution of power. There is a struggle and a reversal of forces, but that struggle leads not necessarily to domination, but to a different form of arranging the sharing of the 'to come' in which the 'sentiment of compassion' is not violated. This other coming would depart from, yet without assurances, the violation of compassion characteristic of a system of exploitation and exclusion (rather than oppose, it departs from, for another 'coming' creates within a system of exploitation the conditions for its dislocation).

Moreover, if this coming is to come in a sphere of experience in which coming already happens, then law—differential, contaminating, restless—can be more fully enjoyed and played with. Law becomes a good space (a theatre to be experienced rather than merely watched) for exercising the call, the postulation, to other forms of enjoying sociability.[88] It is not that playing with law is the only way forward, nor that this play happens in an altogether different time. On the contrary, playing with law is already happening, in law courts (in the allegedly instrumental use of law by social movements), in literature, and in legal theory.[89] What is needed, along with other forms of playing with differential and restless spaces, is a more radical playing with law, in order to bring to fruition the exposure of law.

I shall come back to the issue of the passion that grounds sovereignty itself. I shall come back to problem of fear. For if one perceives in Derrida a certain return to affections, one has to take into account that there is also a passion in play in the sovereign drive. If this affection were the true reason for the sovereign abusive drive to exploitation and accumulation, then a return to affections would be rather naïf.

Let it be clear there is no easy return to affections here as opposed to reason. Derrida in no way espouses dispensing with reason, rather he finds in reason also a passion for the unconditional, or, to be more precise, in what he calls 'the reasonable,' which articulates the exigency to calculation and the exigency to the incalculable.[90]

4.4. Encountering Fears

I shall now dwell on Derrida's last two seminars, which also refer to the question of sovereignty. Yet, it is a sovereignty that comes in a new light. The nature of these texts is one of close readings of other texts. To discuss all of them in detail would require another entire book that also deals with Schmitt, Hobbes, Heidegger, and Daniel Defoe's Robinson Crusoe. I shall therefore limit myself to fleshing out the aspects most relevant to my argument. The question here is fear. Fear will be discussed as the exploitation of the 'to come,' which is crucial for the dominant discourse of democracy, for sovereign democracies. But I shall also envisage a certain courage to face fear itself—key for another 'to come.'

Derrida's last seminars in Paris and Irvine dealt with the relationship between fear and autoimmunity (entitled 'The Beast and the Sovereign,' these seminars inform a great deal of his late published writings). In the seminars of December 2001, Derrida takes on the question of the Leviathan. Like Schmitt long before him, Derrida emphasizes the bond between protection and obedience, and the continuity of fear from before until after the covenant. For Schmitt, *'protego ergo obligo* [I protect therefore I command obedience] is the *cogito ergo sum* of the state.'[91] Fear is at work both for the sake of the covenant, and, through criminal law, as pervasively mobilized so as to warrant obedience.

For a start, Derrida opens the possibility that legal obedience is not only a function of debt for protection or guilt for non-self-protection (guilt of simply existing, as Agamben would rather have it).[92] The fear of anarchy and death, the anxiety and uncertainty of the future, cannot be simply equated with the fear generated by the monstrous *art* of the political unity (be it bodily or representative). The former is fear simply put, 'true' fear; the latter is fear generated by the 'monstrous' inventions of the political unity. The second, this machine-like man-made fear, is *posited* as the same, as undivided, as conventional and immortal. The unity of sovereignty is predicated on the unity of protection and obedience, the unity of fear (when, in fact, as Benjamin once claimed, it is altogether improbable that the malaise of existence led to law, he says that rather the opposite seemed the case; and one cannot be so sure about this opposite either, but simply that divisibility strikes at the heart of law's claim to a higher unity of existence).[93]

Derrida highlights, furthermore, that if Hobbes makes fear 'the political passion *par excellence*' fear may also be the cause of crime.[94] Derrida insists that, even for Hobbes, fear is only 'of all passions, that which inclineth men least to break the laws' (even if also the only 'thing' that deters men).[95] Derrida emphasizes then that the intense passion on which Hobbes relies to produce the spark of reason is itself divisible (for Hobbes it is fear of death and anarchy that lead to the rational decision to attribute one's 'natural' rights to an overarching entity). That is, the ultimate ground of sovereignty, that which *posits* itself as indivisible, is itself divisible (in insisting on that positing, and its shared fiction [see ch. 1.1] one notices the importance of exposure).

Derrida indicates, moreover, that Hobbes privileges bodily fear, corporeal punishments, and the presence of fear. It is like that, as immediate and incarnate presence, that fear may warrant obedience to the laws. Derrida, however, claims that fear has always a non-bodily element, what makes fear fear is precisely a delay, a protracted threat (all fear conceals fear of fear):

> There is in all fear something that refers, essentially, to the non-body and non-present, if only the *to-come* of a threat: what causes fear is never fully present nor fully corporeal, in the sense that the purely corporeal is supposed to be saturated with presence [my emphasis].[96]

These spectres, this spectrality of fear, is one of the many instances of the ruin of the Leviathan. Its invidisibility is *posited* precisely *before* the divisibility which constitutes it.

This is clearly put in Derrida's characterization of sovereignty: '[Sovereignty] is posited as immortal and indivisible precisely because it is mortal, and divisible, contract and convention being destined to ensure for it what it does not have, or is not, naturally.'[97] However, by emphasizing this 'position' of sovereignty, Derrida is not endorsing the strict separation between nature and convention, the natural and the artificial. On the contrary, he suggests that the indivisible cannot finally escape divisibility, and conversely that the divisible cannot sustain itself without a spark of indivisibility. This is not to maintain that they are tantamount to each other. Rather Derrida's work suggests that they can neither be easily contained within themselves, nor opposed to each other:

> I have been emphasizing for a long time the fragility and porosity of this distinction between nature and culture ... Every time one puts an oppositional limit in question, far from concluding that there is identity, on the contrary, we must [*il faut*] multiply attention to differences, refine the analysis in a restructured field.[98]

What Derrida does with sovereignty in this instance is not very different from what he did to visibility, autonomy, friendship and other concepts in the texts which I have analyzed so far.

Precisely here (in Derrida's complication of oppositions, and reinvention of differences) may lie Derrida's fragile alternative to the order of sovereignty. Certainly not by merely inverting a hierarchic ordering, but by radically exposing oneself to it, to a differentiation that involves the making of structures, and exposing in the making. Rather than a purely theoretical and cognitive enterprise, his writing stimulates sensitivities to conditions of hierarchy, exclusion, and suffering. The alternative can be formulated in the following way.

On the one hand, one could resign oneself to the sovereign power to make ever more hierarchic distinctions in fear of fear, that is, to radically attempt to evade passion and affection (and most common sense orientations tend to warrant against fear and anxiety, pursuing a stabilization of expectations) in the name of possibility and survival.[99] On the other hand, there may be an opportunity to launch an endurance of fear in the joy of the 'coming' passions of constitution and deconstruction, where strong normative and stabilizing orientations turn into more fragile and exposed postulations. In this instance, there is survival, but not the over-determination of survival. And facing fear means fundamentally to come to taste a life of living–dying; that is where the condition of living is spectral (hence on the border between life and death, reality and illusion, certainty and uncertainty), and where one's very fears are exposed.[100]

In fact, as we shall see, Derrida's distinctions pose the question of his inclinations, and one cannot evade them entirely. Derrida certainly proceeds without a mere positivist description of what happens. Hence, he is also dedicated to 'something.' He expresses his dedication to this 'something' strategically initially through a side of the 'opposition' (the one that is most weakened); the unconditional or the incalculable, for instance, as opposed to the prevalence of 'conditions' and 'calculations.' But at bottom he always moves towards rearranging the opposition at the space of its internal borders. His strategy moves towards the exposure of what already 'is.' My only concern with this strategy is that one must take the end-game of exposure seriously. In other words, accepting the 'initial' opposition or dichotomy at worst reinforces an oppressive dichotomy, and at best is of little effect in mobilizing the forces towards that rearrangement, for it simply beggars belief. Yet, even this exposure happens already, but through a cognitive and power-grabbing manner, which could even be capable of controlling the blind spot of exposure: one can know that one cannot be entirely exposed. That is why it is necessary to say that, in my reading, the Derridean exposure is an exposure of the exposure, an overexposure that threatens one's condescension with cognitive exposure (with acknowledgment) and one's own predicaments.

Indeed my true objection, beyond the range of possible interpretations of Derrida's work, lies on that strategic level. One must not keep treating what is already perceived as intertwined as if it were not. The already classical example has been treated in chapter three: why oppose law to justice before further complicating the distinction and showing a mutual contamination of terms? There is no legal force without authority, and there is no authority without some type of 'force,' whether material or symbolic. There is no law without appeal to justice, in which case the reference to justice must belong to the very understanding, not to say the 'concept' of law. And that is still very different from saying that law is 'just' or tantamount to justice.

What one needs to highlight and expose is the extent to which law and justice are already intertwined, and the extent to which there may be a form of mastery of this intertwinement itself that is hierarchical and often causes distress and unequal suffering. Strategically this calls for complex social discourses and narratives that make difficult decisions concerning description and emancipation, and not the simplistic setting of oppositions: law and justice, calculable and incalculable, conditional and unconditional. The narrative element intends to respond to Derrida's attempt to escape the risk of a positivistic discourse about 'society.' Within narratives, the autobiographical element is apt to avoid the 'power' of fiction, its power to make worlds, rejoicing in its 'own' success, and hence without self-questioning.

In spite of that, Derrida's own 'exposure' happens (see ch. 1), in a way that is itself indisputably cognitive; but also more than that, sensitive and sensorial. It affects the reader. It calls upon an autobiographic machine. It calls upon the struggle against the most acute, but often-neglected agonies. In the seminars on 'The Beast and the Sovereign,' however, one does not find explict indications to the further *postulatory* effects of such agonies, unless perhaps through his style and incisive auto-bio-graphical approach (see ch. 1.1).

Courage

In Derrida's seminars of the following academic year (2002–3), he addressed more directly the problem of 'the sovereign' in itself, in its fear of itself.[101] I shall address the seminars to the extent that they indicate a subtle type of courage not foreign to fear, different from the pursuit of 'possibility' and grandeur (but not of course immune to them). In a parallel reading of Defoe's *Robinson Crusoe* and Heidegger's seminars of the years 1929–30, Derrida exposes the sovereign in its fear of itself, and supposedly in its attempt to destroy the spectral conditions for itself.[102] Crusoe is profoundly disturbed by his own fears. He is afraid of being buried alive, being swallowed up alive. And he who is about to swallow him up is another, another very close to himself, perhaps himself indeed. Derrida dwells on Crusoe's encounters with 'the other's footprints.[103]

Crusoe had always been terrified of the beasts who were not alone; later he seemed himself not to be alone.[104] Footprints enter the stage, and someone else, another one, much closer to Crusoe himself. And yet the other could be himself, his own footprint.[105] It is, for Derrida, an essay on sovereignty. On 'man' alone with himself, present to himself, sovereign alone, in his relation to the sun, the highest source of power and animus, and his subjugation of others—of stones, animals, and persons, and most importantly, of himself. But Crusoe is also, always, the very living dead, buried in an island of himself. What is necessary for Derrida is a work of thinking the living–dead, of addressing it. In the seminar, he touches upon the point of courage, crucial to the coming:

> Courage! Courage, then! Heart and courage are necessary [*il faut du coeur et du courage*, where 'il faut' is also the necessity in the void of the lack itself, a faith, *foi*] in order to think, contrary to what many would be tempted to think—necessary, for instance, in order to think the living-dead. Being for or against, accepting or not this possibility, or impossibility, courage is necessary to think about *this* [*ça*] ... Courage without fear is no courage ... What is the affinity, proximity, the obscure alliance between courage *of* fear, this fear *of* courage and the *ghost*? ... What I have just called 'the ghost' is well the inconceivable, the contradictory, the unthinkable, the impossible. But I have insisted on this zone where the impossible is named, desired, apprehended—where it affects us.[106]

That is Derrida's response to Defoe and 'Crusoe' (but also to Heidegger): there is no reason to fear fear.[107] What Derrida puts forward is another type of affection. He wishes to welcome not only the other 'other,' but also this other that is the most difficult to acknowledge as other, the closest, the brother, and even oneself. Derrida's efforts are directed towards an as yet unforeseen experience of hetero-auto-affection, in which self and other are catered for and exposed to their restless coming. Fear can only be part and parcel of this sensitivity. It is another passion that affects one here and, if well catered for, one that builds confidence and faith in another organization of relations of one and other (no longer knowledge simply, but a knowledge that includes the force and the fragility of faith).[108]

This reminds us of what we have said about compassion. Yet it must be even clearer now that one cannot share a passion directly, only obliquely as a passion of sharing an experience with that which by definition cannot be shared. Com-passion must be understood in that way, in that subtle form of auto-hetero-affection.[109] The experience of the ghost that is in fear but without fear of fear is precisely this one: 'a reflection about the acute specificity of the ghostly [*phantasmatique*] must go through an experience of living–death, through affection, imagination, and sensibility (space and time) as auto-hetero-affection.'[110]

Yet, one may still ask how exactly is this experience abused, violated, exploited? Can one not now say that sovereignty differs from unconditionality given its denegation and destruction of its own conditions? Unfortunately the same aporias that I have shown persist. No one unconditional can be by definition receptive to conditions—exactly like sovereignty. But if one wishes to show how the unconditional depends on conditions, and in fact, directly employs them, one would have again to include sovereignty. Derrida does not refer to this, but Crusoe is not simply delusional in his sovereign affirmation (Crusoe calls himself King in a kingdom of three or four subjects, and Derrida refers to him as delusional).[111] There is almost as much rationality and calculation as there is delusion and incalculability.[112] It is this calculation amidst fear of fear that leads to the subjection and exploitation of all others around him.

In addition, one should not turn a blind eye to the socio-economic *conditions* in which Defoe's novel locates itself. Crusoe, after all, is a plantation owner in what he calls 'the Brasils.' Since he lands in the Bay of All Saints, Defoe must have had in mind what is today indeed Brazil (more specifically in what is today the State of Bahia).[113] Benefiting from a wealthy upbringing, and after adventures in North-west Africa, Crusoe settles in Brazil. There he benefits from the favours of an 'honest man' owner of a plantation (the pinnacle of Brazilian traditionalism, 'honest man' means a member of the local elite; this figure of 'honesty' is inextricable from local corruption and domination over slaves and later poor workers). With the profit of the sale of his invaluable English goods, he decides to set up his own plantation. And he ends up stranded on a desert island because he sets sail to catch African slaves for his plantation, where he grows tobacco and later sugar cane. Upon his escape he is surprised by the continuous success of his enterprise, and becomes very well off with the sale of his estate in Brazil.

Most crucially, Crusoe's story is not the abstract tale about 'human' control over nature. This 'sovereign' teaches Friday to call him 'master' and subjects all around him (men and beast alike) to his dominions. Such a sovereign is also the owner of an enterprise of profit-making which requires the work of others to thrive at all. The problem lies there in the form of articulation of calculation and the incalculable, of the many and the one. The problem, as I have been arguing, lies there, and not in the suppression of division, which after all is relative.

The predicament to which Derrida alludes is not simply one of the abuse of power; more deeply, his whole performative efforts show the problem of an abuse of the 'to come' itself, that is, an abuse of the living–dying demeanour which all sensitive beings experience. The equality of that experience is nonetheless not translated into shared enjoyment. This widespread abuse is possible ultimately because of a very crucial abuse: the abuse of the unconditional itself, which does not destroy but exploits material and symbolic conditions. This is, in a sense, the abuse *of* humanity, intensified infinitely in modernity; the abuse of extracting itself from the living–dying beings of the world, but above all the abuse in creating 'worlds' of constraining orders that, no matter how flexible and accelerated, always reinforce the borders of their own divisions. Derrida truly comes to shuffle the cards, to mount a ceaseless battle against the agony of oppositions, the agony of common sense, the agony of 'reason' in its doubly fearful attempt to warrant overarching survival through all types of orientations. Derrida exposes one to survival from the start (that is before the fearful threat or exposure to violent death). If there is a fragile distinction to be made between sovereignty and unconditionality, it must rest in two, but perhaps more, different ways to relate to the other, namely exploitation and exposure.

There is certainly exposure in exploitation. This exposure is exploitative in at least two ways. On the one hand, it can signify the actual entrapment of 'social' forces in a chain of material and symbolic extraction of the spark or the working trauma that each living–dying trace can inflict upon its environment (the plantation, the production line, the office, the information network; and, at bottom, all hierarchic binary machines are forms of direct exposure to exploitation). On the other hand, this exposure is not simply material or symbolic. It is also cognitive. That is, what Hobbes indicates upon reflection of existing social processes (in fact hardly extricable from the colonial enterprise) is also the cognitive aspect of exposure to exploitation. One inscribes oneself into a system of sovereign exploitation because there is a rational gain, that is, to stave off death.

What Derrida proposes with the 'to come' is a postulation towards the exposure of a generalized restlessness. That is the equal exposure of the living–dying to the restless and, in this sense, free environment of experiences of suffering and joy. A postulation always poses a certain subtle law. This is not to say that Derrida has 'laid down the law' of deconstruction, or anything of this nature (like Bennington's *Legislations*).[114] Yet, every writing—every inscription, description, or performance—that provides an incision onto the sediments of normality will also, albeit minimally be a postulation. The postulation of the 'to come' is a subtle but unmistakeable one. One in which the restless movement of *coming* comes to the fore, and requires the enjoyment of *coming* in all its contours, beyond the common sense of binary distinctions. Yet, as a law, albeit a dim one, the 'to come' cannot avoid the risk of turning back against itself, and violating 'itself,' exploiting and concentrating its forces, and even turning itself into a guidance: 'this risk is ineluctable' (as in the phenomenon of law's corruption of autoimmunity).[115] In this sense it can always revert to sovereignty, and as sovereignty, it can turn into normalized calculability, but these risks remain crucial for it to be 'to come,' and not any type of predictable or settled enterprise.

We have seen once again that sovereignty cannot be easily distinguished from unconditionality. Further, in Derrida, one can see at work a pursuit of exposure to fear, to a passion and affection, with the purpose of warranting against, cautioning against the ceaseless move towards survival that leads to so entrenched and hierarchic distinctions. I have struggled to show the complexity of the deconstruction of sovereignty, towards another 'to come.'

∽

I have enquired whether the role of the unconditional would not be better and more aptly rendered through the notion of the 'to come' itself (the role of the unconditional is the role of a postulation towards intense exposure; I do not see that in the ultimate distinction between unconditionality and sovereignty). One may think of the 'to come' as the unconditional, but that in my reading is very reductive of the 'to come' in its full linguistic, literary, temporal, and spatial connotations. The only way to depart from sovereignty is to put forward overexposure, in a sustained commitment to the 'to come.' Sovereignty is a principle of exploitation of the 'to come.' Instead of letting the 'to come' come, sovereign powers extract the forces of 'coming,' accumulating in themselves such enjoyment, violating compassion and the experience of possibility and impossibility of shared-out enjoyment.[116] What is necessary is a new strategic discourse that takes into account the pre-existence and wide dissemination of sovereign exposure.

In light of this complication of the distinction between sovereignty and unconditionality, one could still question whether the earlier distinction between future and 'to come' should not be forsaken. As I have explained, this very distinction is also fragile. Future and ideals represent a minimum form of the underexposed constitution. They are not entirely debunked with the widening of sovereignty and sovereign subjectivities. In fact, there are many ways in which the future is employed in a sovereign way, without any legal, moral, or ethical commitment to it. Exposure and underexposure (in a certain way 'roguishness' and idealism) keep playing an infinite game. That is not to say there is not something worth fighting for in sovereign exposure. In a sense what I do is to rehabilitate in a different way this something for which Derrida also attempted to fight.

Instead of placing this Derridean discourse of exposure in the realm of the unconditional, I propose to fight for another articulation of the conditional and the unconditional, one that strives against the agony of this very form or articulation, the binary machines, the walling up and wheeling of exclusion and exploitation. Yet to strive against that agony, one has to account for what is keeping that game of agonies in play. 'Exposing' or identifying it simply, I maintain, is no way forward, no good strategy. The game of agonies includes exposing them, roguishly condoning them in the minimum pleasure of the knowledge of their existence. It is necessary rather to promote a shift in the quality of exposure. But a shift in quality can also be achieved through a dramatic shift in quantity. That is why a careful experience of the 'to come'—catering for its delicate equal coming—requires an overexposure and a different form of commitment to it.

This is not to defend the coming of a presence, the authentic presence to the life of enjoyment and even suffering. Rather, I have attempted a fine-tuning of an affection exposed to living with the 'ghost,' the 'spectres' themselves; an attempt to confront survival (life–dying, and death–living) itself. This is not an attempt to find the truth or the life behind the spectres. Rather it is an attempt to be sensitive to the truth of the spectres themselves, of the sense-making and hyper-theatricality (more than in the 'view' of the theatre, but still staged) of surviving amidst spectres of spectres, without barring arbitrarily any supposed presence of the living. In this tuning and in this sensitivity to the struggles for a fuller enjoyment of the to come, one cannot bar the possibility that 'outdated' or 'dangerous' vocabularies might be used by those who experience the wheel of exploitation and/or exclusion (one may think of notions such as 'people,' 'hope,' 'utopia,' 'dignity,' 'honesty,' 'authenticity,' 'nationhood,' 'privacy' and even 'sovereignty' itself). Pending their irreducible contexts and their capacity to open themselves to their own frailties and fears, such notions can and have been useful to various concrete struggles in recent years. Such openness is an element of the overexposure here called to the fore.

The truthful experience of living with spectres—this is the challenge of the 'to come.' Here the true 'come' is distinguishable from the future and from sovereignty. On the one hand, the future is a form of underexposure (or concealment, understood in this way, and even in concealment, even in the great concealment of ideals, there is never an absolute closing off; rather, an underexposure). On the other hand, the knowledgeable demeanour of sovereign exposure is one that is not entirely devoid of underexposure. Sovereign exposure is still a form of concealment, a concealment of its own sensibility whose greatest example is the exploitation of fear of fear and the rejection of fear as such. Sovereignty, rational and passionate, is the exploitation of the spectre of passions (their ruin, uncertainty, im-possibility). If there is a move towards exposure in sovereignty, that is what needs to be retained. Yet in Derrida, and in this book, such exposure must happen in a different way, without fear of fear, within the tension of passion, uncertainty, and im-possibility; in brave 'conversation' (or deliberation) with the spectres.[117]

One can realize now the intense exposure, the intense 'constitutional' charge that Derrida's expression 'democracy to come' involves. Democracy has a restless core in its constant process of exposure to the constitutions and deconstitutions of law; in the experience that democracy entails of the very lines and divides of sociability. The 'to come,' in turn, is not a term to warrant the place of an ideal, which would stabilize the restlessness of democracy, of that very restless core. In my reading, the 'to come' is not even pure unconditionality. It is rather a generalized exposure to the restlessness of living–dying, including of course also its unconditional element that is often concealed or underexposed and which must be for that reason emphasized (but even the radical 'to come' is not immune to underexposure; what happens is that in this articulation the 'to come' advances, comparatively, a more intense exposure).

Do I mean that 'democracy' and 'to come' are merely coterminous? Far from it. If the 'to come' is generalized exposure, democracy, more specifically, pertains to the tradition of exposure to the law in ruins, to the dividing lines of sociability. To be sure, however, the latter may disclose more generalized issues and the 'to come' itself. In addition, my approach to the 'to come' is an interested one; I develop it with legal-ethical-political questions in mind (a more literary or theological-eschatological approach would also be possible). It is already an attempt to highlight the restless character of democracy. For that, it was important to differentiate the 'to come' from the future and from sovereignty which operate concealment and exploitation, with emphasis on concealment for the first and on exploitation for the second. This is concealment and exploitation of the restless character of living–dying, of the spectres of the world that 'make' the 'world.' If they are not exactly coterminous, there may be no democracy without the 'to come,' and there may be no 'to come' without democracy.

As I have maintained throughout this book, Derrida favours the paradox of paradox, the clash of different universalizing experiences. Yet I have used this 'strategy' to reactivate the 'to come' itself. That is, the 'to come' is wrested from the pure sphere of unconditionality, and brought back to the more dangerous and menacing site of the border between conditionality and unconditionality; in the movement of its own performativity and in the joy that overrides it. And thus, this is the opportunity for a different articulation of the latter, struggling against situations of exploitation and exclusion; opening the avenue for the clash of universalizing experiences, for the raising of different voices and their appraisal through a novel 'theoretical' vocabulary. Here is the chance of another postulation of democracy, in which a different constitutional exposure is pursued, one that is more truthful, more radical, more exposed—an overexposure.

POSTULATING FORMALIZATIONS

By definition, this call to interpret and intensify a postulation of democracy should not have an end. For it is intertwined with endless legal-political-ethical problems. This postulation requires a continuation. If there is a conclusion to be thought, it can but be provisional or tentative because the book pleas, more than anything, for further thinking, practical instantiations, and political action.

I have argued that democracy to come can be interpreted as constitutional exposure. Moreover, I have sought to intensify that very exposure towards a more radical experience of democratic exposure, an overexposure. I have performed this task by means of addressing each constitutive element of the phrase in question: democracy, law, and 'to come.' I have *interpreted* Derrida's postulation in the first two chapters and *intensified* it in the last two chapters. In all, I disclose a journey of thought and research that contributed to furthering the postulation of 'democracy to come.' Democracy to come emerges as the exposure of exposures, the hyperbole of exposures, as a discourse of constitutional exposure that opens the way for an overexposure, for a radical deconstitution, for a 'true' coming of democracy.

∽

I can now propose a few formalizations. These propositions do not belong 'logically' to the book. That is, their inclusion here is not a direct consequence of what came before. Yet, they do resonate with what came before, and, more importantly, they are open to new ways of articulating the topics of this book. They are ready to support coming journeys of research, thinking, and political action. Let us check, then, these *interested* formalizations, these formal postulations, on three interrelated dimensions, which further my contribution to the Derridean discourse of *constitutional exposure* and shape an intense postulation:

exposure, constitutionality, and 'to come.'

Exposure

I have systematically related the place of democracy to the quality-quantity of exposure. I discern three intertwined moments here. The first moment is that of underexposure. In this instance, the ruins of law are concealed. Yet, in this very concealment, there is never a final closing off; there may well be opportunities for heightening the perception of these gaps or fractures in the structure of concealment. Such an underexposure leads to experiences of suffering and subjection, inscribing people into a hierarchical apparatus of power. Thus, if the primary experience of this moment is concealment, there is also exploitation in concealment. As seen in chapter two, monarchy is the symbolic name of this underexposure. One could yet conceive of several other experiences; reliance on predetermined visions of the future, ideals, and hope simply tend to protract the order of concealment into a linear time frame.

The second instance is that of exposure. Here the ruins of law are exposed; exposed as exploitation in the material sense and as awareness in the cognitive sense. There is wide inscription of material exposure of people into several codes of exploitation and extraction of social forces (the capitalist code in the Marxist tradition, but not only this: patriarchy, racism, and anthropocentrism may also be deemed such codes). There is also, almost concomitantly, perception of this heightened process. Often, the knowledge of exploitation can lead to a degree of complacency (when one is subjected to it), and to a degree of enjoyment (when it is the suffering of the other that is exposed). Material (to include the passionate affection to social symbols) and cognitive exposures are not incompatible with exploitation, and yet there is a degree of concealment, an element of underexposure.

This element manifests itself in the extent to which people condone a limited exposure, when one's corporeity is included in social codes in necessarily only partial ways, severing the vicariousness of one's social experience, for such vicarious restlessness would unsettle the code. Underexposure also appears in the lack of exposure to one's own role, complacent or joyful in the social process of exploitation. This is the instance of sovereign democracies, as I have argued in chapters two, three, and four.

The third instance is that of a conceivable overexposure. Here one radicalizes both processes of exposure, bringing them to their ultimate consequences, that is, producing an exposure of the exposure. This is conceivable by means of the elaboration of a discourse that brings together the several codes of exploitation. The narrative of exposure is itself a meta-code. This is one that includes the experience of exploitation and the lines of flight from the code. In the third moment of this elaboration, one does not simply destroy all underexposure towards pure exposure. Rather, one reaches a delicate sensibility of the interplay between exposure and underexposure, where the truth of this very interplay is carefully experimented.

Finally, one can read this overexposure in the relational sense of a heightened sensibility that threatens the attempted closures of both underexposure and exposure. Here, without claiming to do away with all underexposure, one challenges the current experiences of underexposure in one's faithfulness to a more radical experience of exposure. The process that has already started is reclaimed, brought to its ultimate consequences, and instead of a difference in degree, precisely because of its intensity, one can perceive a difference of quality between underexposure and exposure on the one hand, and overexposure, on the other hand. This third moment or instance is that of democracy to come.

Law and Constitutionality

Another explanatory bipolarity that I have articulated is that between constitution and deconstitution. This is intimately linked to underexposure and exposure; for a constitution is achieved precisely by concealing its own ruins. Furthermore, in a world always already pervaded by the process of constitution, deconstitution is achieved by means of exposing the fragility of constitutions. Law itself is caught between these two moments. On the one hand, law requires a constitution to posit itself, to affirm itself radically in a space of deconstitution. On the other hand, in order to affirm itself radically law needs to mobilize deconstitution, and it cannot by any means destroy it if it strives to survive. In addition, by means of this process, the space of law is one pervaded by both constitution and deconstitution. One can find 'law' always in ruins, which means that it is always posited and deposed, constituted and deconstituted. Yet, there are social formations in which deconstitution prevails, as those in which exposure prevails (modernity is marked by the prevalence of deconstitution and exposure).

What is the role of democracy to come in this regard? It can be perceived as an intensification of deconstitution. Democracy to come fights the minimum of constitution that always subsists in even the most heightened deconstituton. Yet, since there can be no pure deconstitution, what democracy to come does is to bring the interplay itself to fruition, exposing this very game. In the realm of constitutionality, the name one can give to this third moment is hyperbolic constitution. Democracy to come operates a hyperbolic effect. It brings together two intense processes of 'constitutional' setting, that is, both processes that involve constitution and deconstruction. This hyperbolic moment may be seen as a third moment, after historical experiences of constitution and deconstruction (provided that one notices that though there is a link, it is not one of necessity between them, and provided that one notices that each one does not close off the other).

Yet, one can also take this 'constitutional' hyperbole in relation to constitution and deconstruction as a second moment. This is the moment in which the differential alliance between constitution and deconstruction is exposed and brought to fruition. Here the constitutional experience is brought to a new level. Not that constitution and deconstruction will disappear, but that they may be more truthfully experienced. This hyperbole would be more truthful to the equality of exposure, towards a greater equality of forces (in the struggle against hierarchy, or subordination, but not against all dissymmetry). The hyperbole does not belong only to a symbolic level of constitutional struggles; it reaches the very sensibility to one's exploitation and non-exploitation, one's submission into a symbolic structure or to the gap within it. The hyperbolic moment is not entirely novel, though. As overexposure, it has already commenced in all radicalizations of the sense of the experience of what is (coming) and in all radical democratic deliberation on the dividing lines of sociability, on the law.

'To Come'

Finally, on the level of the 'to come,' one can speak of three experiences: the denegation of the 'to come' in the legal-political-ethical use of 'the future' or of 'ideals,' its abuse or exploitation in sovereign democracies, and its truth in democracy to come, or more briefly, in the *true to come* (true here not as revelation, but as insistence, adherence, and faith in it; true, akin to the German *trauer*, to trust; truth as the hyperbole of trust).[1] That denegation is possible also by a careful manipulation of the 'to come,' contorted into the future present, devoid of more challenging modes of time. An exploitation occurs by means of an exposed intensification of the movement of the 'to come,' where an equality of forces is elevated as the very mechanism for wide-ranging subjection into hierarchical and often systemic binary codes, such as 'have/not-have' (hardly any solid 'tradition' remains in this instance).

The *true to come*, the 'to come' to which democracy to come aspires is both akin to and distinguishable from the 'to come' of sovereign democracies. In these social formations, the 'to come' is mobilized, time is restless, speed and acceleration are intensified. Spatial restlessness also happens and delocalization becomes the norm. Yet, in exploiting the 'to come' to the extreme, there remains a minimum order of its denegation which the future holds often in a 'roguish' or contemptuous way. 'The future' is one way of settling the restless, temporal, and spatial experiences of sovereign democracies. Ultimately, though, every exploitation of the 'to come,' every instance of its violation by a hierarchical code has recourse to fear, and mainly to social structures that exploit the fear of fear. Thus, on the one hand, the *true to come* intensifies an experience of the 'to come' existent in sovereign democracies; on the other hand, it is distinguishable from that experience for it rejects exploitative orders that thrive within democracies and through democratic forms.

There is no direct political project behind this postulating vocabulary. But it lends itself to thinking democracy and politics in more radical and unheard-of ways: beyond 'democratic' complicity with exploitative and hierarchical social orders (including the global one), beyond 'democratic' complacency with established forms and legitimation mechanisms, beyond rationalistic reductions of political or social goals. Such new thinking in turn may be an element of contemporary political action. Perhaps the exposed truth of democracy—to, with and beyond its people—imports its constitutional *salvation*, or salutation, its *coming*.

BIBLIOGRAPHY

Works by Derrida

Derrida, Jacques. 'Introduction.' In Husserl, Edmund, *L'origine de la géométrie*. 3–171. Paris: PUF, 1962; *Edmund Husserl's 'Origin of Geometry.'* Translated by J. P. Leavy. Lincoln, NE: University of Nebraska Press, 1989.

———. 'Force et signification.' In *L'Écriture et la différence*, 9–49. Paris: Éditions du Seuil, 1967; 'Force and Signification.' In *Writing and Difference*, translated by A. Bass, 3–30. London: Routledge & Kegan Paul, 1978.

———. 'De l'économie restreinte à l'économie générale: Un hégelianisme sans réserve.' In *L'écriture et la difference,* 369–408. Paris: Éditions du Seuil, 1967; 'From Restricted to General Economy: A Hegelianism Without Reserve.' In *Writing and Difference, 251–77*. London: Routledge & Kegan Paul, 1978.

———. *L'Écriture et la différence.* Paris: Éditions du Seuil, 1967; *Writing and Difference.* Translated by A. Bass. London: Routledge & Kegan Paul, 1978.

———. *De la grammatologie.* Paris: Galilée, 1967; *Of Grammatology*. Translated by G. C. Spivak. Baltimore: Johns Hopkins University Press, 1997.

———. *Positions.* Paris: Minuit, 1972; 'Interview: Jacques Derrida—Positions.' Translated by G. Scarpetta and J. L. Houdebine. *Diacritics* 2/4 (1972), 35–43.

———. 'Les fins de l'homme.' In *Marges de la philosophie,* 129–64. Paris: Éditions de Minuit, 1972; 'The Ends of Man.' In *Margins of Philosophy*, translated by A. Bass, 108–36. Chicago: The University of Chicago Press, 1982.

———. 'Signature Événement Contexte.' In *Marges de la philosophie*. Paris: Les Éditions de Minuit, 1972, 365–93; 'Signature Event Context.' In *Margins of Philosophy*, translated by A. Bass, 307–30. Chicago: University of Chicago Press, 1985.

———. *Marges de la philosophie.* Paris: Les Éditions de Minuit, 1972; *Margins of Philosophy*. Translated by A. Bass. Brighton. Sussex: The Harvester Press, 1982.

———. *La dissémination.* Paris, Éditions du Seuil, 1972; *Dissemination*. Translated by B. Johnson. London: Continuum, 2004.

———. 'Fors: Les mots anglés de Nicolas Abraham and Maria Torok.' In

N. Araham and M. Torok, *Le Verbier de l'homme aux loups*, 9–73. Paris: Flammarion, 1976; 'Fors: The Anglish words of Nicolas Abraham and Maria Torok.' *Georgia Review* 31/1 (1976), 64–116.

———. 'Préjugés—Devant la loi.' In *La Faculté de juger*, edited by J. Derrida et al., 87–139 Paris: Les Éditions de Minuit, 1985; 'Before the law.' In *Acts of Literature*. translated by A. Ronell, 181–220. New York: Routledge, 1992.

———. 'Lettre à un ami japonais.' *Le Promeneur*, XLII (1985), 2–4; 'Letter to a Japanese Friend.' In *Derrida and Difference*, edited by D. Wood and R. Bernasconi, 1–5. Coventry: Parousia Press, 1985.

———. 'Désistance.' In *Psyché: Inventions de l'autre*, 597–638. Paris: Galilée, 1987; 'Introduction: Desistance.' In P. Lacoue-Labarthe, *Typography—Mimesis, Philosophy, Politics*, 1–42. Cambridge, MA: Harvard University Press, 1989.

———. 'Privilège. Titre justificatif et remarques introductives.' In *Du droit à la philosophie*, 9–108. Paris: Galilée, 1990; 'Privilege: Justificatory Title and Introductory Remarks.' In *Who's Afraid of Philosophy? Right to Philosophy 1*, translated by J. Plug, 1–66. Stanford: Stanford University Press, 2002.

———. 'Mochlos ou le conflit des facultés.' In *Du droit à la philosophie*, 397–438. Paris: Galilée, 1990; 'Mochlos, or The Conflict of the Faculties.' In *Eyes of the University: Right of Philosophy II*, translated by J. Plug et al., 83–112. Stanford: Stanford University Press, 2004.

———. 'Ponctuations: le temps de la thèse.' In *Du Droit à la philosophie*, 439–60. Paris: Galilée, 1990; 'Punctuations: The Time of a Thesis.' In *Eyes of the University: Right of Philosophy II*, translated by J. Plug et al., 113–28. Stanford: Stanford University Press, 2004.

———. *Du droit à la philosophie*. Paris: Galilée, 1990; *Who's Afraid of Philosophy? Right to Philosophy 1*. Translated by J. Plug. Stanford: Stanford University Press, 2002; *Eyes of the University: Right to Philosophy 2*. Translated by J. Plug et al.. Stanford: Stanford University Press, 2004.

———. *La genèse dans la philosophie de Husserl*. Paris: PUF, 1991 [dissertation, 1954]; *The Problem of Genesis in Husserl's Philosophy*. Translated by M. Hobson. Chicago: The University of Chicago Press, 2003.

———. 'La démocratie ajournée.' In *L'Autre cap*, 103–124. Paris, Les Éditions de Minuit, 1991; 'Call It a Day for Democracy.' In *The Other Heading*, translated by A-P. Brault and M. Naas, 84–109. Bloomington: Indiana University Press, 1992.

———. *L'Autre Cap*. Paris: Les Éditions de Minuit, 1991; *The Other Heading*. Translated by A-P. Brault and M. Naas. Bloomington: Indiana University Press, 1992.

———. *Acts of Literature*. Translated by A. Ronell. New York: Routledge, 1992.

———. 'Y a-t-il une langue philosophique?' In *Points de Suspension—Entretiens*, 229–240. Paris: Galilée, 1992; 'Is There a Philosophical Language?' In *The Derrida–Habermas Reader*, edited by L. Thomassen, translated by P. Kamuf, 35–45. Edinburgh: Edinburgh University Press, 2006.

———. *Passions: 'L'offrande oblique.'* Paris: Galilée, 1993; 'Passions: "An Oblique Offering".' In *On the Name*, translated by T. Dutoit, 3–34. Stanford: Stanford University Press, 1995.

———. *Apories: Mourir—s'attendre aux 'limites de la vérité.'* Paris: Galilée, 1993; *Aporias*. Translated by T. Dutoit. Stanford: Stanford University Press, 1993.

———. *Spectres de Marx—L'état de la dette, le travail du deuil et la nouvelle Internationale*. Paris: Galilée, 1993; *Specters of Marx—The State of the Debt, the Work of Mourning, and the New International*. Translated by P. Kamuf. New York: Routledge, 1994.

———. *Force de loi—le fondement mystique de l'autorité*. Paris, Galilée, 1994; 'Force of Law—The "Mystical Foundation of Authority".' In *Acts of Religion*, edited by G. Anidjar. New York: Routledge, 2002.

———. 'L'oreille de Heidegger: Philopolémologie (*Geschlecht* IV).' In *Politiques de l'amitié*, 341–419. Paris: Galilée, 1994; 'Heidegger's Ear: Philopolemology (*Geschlecht* IV).' In *Reading Heidegger: Commemorations*, edited by J. Sallis, translated by J. P. Leavey, 163–218. Bloomington: Indiana University Press, 1993.

———. *Politiques de l'amitié*. Paris: Galilée, 1994; *Politics of Friendship*. Translated by G. Collins. London: Verso, 1997.

———. *Le monolinguisme de l'autre, ou la prothèse d'origine*. Paris: Galilée, 1996; Monolingualism of the Other, or the Prosthesis of Origin. Translated by P. Mensah. Stanford: Stanford University Press, 1998.

———. 'Remarks on Deconstruction and Pragmatism.' In *Deconstruction and Pragmatism*, edited by C. Mouffe, translated by S. Critchley, 77–88. London: Verso, 1996.

———. 'Performative powerlessness.' *Constellations* 7/4 (2000), 466–8.

———. *Le toucher, Jean-Luc Nancy*. Paris: Galilée, 2000; *On Touching—Jean-Luc Nancy*. Translated by C. Irizarry. Stanford: Stanford University Press, 2005.

———. *Foi et Savoir—Les deux sources de la religion aux limits de la simple raison*. Paris: Éditions du Seuil, 2000; 'Faith and Knowledge.' In *Acts of Religion*, translated by S. Weber, 42–101. New York: Routledge, 2002.

———. 'Performative Powerlessness.' *Constellations* 7/4 (2000), 467–8.

———. 'Une certaine possibilité impossible de dire l'événement.' In *Dire l'événement, est-ce possible?* edited by G. Soussana, J. Derrida and A. Nouss, 79–112. Paris: L'Harmattan, 2001; 'A Certain Impossible Possibility of Saying the Event.' Translated by G. Walker. *Critical Inquiry* 33 (2007), 441–61.

———. 'La machine à traitement de textes.' In *Papier Machine,* 151–66. Paris: Galilée, 2001; 'The Word Processor.' In *Paper Machine*, translated by R.

Bowlby, 19–32. Stanford: Stanford University Press, 2005.

———. 'Pour José Rainha. *Ce que je crois et crois savoir ... .*' In *Papier Machine*, 333–6. Paris: Galilée, 2001; 'For José Rainha: What I Believe and Believe I know.' In *Paper Machine*, translated by R. Bowlby, 109–11. Stanford: Stanford University Press, 2005.

———. *Papier Machine*. Paris: Galilée, 2001; *Paper Machine*. Translated by R. Bowlby. Stanford: Stanford University Press, 2005.

———. *L'Université sans condition*. Paris: Galilée, 2001; 'University without Condition.' In *Without Alibi*, edited by P. Kamuf, 202–37. Stanford: Stanford University Press, 2002.

———. *Without Alibi*. Translated by P. Kamuf. Stanford: Stanford University Press, 2002.

———. Nancy, Jean-Luc, 'Responsabilité—du sens à venir.' In *Sens en tous sens—Autour des travaux de Jean-Luc Nancy*, edited by F. Guibal and J-C. Martin, 165–200. Paris: Galilée, 2002.

———. 'Declarations of Independence.' In *Negotiations—Interventions and Interviews, 1971–2001*, 46–54. Stanford: Stanford University Press, 2002.

———. 'Open Letter to Bill Clinton.' In *Negotiations: Interventions and Interviews 1971–2001*, 130–2. Stanford: Stanford University Press, 2002.

———. 'Politics and Friendship.' In *Negotiations: Interventions and interviews 1971–2001*, 147–98. Stanford: Stanford University Press, 2002.

———. 'As If It Were Possible, "within Such Limits".' In *Negotiations: Interventions and Interviews 1971–2001*, 343–70. Stanford: Stanford University Press, 2002.

———. *Negotiations—Interventions and Interviews, 1971–2001*. Stanford: Stanford University Press, 2002.

———. *Acts of Religion*. Translated by G. Anidjar *et al.* New York: Routledge, 2002.

———. 'Pas.' In *Parages*, 2nd edn, 19–116, Paris: Galilée, 1986–2003.

———. *Parages*, 2nd edn. Paris: Galilée, 1986–2003.

———. 'Abraham, l'autre.' In *Judéités—Questions pour Jacques Derrida*, edited by J. Cohen and R. Zagury-Orly, 11–42. Paris: Galilée, 2003.

———. *Chaque fois unique, la fin du monde*. Paris: Galilée, 2003; *The Work of Mourning*. Chicago: University of Chicago Press, 2001.

———. *Béliers. Le dialogue ininterrompu: Entre deux infinis, le poème*. Paris: Galilée, 2003; 'Rams: Uninterrupted dialogue—between two infinities, the poem.' In *Sovereignties in Question*, translated by T. Dutoit *et al.*, 135–63. New York: Fordham University Press, 2005.

———. *Voyous—deux essais sur la raison*. Paris: Galilée, 2003; *Rogues—Two Essays on Reason*. Translated by A-P Brault and M. Naas. Stanford: Stanford University Press, 2005.

———. 'Le lieu dit: Strasbourg.' In J. Derrida *et al.*, *Penser à Strasbourg*, 31–58.

Paris: Galilée-Ville de Strasbourg, 2004.

Derrida, Jacques *et al.*, *Penser à Strasbourg*. Paris: Galilée-Ville de Strasbourg, 2004.

———. 'La bête et le souverain.' In *La démocratie à venir*, edited by M-L. Mallet, 433–476. Paris: Galilée, 2004.

———. 'La vérité blessante, Ou le corps à corps des langues—Entretien avec Jacques Derrida.' *Europe* (May 2004), 8–28; 'The truth that wounds: From an interview.' In *Sovereignties in Question: The poetics of Paul Celan*, translated by T. Dutoit *et al.*, 164–9. New York: Fordham University Press, 2005.

———. *Sovereignties in Question: The Poetics of Paul Celan*. Translated by T. Dutoit *et al.* New York: Fordham University Press, 2005.

———. *D'un ton apocalyptique adopté naguère en philosophie*. Paris: Galilée, 2005; 'On a Newly Arisen Apocalyptic Tone in Philosophy.' In *Raising the Tone of Philosophy*, edited by P. Fenves, 117–71. Baltimore: The Johns Hopkins University Press, 1993.

———. and De Cauter, Lieven, 'For a Justice to Come: An Interview with Jacques Derrida.' In *The Derrida-Habermas Reader*, edited by L. Thomassen, 259–69, Edinburgh: Edinburgh University Press, 2006.

———. *L'animal que donc je suis*. Paris: Galilée, 2006; 'The Animal that Therefore I Am (More to Follow).' *Critical Inquiry*, 28 (2002), 369–418.

———. 'Le souverain bien—ou l'Europe en mal de souveraineté.' *Cités*, 30 (2007), 103–40.

———. *Séminaire La bête et le souverain*, vol. I (2001–2). Paris: Galilée, 2008; *The Beast and the Sovereign*, vol. 1. Translated by G. Bennington. Chicago: Chicago University Press, 2009.

———. *Séminaire La bête et le souverain*, vol. II (2002–3). Paris: Galilée, 2010.

Works by Other Authors

Abensour, Miguel. La démocratie contre l'Etat—Marx et le moment machiavélien. Paris: Editions du Félin, 2004.

———. Rire des Lois, des Magistrats et des Dieux—L'impulsion Saint Just. Paris: Horlieu, 2004.

Agacinski, Sylviane, Jacques Derrida, Sarah Kofman, Ph. Lacoue-Labarthe, Jean-Luc Nancy, and Bernard Pautrat. *Mimesis des articulations*. Paris: Aubier-Flammarion, 1975.

Agamben, Giorgio. *Language and Death: The Place of Negativity*. Translated by K. E. Pinkus. Minneapolis: University of Minnesota Press, 1991.

———. *Homo Sacer: Sovereign Power and Bare Life*. Translated by D. Heller-Roazen. Stanford: Stanford University Press, 1998.

———. 'Pardes: The Writing of Potentiality.' In *Potentialities—Collected Essays in Philosophy*. Translated by D. Heller-Roazen, 205–19. Stanford: Stanford University Press, 1999.

———. 'Friendship.' *Contretemps* (December 2004), 2–7.

———. *State of Exception*. Chicago: University of Chicago Press, 2005.

———. Il Regno e la Gloria: Per una Genealogia dell'economia e del governo. Vicenza: Neri Pozza, 2007.

Agamben, Giorgio, Alain Badiou, Daniel Bensaïd, Wendy Brown, Jean-Luc Nancy, Jacques Rancière, Kristin Ross & Slavoj Žižek, eds. *Démocratie, dans quel état?* Paris: La fabrique, 2009.

Arendt, Hannah. *The Human Condition*. Chicago: The University of Chicago Press, 1958.

Aristotle. *Ethics to Eudeme*. London: William Heinemann LTD, 1952.

———. *The Politics and The Constitution of Athens*. Cambridge: CUP, 1996.

Arnaud, André-Jean. *Le droit trahi par la philosophie*. Rouen: Bibliothèque du Centre d'Études Juridiques et Politiques de Rouen, 1977.

———. Critique de la Raison Juridique 2, Gouvernants sans frontières—Entre mondialisation et post-mondialisation. Paris: L.G.D.J., 2003.

———.Entre modernité et mondialisation—Leçons d'histoire de la philosophie du droit et de l'état, 2nd edn. Paris: LGDJ, 2004.

Badiou, Alain. 'Of an Obscure Disaster.' Translated by B. P. Faulks. *Lacanian Ink*, 22 (2004), 58–89.

Balibar, Etienne. '"Possessive Individualism" Reversed, From Locke to Derrida.' *Constellations* 9/3 (2002), 299–317.

———. 'Prolegomena to Sovereignty.' In *We, the People of Europe? Reflections on Transnational Citizenship*. 133–154. Princeton: Princeton University Press, 2004.

———. *We, the People of Europe? Reflections on Transnational Citizenship*. Princeton: Princeton University Press, 2004.

———. Violence et civilité : Wellek Library Lectures et autres essais de philosophie politique. Paris: Galilée, 2010.

Barreto, José Manuel. 'Human Rights and Emotions from the Perspective of the Colonized: Anthropophagi, Legal Surrealism and Subaltern Studies.' *Revista de Estudos Constitucionais, Hermenêutica e Teoria do Direito (RECHTD)* 5/2, julho-dezembro (2013), 106–15.

Bateson, Gregory. *Steps to an Ecology of Mind*. Chicago: University of Chicago Press, 1972.

Baudrillard, Jean. *Paroxysm—Interviews with Philippe Petit*. London: Verso, 1998.

Bauman, Zygmunt. *Liquid Modernity*. Cambridge: Polity, 2000.

Beato, Zelina. Transcription of Derrida's course in the EHESS (École des Hautes Études en Sciences Sociales), academic year 2002–3, in http://www.unicamp.

br/iel/traduzirderrida/Ecole_2002.htm#26mar, accessed on 30 June 2004.

Benjamin, Walter. 'Schicksal und Charakter.' In *Walter Benjamin Gesammelte Schriften*, IIi, edited by R. Tiedemann and H. Schweppenhäuser, 171–9. Berlin: Suhrkamp, 1977); 'Fate and Character.' In *Walter Benjamin—Selected Writings*, vol. 1, edited by M. Bullock and M. W. Jennings, 201–6. Cambridge: MA, Harvard University Press, 1996.

———. 'Über Sprache überhaupt und über die Sprache des Menschen.' In *Walter Benjamin Gesammelte Schriften*, IIi, edited by R. Tiedemann and H. Schweppenhäuser, 140–57. Berlin: Suhrkamp, 1977); 'On Language as Such and on the Language of Man.' In *Walter Benjamin—Selected Writings*, vol. 1, edited by M. Bullock and M. W. Jennings, 62–74. Cambridge, MA: Harvard University Press, 1996.

———. 'Zur Kritik der Gewalt.' In *Walter Benjamin Gesammelte Schriften*, IIi, edited by R. Tiedemann and H. Schweppenhäuser, 179–203. Berlin: Suhrkamp, 1977); 'Critique of Violence.' In *Walter Benjamin—Selected Writings*, vol. 1, edited by M. Bullock and M. W. Jennings, 236–52. Cambridge, MA: Harvard University Press, 1996.

———. 'Ursprung des deutschen Trauerspiels.' In *Walter Benjamin Gesammelte Schriften*, IIi, edited by R. Tiedemann and H. Schweppenhäuser, 203–430. Berlin: Suhrkamp, 1977; *The Origin of German Tragic Drama*. Translated by J. Osborne. London: Verso, 1998.

———. 'Über den Begriff der Geschichte.' In *Walter Benjamin Gesammelte Schriften*, Iii, edited by R. Tiedemann and H. Schweppenhäuser, 255–66. Berlin: Suhrkamp, 1977; 'On the Concept of History.' In *Walter Benjamin—Selected Writings*, vol. 1, edited by M. Bullock and M. W. Jennings, 389–400. Cambridge, MA: Harvard University Press, 1996.

———. 'The Right to Use Force.' In *Walter Benjamin—Selected Writings*, vol. 1, edited by M. Bullock and M.W. Jennings, 231–4. Cambridge, MA: Harvard University Press, 1996.

Bennington, Geoffrey. *Legislations—The Politics of Deconstruction*. Verso: London, 1991.

Benvindo, Juliano Zaiden. On the Limits of Constitutional Adjudication: Deconstructing Balancing and Judicial Activism. Heidelberg: Springer, 2010.

Bernstein, Richard. 'Serious Play: The Ethical-Political Horizon of Derrida.' In *The New Constellation: The Ethical-Political Horizons of Modernity/Postmodernity*. 172–98. Cambridge, MA: MIT, 1992.

———. *The New Constellation: The Ethical-Political Horizons of Modernity/Postmodernity*. Cambridge, MA: MIT, 1992.

———. 'Derrida: The Aporia of Forgiveness?' *Constellations* 13/3 (2006), 394–406.

Blanchot, Maurice. *Le pas au-delà*. Paris: Gallimard, 1973.

Bodin, Jean. *On Sovereignty*. Translated by J. H. Franklin. Cambridge: CUP, 1992.

Bosteels, Bruno. 'Force of Nonlaw: Alain Badiou's Theory of Justice.' *Cardozo Law Review* 29/5 (2008), 1905–26.

Bourdieu, Pierre. 'La force du droit: Eléments pour une sociologie du champ juridique.' *Actes de la recherche en sciences sociales* 64/1 1986, 3–19; 'The Force of Law: Towards a Sociology of the Juridical Field.' *The Hastings Law Journal* 38 (1987), 805–53.

———. *Language and Symbolic Power*. Translated by M. Adamson and G. Raymond. Cambridge: Polity Press, 1992.

Cabo Martín, Carlos de. *Teoría Constitucional de la Solidariedad*. Madrid: Marcial Pons, 2006.

Châtelet, François *et al.* 'Titres.' In J. Derrida, *Du droit à la philosophie*, 551–76; 'Titles.' In J. Derrida, *Eyes of the University: Right to Philosophy 2*, translated by J. Plug *et al.*, 195–215. Stanford: Stanford University Press, 2004.

Cohen, Felix. 'Transcendental Nonsense and the Functional Approach.' *Columbia Law Review* 35/6 (1935), 809–49.

Côrtes, Norma. *Esperança e Democracia—As idéias de Álvaro Vieira Pinto*. Belo Horizonte: UFMG, 2003.

Cotta, Sergio. *Il diritto nell'esistenza*, 2nd edn. Milano: Giuffé Editore, 1991.

Critchley, Simon. *Ethics, Politics, Subjectivity*. London: Verso, 1999.

Defoe, Daniel. *Robinson Crusoe*. Oxford: OUP, 1983.

Dejanovic, Sanja, ed. *Nancy and the Political*. Edinburgh: Edinburgh University Press, 2015.

Deleuze, Gilles. *La philosophie critique de Kant*. Paris: PUF, 1963.

Devisch, Ignaas. 'Doing Justice to Existence: Jean-Luc Nancy and "the Size of Humanity".' *Law and Critique* 22 (2011), 1–13.

Dewey, John. 'Creative Democracy: The Task before Us.' In *The Later Works of John Dewey, 1925–1953, vol. 14: 1939–1941, Essays,* edited by J. A. Boydston, 224–30. Carbondale, Ill.: Southern Illinois University Press, 1981.

Douzinas, Costas, and Adam Gearey. *Critical Jurisprudence: The Political Philosophy of Justice*. Oxford: Hart Publishing, 2005.

Dyzenhaus, David. *The Constitution of Law: Legality in a Time of Emergency*. Cambridge: CUP, 2006.

Ewald, François. *L'État providence*. Paris: Grasset, 1986.

Fitzpatrick, Peter. *Modernism and the Grounds of Law*. Cambridge: CUP, 2001.

———. 'Bare Sovereignty: *Homo Sacer* and the Insistence of Law.' Theory and Event 5(2) (2001), 34–67.

———. 'Access as justice.' *Windsor Yearbook of Access to Justice* 23/1 (2005), 3–16.

———. '"New Constitutionalism": Globalism and the constitution(s) of nations.' *Law, Democracy and Development* 10/2 (2006), 1–20.

———. 'Righteous Empire.' *Unbound* 2/1 (2006), 1–18.

———. "What Are the Gods to Us Now?": Secular Theology and the Modernity of Law, *Theoretical Inquiries in Law* 8/1 (2007), 161–90.

Fritsch, Matthias. 'Derrida's Democracy to Come.' *Constellations* 9/4 (2002), 574–97.

Gasché, Rodolphe. *The Tain of the Mirror—Derrida and the Philosophy of Reflection*. Cambridge, MA: Harvard University Press, 1986.

Ghetti, Pablo. 'Às Margens da Deliberação: Por uma política deliberativa *por vir*.' In *Temas de Constitucionalismo e Democracia*, edited by J. R. Vieira, 20–39. Rio de Janeiro: Renovar, 2003.

———. 'Laws of Deliberation: From Audaciousness to Prudence... and Back.' *Law and Critique* 16/3 (2005), 255–75.

———. 'From the Posthumous Memoirs of Humanity: "Democracy *to come*".' *Law, Culture and the Humanities* 1/2 (2005), 208–20.

———. 'World and Waste, or the Law of Liquidity.' In *Liquid Society and its Law*, edited by P. Jiri, 61–77. Aldershot: Ashgate, 2007.

———. Direito e Democracia sob os Espectros de Schmitt: Contribuição à Crítica da Filosofia do Direito de Jürgen Habermas. Rio de Janeiro: Lumen Juris, 2006.

Giddens, Anthony. *The Consequences of Modernity*. Cambridge: Polity, 1991.

Goodrich, Peter. 'Satirical Legal Studies: From the Legists to the Lyzard.' *Michigan Law Review* 103 (2004), 397–517.

———. 'Specters of Law: Why the History of the Legal Spectacle Has Not Been Written.' *UCIRVINE Law Review* 1/3 (2011), 773–812.

Guattari, Felix, and Suely Rolnik. *Molecular Revolution in Brazil*. Los Angeles: Semiotext(e), 2008.

Habermas, Jürgen. *The Theory of Communicative Action*. Boston: Beacon Press, 1987.

———. *Justification and Application: Remarks on Discourse Ethics*. Translated by C. P. Cronin. Cambridge, MA: MIT Press, 1994.

———. *Between Facts and Norms*. Cambridge, MA: MIT Press, 1998.

———. *The Inclusion of the Other: Studies in Political Theory*. Translated by C. Cronin and P. De Greiff. Cambridge, MA: MIT Press, 1999.

———. 'Constitutional democracy: A Paradoxical Union of Contradictory Principles?' *Political Theory* 29/6 (2001), 766–81.

———. 'A Last Farewell: Derrida's Enlightening Impact.' In *The Derrida-Habermas Reader*, edited by L. Thomassen, 307–8. Edinburgh: Edinburgh University Press, 2006.

Harrington, James. *The Commonwealth of Oceana* and *A System of Politics*. Cambridge: CUP, 1992.

Heidegger, Martin. *Fundamental Concepts of Metaphysics: World, solitude, finitude*. Indianapolis: Indiana University Press, 2001.

———. *la pauvreté (die Armut)*. Translated by P. Lacoue-Labarthe and A. Samardzija. Strasbourg: Presses Universitaires de Strasbourg, 2004.

Hirvonen, Ari, ed. *Policentricity—The Multiple Scenes of Law*. London: Pluto Press, 1998.

Hobbes, Thomas. *Leviathan*. Oxford: OUP, 1996.

Holston, James. *Insurgent Citizenship: Disjunctions of democracy and Modernity in Brazil*. Princeton: Princeton University Press, 2008.

Honig, Bonnie. 'Dead Rights, Live Futures: A reply to Habermas's "Constitutional democracy".' *Political Theory* 29/6 (2001), 792–805.

Honneth, Axel. 'The Other of Justice: Habermas and the Ethical Challenge of Postmodernism.' In *Cambridge Companion to Habermas*, edited by S. K. White, 289–324. Cambridge: CUP, 1995.

———. 'Democracy as Reflexive Cooperation: John Dewey and the Theory of Democracy Today.' Political Theory 26/6 (1998), 763–83.

Hutchens, B. C., ed. *Jean-Luc Nancy: Justice, Legality and World*, 11–18. London: Continuum, 2012.

Jennings, Theodore W. JR. *Reading Derrida / Thinking Paul*—On Justice. Stanford: Stanford University Press, 2006.

Kant, Immanuel. 'Perpetual Peace: A Philosophical Sketch.' In *Political Writings*, 112–13. Cambridge: CUP, 1991.

———. *Political Writings*. Cambridge: CUP, 1991.

———. *Metaphysics of Morals*. Translated by M. Gregor. Cambridge: CUP, 1996.

———. *Groundwork of the Metaphysics of Morals*, M. Gregor. Cambridge: CUP, 1998.

———. *Critique of Pure Reason*. Translated by P. Guyer and A. W. Wood. Cambridge: CUP, 1998.

———. *Critique of Judgement*. Translated by N. Walker and J.C. Meredith. Oxford: OUP, 2007.

Keeley, Brian L. 'Making Sense of Senses: Individuating Modalities in Humans and Other Animals.' *The Journal of Philosophy* XCIX/1 (2002), 5–28.

Kelsen, Hans. *Pure Theory of Law*, 2nd edn. Translated by M. Knight. Berkeley: University of California Press, 1967.

Kennedy, Duncan. *A Critique of Adjudication {fin de siècle}*. Cambridge, MA: Harvard University Press, 1998.

Kirchheimer, Otto. 'Weimar—And What Then? An Analysis of a Constitution.' In Burin, F.S. Shell, K.L. *Politics, Law, and Social Change—Selected Essays of Otto Kirchheimer*, Columbia University Press: New York, 1969, 33–74.

Laclau, Ernesto, and Chantal Mouffe. *Hegemony and Socialist Strategy*. London: Verso, 1986.

Laclau, Ernesto. *On Populist Reason*. London: Verso, 2005.

Lacoue-Labarthe, Philippe. 'Typographie.' In Agacinski *et al.*, *Mimesis des articulations*, 168–246. Paris: Aubier-Flammarion, 1975.

———. 'Présentation.' In Martin Heidegger, la pauvreté (die Armut), translated by P. Lacoue-Labarthe and A. Samardzija, 5–65. Strasbourg: Presses Universitaires de Strasbourg, 2004.

———. 'La philosophie fantôme.' *Lignes* (mai 2007), 205–14.

Lawlor, Leonard. *Derrida and Husserl: The Basic Problem of Phenomenology*. Indianapolis: Indiana University Press, 2002.

Lefort, Claude. 'La question de la démocratie.' In *Essais sur le politique, XIX-XX siècles*, 17–30. Paris: Éditions du Seuil, 1986.

———. *Complications: Communism and the Dilemmas of Democracy*. Translated by J Bourg. New York: Columbia University Press, 2007.

Lipovetsky, Gilles. *Hypermodern Times*. Cambridge: Polity, 2005.

Llewelyn, John. *Derrida on the Threshold of Sense*. London: Macmillan 1986.

Luhmann, Niklas. *Law as a Social System*. Translated by K. A. Ziegert. Oxford: OUP, 2004.

Machiavelli, Niccolo. *The Prince*. Cambridge: CUP, 1988.

———. *Discourses on Livy*. Oxford: OUP, 2009.

McCormick, John P. 'Derrida on Law: or Poststucturalism Gets Serious.' *Political Theory* 29/3 (2001), 395–423.

Mallet, Marie-Louise, ed. *La démocratie à venir*. Paris: Galilée, 2004.

Marin, Louis. *Politiques de la représentation*. Paris: Kimé, 2005.

Marx, Karl. *Capital, Volume I: A Critique of Political Economy*. Translated by B. Fowkes. Harmondsworth: Penguin, 1976.

McDonald, Angus. 'The Noble Lie: Critical Constitutionalism, Criticised.' In *Policentricity—The Multiple Scenes of Law*, edited by A. Hirvonen, 61–96. London: Pluto Press, 1998.

Meili, Stephen. 'Cause Lawyers and Social Movements: A Comparative Perspective on Democratic Change in Argentina and Brazil.' In *Cause Lawyering: Political Commitments and Professional Responsabilities*, edited by A. Sarat, 487–522. Oxford: OUP, 1998.

Menke, Christoph. 'Ability and Faith: on the Possibility of Justice.' *Cardozo Law Review* 27 (2005), 595–612.

Michelman, Frank. *Brennan and Democracy*. Princeton: Princeton University Press, 1999.

Montaigne. Michel de, *Essais*, vol. III. Paris: Garnier, 1959.

Montesquieu. *De l'esprit des lois*. Paris: Librairie Garnier Frères, 1944.

Mouffe, Chantal, ed. *Deconstruction and Pragmatism*. London: Routledge, 1999.

Mouffe, Chantal. *The Democratic Paradox*. London: Verso, 2000.

Nancy, Jean-Luc. *Le discours de la syncope*. Paris: Aubier-Flammarion, 1976.

———. 'Lapsus judicii.' In *L'impératif catégorique,* 43–4. Paris: Flammarion,

1981.

———. *L'impératif catégorique*. Paris: Flammarion, 1981.

———. *The Experience of Freedom*. Translated by B. McDonald. Stanford: Stanford University Press, 1993.

———. 'Menstruum Universale.' In *The Birth to Presence*, 248–65. Stanford: Stanford University Press, 1993.

———. *The Birth to Presence*. Translated by Brian Holmes et al. Stanford: Stanford University Press, 1993.

———. *La communauté desœuvrée*. Paris: Christian Bourgois Editeur, 1999.

———. *Corpus*. Paris: Metaillé, 2000.

———. *Being Singular Plural*. Translated by Robert Richardson and Anne O'Byrne. Stanford: Stanford University Press, 2000.

———. *La communauté affronté*. Paris: Galilée, 2001.

———. *L' 'il y a' du rapport sexuel*. Paris: Galilée, 2001.

———. *La création du monde, ou la mondialisation*. Paris: Galilée, 2002.

———. In *La démocratie à venir*, edited by M.-L. Mallet, 341–59. Paris: Galilée, 2004.

———. *La Déclosion (Déconstruction du christianisme, 1)*. Paris: Galilée, 2005.

———. 'L'indépendance de l'Algérie et l'indépendance de Derrida.' *Cités* 30 (2007), 65–70.

———. *Vérité de la démocratie*. Paris: Galilée, 2008.

———. 'Démocratie finie et infinie.' In *Démocratie, dans quel état?* edited by, G. Agamben et al., 77–94. Paris: La fabrique, 2009.

———. *L'Adoration (Déconstruction du christianisme, 2)*. Paris: Galilée, 2010.

———. 'From the Imperative to Law.' In B.C. Hutchens, ed., *Jean-Luc Nancy: Justice, Legality and World*, 11–18. London: Continuum, 2012.

———. *La possibilité d'un monde*, entretien avec Pierre-Philippe Jandin. Paris: Petits Platons, 2013.

Negri, Toni. 'The Spectre's Smile.' In *Ghostly Demarcations: A Symposium on Jacques Derrida's Specters of Marx*, edited by M. Sprinkler. London: Verso, 1999.

Pascal, Blaise. *Pensées*. Translated by R. Ariew. Indianapolis: Hackett Publishing, 2005.

Perelman, Chaïm. *Logique juridique: Nouvelle rhétorique*. Paris: Dalloz, 1976.

Plato, *Republic*. trans. R. Waterfield. Oxford: OUP, 1993.

Posner, Eric A., and Adrian Vermeule, *Terror in the Balance: Security, Liberty and the Courts*. Oxford: OUP, 2007.

Romano, Bruno. Il Giurista è uno 'zoologo metropolitano'? A partire da una tesi di Derrida. Torino: G. Giappichelli, 2007.

Rawls, John. *Political Liberalism*. New York: Columbia University Press, 1993.

Rials, Stéphane. *Villey et les idoles*. Paris: PUF, 2000.

Rorty, Richard. 'Remarks on Deconstruction and Pragmatism.' In *Deconstruction and Pragmatism*, edited by C. Mouffe, 16–17. London: Routledge, 1999.

———. *Philosophy and Social Hope*. London: Penguin Books, 1999.

Rosenthal, Irena. 'Aggression and Play in the Face of Adversity: A Psychoanalytic Reading of Democratic Resilience.' *Political Theory* (OnlineFirst: 18 August 2014), 1–26.

Sallis, John, ed. *Reading Heidegger: Commemorations*. Bloomington: Indiana University Press, 1993.

Schmitt, Carl. *Political Theology*. Translated by G. Schwab. Cambridge, MA: MIT Press, 1985.

———. *The Concept of the Political*. Translated by G. Schwab. Chicago: University of Chicago Press, 1986.

———. *Verfassungslehre*. Berlin: Duncker & Humblot, 1993.

———. *The Leviathan in the State Theory of Thomas Hobbes: Meaning and failure of a political symbol*. Translated by G. Schwab and E. Hilfstein. Westport, Connecticut: Greenwood Press, 1996.

———. *Hamlet or Hecuba: The Intrusion of Play into Time*. Translated by D. Pan, J. Rust. New York: Telos Publishing, 2009.

Sharkey, Judy. 'Lives Stories Don't Tell: Exploring the Untold in Autobiography.' *Curriculum Inquiry* 34/4 (2004), 495–512.

Sieyès, Emmanuel-Joseph. *Qu'est-ce que le Tiers État?* Paris: Société de l'histoire de la Révolution Française, 1888.

Sloterdijk, Peter, *Derrida, un Égyptien: Le problème de la pyramide juive*. Paris: Maren Sell, 2006.

Smith, Jason. '"A Struggle between Two Infinities": Jean-Luc Nancy on Marx's Revolution and Ours.' In *Nancy and the Political*, edited by S. Dejanovic, 272–89. Edinburgh: Edinburgh University Press, 2015.

Souza Santos, Boaventura. *A Crítica da Razão Indolente—Contra o Desperdício da Inteligência*. São Paulo: Cortez, 2000.

Talisse, Robert B. 'A Farewell to Deweyan Democracy: Towards a New Pragmatist Politics.' SSRN 13 August 2007. Accessed 15 May 2010. http://dx.doi.org/10.2139/ssrn.1005645.

Teubner, Günther. 'The King's Many Bodies: The Self-Deconstruction of Law's Hierarchy.' *Law & Society Review* 31/4 (1997), 763–88.

———. 'Self-Subversive Justice: Contingency or Transcendence Formula of Law.' *The Modern Law Review* 72/1 (2009), 1–23.

Thomassen, Lasse, ed. *The Derrida-Habermas Reader*. Edinburgh: Edinburgh University Press, 2006.

Thorsteinsson, Björn. *La question de la justice chez Jacques Derrida*. Paris: L'Harmattan, 2007.

Thomson, Alex. *Deconstruction and Democracy*. London: Continuum, 2005.

Van der Walt, Johan. *Law and Sacrifice—Towards a Post-Apartheid Theory of Law*. London: Birkbeck Law Press, 2005.

Van der Walt, Johan. 'Immimanence; Law's Language Lesson.' *Law, Culture and the Humanities* 2/1 (2006), 2–16.

Verdú, Pablo Lucas. *El Sentimiento Constitucional: Aproximación al estudio del sentir constitucional como modo de integración política*. Madrid: Reus S.A., 1985.

Viehweg, Theodor. *Topik und Jurisprudenz*. Munich: C.H. Verlag, 2000.

Vieira, José R, ed. *Temas de Constitucionalismo e Democracia*. Rio de Janeiro: Renovar, 2003.

Villey, Michel. *Le droit romain*. Paris: PUF, 1945.

———. 'Préface—La doctrine du droit dans l'histoire de la science juridique.' In Immanuel Kant, *Métaphysique des mœurs—Doctrine du droit*, 5–45. Paris: Librairie Philosophique J. Vrin, 1971.

———. *Le droit et les droits de l'homme*. Paris: PUF, 1983.

———. *La formation de la pensée juridique* moderne. Paris: PUF, 2003.

Viroli, Maurizio. *Niccolò's Smile—A Biography of Macchiavelli.*. London: I.B. Tauris Publishers, 2001.

Warat, Luis Alberto. *Manifesto do Surrealismo Jurídico*. São Paulo: Acadêmica, 1988.

———. *A Ciência Jurídica e seus Dois Maridos*. Santa Cruz do Sul: EDUNISC, 2000.

Weigelt, Markus. 'Introduction.' In Immanuel Kant, *Critique of Pure Reason*, xxxvii–lvii. London: Penguin, 2007.

Winnicott, Donald W. *Playing and Reality*. London: Routledge, 1971.

———. 'Thoughts on the Meaning of the Word Democracy.' In *The Social Engagement of Social Science: A Tavistock Anthology*, edited by E. Trist and H. Murray, 546–57. London: Free Association Books, 1990.

Zarka, Yves-Charles. 'Le souverain vorace et vociférant.' *Cités* 30 (2007), 3–8.

Žižek, Slavoj. *The Paralax View*. Cambridge, MA: MIT Press, 2006.

NOTES

Introduction

1. I am not aware of the thematization of this expression, standing on its own, in previous academic endeavours. It has appeared though to signify the media's engagement with the constitutional system: 'the role played by the media in providing "constitutional exposure" has improved markedly in recent decades.' See Michael G. Kammen, *A Machine That Would Go of Itself: The Constitution in American Culture* (New Brunswick, NJ: Transaction Publishers, 2006), 381.

2. Even if I am aware of Derrida's complex argument (in which justice ends up intertwined with law, see ch. 3), I shall argue that the binary starting point (often perceived as a variation of the transcendental methodology in philosophy) and the structure of the argument misses the point of the functional articulation of rule and justice (or law and justice) that serves the interests of exploitative and exclusionary socio-economic systems.

3. Unconditionality is associated with an imperative exigency in several passages of his work *Voyous*, see Jacques Derrida, *Voyous—Deux essais sur la raison* (Paris: Galilée, 2003), 106, 190, 196, 204, and 210; *Rogues: Two Essays on Reason*, trans. A.-P. Brault and M. Naas (Stanford: Stanford University Press, 2005), 72, 137, 142, 149, and 153. Moreover, Derrida argues that the tradition of a politics of friendship, with an emphasis on Nietzsche, seems marked by 'successive or simultaneous postulations.' See Jacques Derrida, *Politiques de l'amitié* (Paris: Galilée, 1994), 153; *Politics of Friendship*, trans. G. Collins (London: Verso, 1997), 137.

4. Derrida, *Politiques de l'amitié*, 196; trans., 142.

5. Derrida, *Politiques de l'amitié*, 196; trans., 142.

6. Derrida, *Politiques de l'amitié*, 196; trans., 142.

7. Jacques Derrida, *Negotiations: Interventions and interviews, 1971–2001* (Stanford: Stanford University Press, 2002), 21.

8. Derrida, *Negotiations*, 21.

9. See Jacques Derrida, *Le monolinguisme de l'autre, ou la prothèse d'origine* (Paris: Galilée, 1996), 27; *Monolingualism of the Other, or the Prosthesis of Origin*, trans. P. Mensah (Stanford: Stanford University Press, 1998), 11. Derrida's timely allegiances are quite clear also in Jacques Derrida, *Spectres de*

Marx—L'état de la dette, le travail du deuil et la nouvelle Internationale (Paris: Galilée, 1993), 141; *Specters of Marx: The State of the Debt, the Work of Mourning, and the New International*, trans. P. Kamuf (New York: Routledge, 1994), 85.

10. My debt to Nancy here is transparent: exposure points to opening and contact, and to that opening that delineates itself carefully in carnal contact. Here the French term 'exposition' is crucial, for 'po' alludes to *peau*, skin, as in expeausition. This 'po' follows the same pronunciation as French 'peau.' In exposition there is always 'ex*peau*sition.' It happens that this touch of skin, always marginal and never complete, *happens*. Touching exposition never shows completely itself: the entirety of bodies or of body contact or of contacts in bodies. It rather shows the lack of entirety of body and the impossibility of 'final touch.' Cf. Jean-Luc Nancy, *Corpus*, Paris: Métaillé, 2000, 31–4. This sensing of sense, and common-sense, is also in a way a response to key Brazilian and Latin American thinkers whose work informed a great deal of critical endeavours in the region since the 1950's, from the philosophy of development to critical pedagogy and even liberation theology, all of which have partly been predicated on a certain philosophy of consciousness, and a pursuit of truth (or God) to be found in the consciousness of the coming together of the common people, of the poor. This work is reminiscent of that drive even when it attempts to bring it to fruition a different under-standing of knowledge and consciousness, open to the senses of togetherness.

11. Even though one might be tempted to think something like a 'school without school' or a 'post-school' in Derrida's interaction with his friends from Strasbourg: Jean-Luc Nancy, Philippe Lacoue-Labarthe, but also Parisian academic Sarah Kofman, in their common work at the publication series 'Philosophie en effet' (with publisher Galilée) and other figures connected somehow to their proximity to and rejection of Heidegger in and around Strasbourg, such as Maurice Blanchot and Emmanuel Levinas. See Jacques Derrida, 'Le lieu dit: Strasbourg' in J. Derrida et al., *Penser à Strasbourg* (Paris: Galilée-Ville de Strasbourg, 2004), 31–58.

12. Jacques Derrida, *De la grammatologie* (Paris: Galilée, 1967), 18–31; *Of Grammatology*, trans. G. C. Spivak (Baltimore: Johns Hopkins University Press, 1997), 8–18.

13. On that intimate relationship see Jacques Derrida, *Monolinguisme de l'autre* (Paris: Galilée, 1996), 75–114; *Monolingualism of the Other, Or, The Prosthesis of Origin*, trans. P. Mensah (Stanford: Stanford University Press, 1998), 44–94. On the possibility and impossibility of philosophy today, see Lacoue-Labarthe, 'La philosophie fantôme,' *Lignes*, mai (2007), 205–14.

14. Especially relevant here is Derrida's experience of injury and suffering of exploitative inclusion. See the mark, the impact, of the adjective, the injury, 'Jew' on his life: 'This word, this performative address ('Juif,' i.e. almost unavoidably, as if it had been well understood, 'dirty Jew!'), this apostrophe was, and continues [*reste*], and bears [*porte*], older than the statement [*constat*], more archaic than the constative, the figure of a wounding arrow [*flèche*

blessante], of a gun or a projectile that comes once and for all to be lodged and forever rooted in your body, to which it adheres and raises itself from the interior, as a fish hook would do, or an harpoon lodged in yourself, by the equally carving and humid body of each of these letters, j.u.i.f [jew].' Jacques Derrida, 'Abraham, l'autre' in J. Cohen, R. Zagury-Orly, *Judéités—Questions pour Jacques Derrida* (Paris: Galilée, 2003), 19–20.

Chapter 1 'Democracy to Come'

1. The epitomes of the legislative (overtly assumed as a book title and sadly appropriate) type of arguments are those that say what is truth and error about Derrida's writing or, in fact, about Derrida's 'theoretical propositions.' This is not the truth of a practice of *writing*, but the truth of a putative system of thought, one to be mastered and taught. In the name of truth, it comes close to the radical betrayal of a practice of deconstruction and the emergence of a caricatural police of *writing*. See Geoffrey Bennington, *Legislations: The Politics of Deconstruction* (Verso: London, 1991), 1–3, and 11–14.

2. Alex Thomson, *Deconstruction and Democracy* (London: Continuum, 2005). For another important reference on Derrida's democracy to come, see Matthias Fritsch, 'Derrida's Democracy to Come,' *Constellations*, 9/4 (2002), 574–97. Yet, this latter work is less an interpretation or intensification of Derrida's work and more a critique of the lack of normative grounds in his account of democracy. Another, more recent contribution to Derrida's scholarship, despite being sympathetic and truthful to Derrida's take on democracy in many regards, also misses the point of Derrida post-normativism, in an attempt to uncover the normative grounds Derridean positions; see Samir Haddad, *Derrida and the Inheritance of Democracy* (Indiannapolis: Indiana University Press, 2014). My work, on the other hand, assumes that despite Derrida's critique of both normativity and pragmatism, he does not deny their possibility altogether. Instead of being merely groundless, Derrida enjoys a groundlessness that coexists with a plurality of singular grounds. In Derrida, legal-ethical-political postulations seek to *understand* current experiences in this field (as democracy, as the university) to the point of uncovering their truth, but, and this crucial, without effacing, subsuming or sidelining the historical situations in which they can be described. This is akin to a redescription in the sense Mouffe gives it, borrowed from Rorty. See Chantal Mouffe, *The Democratic Paradox* (London: Verso, 2000), 107. I would call 'it,' if I had to, a postulatory or originary redescription. See also Richard Rorty, *Philosophy and Social Hope* (London: Penguin Books, 1999), 87–8.

3. Derrida, *Voyous*, 132; trans., 91.

4. For the more general point of Derrida's experience of oppression and the deep ethical-political-juridical connotations of deconstructive practice, see Jacques Derrida, 'Abraham, l'autre' in J. Cohen and R. Zagury-Orly (eds.), *Judéités: Questions pour Jacques Derrida* (Paris: Galilée, 2003), 11–42.

5. Contrast Derrida's decisive early critique of Levinas with his more obliging comments in 'Force of law.' See Jacques Derrida, 'Violence et Métaphysique' in *L'écriture et la difference* (Paris: Éditions du Seuil, 1967), 117–228; 'Violence and metaphysics' in *Writing and Difference*, trans. A. Bass (New York: Routledge, 1981), 79–153; and Jacques Derrida, *Force de loi* (Paris: Galilée, 1994), 48–61; 'Force of Law: The "Mystical Foundation of Authority"' in *Acts of Religion*, ed. and trans. G. Anidjar (New York: Routledge, 2002), 250–7.

6. See, for instance, Derrida, *Voyous*, 19–24; trans., 1–5.

7. Claude Lefort, 'La question de la démocratie in *Essais sur le politique*, XIX–XX siècles (Paris: Éditions du Seuil, 1986), 17–30.

8. See Richard J. Bernstein, 'Serious play: The ethical-political horizon of Derrida' in *The New Constellation: The Ethical-Political Horizons of Modernity/Postmodernity* (Cambridge, MA: MIT, 1992), 172–98.

9. Jacques Derrida, *Politiques de l'amitié*, 153; trans.,137.

10. Lefort, 'La question de la démocratie,' 18.

11. Lefort, 'La question de la démocratie,' 17.

12. Derrida, *Force de loi*, 63; trans., 257–8.

13. Lefort, 'La question de la démocratie,' 18.

14. Lefort, 'La question de la démocratie,' 27.

15. Derrida, *Voyous*, 51–66; trans., 28–41. See also Derrida, *Politiques de l'amitié*, 339–40; trans., 305–6.

16. Jacques Derrida, *Chaque fois unique, la fin du monde* (Paris: Galilée, 2003), 109–20, and 235–38; *The Work of Mourning* (Chicago: University of Chicago Press, 2001), 77–90, and 189–96.

17. See Yves-Charles Zarka, 'Le souverain vorace et vociférant,' *Cités*, 30 (2007), 8. In this way, Bernstein complains, albeit sympathetically, that Derrida ends up in the realm of the arbitrary when it comes to ethical-political judgement. Such a complaint is off the point. Bernstein misses precisely the relevance of Derrida's performative (and more than performative, see ch. 3) *writing*. See Richard J. Bernstein, 'Derrida: The Aporia of Forgiveness?,' *Constellations*, 13/3 (2006), 394–406.

18. Lefort, 'La question de la démocratie,' 21 (on the risks of judging) and 30 (on philosophy's dependence on democracy).

19. Jacques Derrida, 'Les fins de l'homme' in *Marges de la philosophie* (Paris: Éditions de Minuit, 1972), 134–5; 'The Ends of Man' in *Margins of Philosophy*, trans. A. Bass (Chicago: The University of Chicago Press, 1982), 113–4. See also ch. 2.

20. Translation of Heidegger's 'Destruktion,' in a way that emphasizes the latter's affirmative element, and in a way that conveys the work of translating: caring, bearing, exercising a force on something in order to transpose it to another space. See Jacques Derrida, 'Letter to a Japanese friend' in D. Wood

and R. Bernasconi (eds.), *Derrida and Difference* (Coventry: Parousia Press, 1985), 1–5.

21. Thomson, Deconstruction and Democracy, 2.

22. On the equivalence of Derridean terms see Simon Critchley, *Ethics, Politics, Subjectivity* (London: Verso, 1999), 143–82. This approach to Derrida in turn is highly indebted to the very influential work of Rodolphe Gasché, *The Tain of the Mirror: Derrida and the philosophy of reflection* (Cambridge, MA: Harvard University Press, 1986), 177–251. For the quote, see Thomson, *Deconstruction and Democracy*, 29.

23. Derrida, *Politiques de l'amitiés*, 128; trans., 105 (modified here).

24. Thomson, Deconstruction and Democracy, 54.

25. Derrida, 'La démocratie ajournée,' 103–24; trans., 84–109.

26. The earliest sustained engagement, but not the earliest engagement, as we shall see below—see Jacques Derrida, *La dissémination* (Paris: Éditions du Seuil, 1972), 165–8; *Dissemination*, trans. B. Johnson (London: Continuum, 2004), 144–6, and 182–3.

27. Derrida, 'La démocratie ajournée,' 114; trans., 98 (for the first quote) and 104; trans., 85 (for the issue of public opinion).

28. Derrida, 'La démocratie ajournée,' 116; trans., 99–100.

29. Derrida, 'La démocratie ajournée,' 115; trans., 98.

30. Derrida, 'La démocratie ajournée,' 115' trans., 98.

31. Derrida, 'La démocratie ajournée,' 112; trans. 95; for the reference to public opinion as 'ghost,' 103–5 and 107; trans., 84–7.

32. Derrida, 'La démocratie ajournée,' 104; trans., 85–6.

33. Derrida, 'La démocratie ajournée,' 121–2; trans., 105–7.

34. We are perhaps moving too fast here on the question of responsibility. Yet it is necessary to do so, given that Derrida's terms are highly interconnected. One cannot stop simply at one particular point, since this reading sends the reader off to so many other intimately related junctures. Let me make myself clearer: responsibility in the inherited juridical-philosophical sense may not be simply the ability to respond. Responsibility, in this context of Derrida's writing, requires an element of irresponsibility that gives itself to the non-presence (non-ordinary) without which the day cannot come about. A new language needs to be found to express this new response or responsivity to the complex event of the 'day.' See Derrida, 'La démocratie ajournée,' 123; trans., 107–8. In fact a true response, the response that Derrida has been giving, the response of his writing, has to acknowledge also a right not to respond—the right not to be subsumed in an economy of giving and taking, the courtesy of the right moment to speak. As we shall later see, here rests a question of the secret. This secretive non-response is also part of Derrida's constellation of texts on 'democracy to come.' An author, for instance, who in a democracy has 'the right to say everything' (*droit de tout dire*) should not be legally answerable

for his writings or ideas, and this is crucial to democracy: 'this authorization to say everything ... acknowledges a right to absolute nonresponse, just where there can be no question of responding, of being able to or having to respond ... We find there a hyperbolic condition of democracy which seems to contradict a certain determined and historically limited concept of such a democracy, a concept which links it to the concept of a subject that is calculable, accountable, imputable and responsible ... This contradiction also indicates the task (task of thought, also a theoretical-practical task) for any democracy to come.' Jacques Derrida, *Passions: 'L'offrande oblique'* (Paris: Galilée, 1993), 65–7; 'Passions: "An Oblique Offering",' trans. T. Dutoit, in *On the Name* (Stanford: Stanford University Press, 1995), 29.

35. Derrida, 'La démocratie ajournée,' 122; trans., 107.

36. Derrida, 'La démocratie ajournée,' 124; trans., 109 (modified). This epistemic move aims to escape self-reflection, reflection transparent to itself, and thus also a move away from the 'constitution' of the subject. Derrida is careful to resist the processes of transcendental reflection and totalizing speculation of an auto-positioning move. See for this the extraordinary work of Gasché: *The Tain of the Mirror*, 79–105. One of my only reservations with Gasché's approach is that he puts too much emphasis on the move away from reflection as a 'philosophical quest' for the conditions of possibility and impossibility of reflection, where 'philosophical' plays a predominant role. This not a problem simply because Derrida would be non-philosophical in many respects, but because 'the tradition of philosophy' is conceived in an almost autonomous fashion with little room for the social and political conditions of its constitution. In fact, in this process, in this move away from reflection, it is a troubled tension of sense, sensing, and its impossibilities that comes across—from the epistemic to the threshold between knowledge and sense, from the epistemic to the hyperepistemic, from consciousness to exposure. In that regard, but with a different terminology, a good work to reckon with is John Llewelyn, *Derrida on the Threshold of Sense* (London: Macmillan 1986), 119–23. Yet one finds by far the best indications on the matter of sense in Derrida's work on Nancy: Jacques Derrida, *Le toucher, Jean-Luc Nancy* (Paris: Galilée, 2000), 129–49.

37 Paul Valéry (1871–1945) was one of the greatest French poets of the 20th century; initially close to the symbolist movement and to Mallarmé. Also renowned as an essayist and society figure, he devoted himself to a wide variety of subjects, with special attention to France's and Europe's role in the world.

38. Jacques Derrida, *L'Autre Cap* (Paris: Les Éditions de Minuit, 1991), 62; *The Other Heading*, trans. P.-A. Brault and M. Naas (Bloomington: Indiana University Press, 1992), 62.

39. Derrida, *L'Autre Cap*, 18; trans., 12.

40. Jacques Derrida, *Negotiations*, 36.

41. Derrida, *L'Autre Cap*, 71; trans., 72–3.

42. Derrida, *Voyous*, 204–8; trans., 148–50. Less audaciously, but in the

same token, see Derrida, *Force de Loi*, 44; trans., 248.

43. Derrida, *L'Autre Cap*, 73; trans., 75.

44. See also Derrida, *Voyous*, 35; trans., 14–15. And: 'It [Europe, the Capital, the Heading] has begun to open itself, or rather to let itself open, or, better yet, to be affected with opening without opening *itself* onto an other, onto an other that the heading can no longer even relate to itself as *its* other, *the other with itself*.' Derrida, *L'Autre Cap*, 75; trans., 76.

45. Derrida, *L'Autre Cap*, 76; trans., 78.

46. Derrida, *L'Autre Cap*, 76; trans., 78.

47. Jacques Derrida, 'Privilège. Titre justificatif et Remarques introductives' in *Du droit à la philosophie* (Paris: Galilée, 1990), 9–108; trans., 1–66.

48. Derrida, 'Privilège,' 24 and 39; trans., 10 and 20.

49. Derrida, 'Privilège,' 39; trans., 20.

50. Derrida, 'Privilège,' 41; trans., 22.

51. Derrida, 'Privilège,' 53; trans., 29.

52. Derrida, 'Privilège,' 53; trans., 29.

53. Derrida, 'Privilège,' 53; trans., 30. This is the first textual appearance of 'democracy to come.' There is another one in the same chapter, but it is a title of the section in which the phrase appears: 'La démocratie à venir: droit à la langue, droit de la langue'; 'The Democracy to Come: Right of Language, Right to Language.' Derrida, 'Privilège,' 41; trans., 22.

54. Derrida proposes the distinction between affirmation and position. Affirmation is associated with the promise, the unconditional, but it always requires a position, an institution—it requires becoming determinate, positioned. Positions, on the other hand, cannot simply be positions if they do not yet yield to some affirmation, if they do not 'decay' in some way. The second part of the reasoning is only implicit in this instance of Derrida's writing, but the same 'logic' has been applied in many other instances. See Derrida, *Negotiations*, 25–6.

55. Thomson, *Deconstruction and Democracy*, 28 and 31–2. Critchley, *Ethics, Politics, Subjectivity*, 254–86 (the latter as to the supposed lack of the question of power).

56. Richard Rorty, 'Remarks on deconstruction and pragmatism' in *Deconstruction and Pragmatism*, ed. Chantalle Mouffe (London, Routledge, 1999), 16–17.

57. Derrida, *Politiques de l'amitié*, 19; trans., 3.

58. Derrida, *Politiques de l'amitié*, 59, 86–8; trans., 39, 68–9.

59. 'It is not the number that is interdicted, nor the more than one, but the numerous, if not the crowd.' Derrida, *Politiques de l'amitié*, 39; trans., 21.

60. Derrida, *Politiques de l'amitié*, 34 ; trans., 16.

61. Derrida, *Politiques de l'amitié*, 37; trans., 19–20.

62. Derrida, *Politiques de l'amitié*, 281; trans., 251.

63. For the strong link between friendship and virtue, see Derrida, *Politiques de l'amitié*, 207; trans., 191–2.

64. Derrida, *Politiques de l'amitié*, 40–1; trans., 22–3.

65. Derrida, *Politiques de l'amitié*, 18–22 trans., 2–6.

66. Derrida, *Politiques de l'amitié*, 19–20; trans., 3–4.

67. Derrida, *Politiques de l'amitié*, 114–15; trans., 93–4.

68. Derrida, *Politiques de l'amitié*, 116; trans., 94–5.

69. Derrida, *Politiques de l'amitié*, 29–32; trans., 9–12. It is a sentence by Aristotle that serves as epigraph to the book. As received by a certain tradition (Diogenes Laertius, Cicero, Montaigne, Nietzsche) Aristotle's sentence can only become clear in this context. 'Oh my friends, there are no friends' has to be understood as the unconditional, pure moment of friendship that sustains it, even if only as a ghost, as a prospect—the prospect of the dead friend and of loving the dead friend in his absence. The true virtuous, active friend need not be loved back in order to love. Death, transcendence, dissymmetry, are inscribed in the most 'reciprocal' of all relationships. Such a reciprocal relationship is itself the ground of all universalizations. Yet, this sentence's wording is highly contested. Derrida discusses this extensively in ch. 8 of *Politics of Friendship*. Everything revolves around the initial omega. The difference is between a vocative and pronominal omega, between 'oh my friends,' and 'he who has friends.' The first yields the paradoxical sentence so relevant to Derrida. The second leads to a much more straightforward reading: 'he who has many friends has no friends.' The authoritative edition in English has the omega in the pronominal form, and translates accordingly: ω φίλοι ούδείζ φίλος (yet, the translation is not as straightforward as it could have been, adding a few important words inexistent in the original, 'true' for instance: 'he who has friends can have no true friend'). Derrida is in no doubt about which version is historically right (vocative omega or pronominal omega). He pursues an interpretation of the broad framework of Aristotle's work, and Diogenes Laertius reference to book seven of 'Ethics' (the *Ethics to Eudeme*). The conclusion is evidently for the pronominal version of the omega, and the more 'natural' interpretation. Yet, all this only confirms Derrida's thesis of the 'rarefaction' of friends—a pursuit of absolute symmetry that ends up in absolute dissymmetry, the love for the dead friend. In an article called 'On Friendship,' Agamben writes as if he were making a great revelation about the true nature of this sentence attributed to Aristotle, and about Derrida's disregard for this 'settled' version (Agamben complains also that he made this revelation to Derrida, and that no reference of the matter appears in Derrida's work). In his book, however, Derrida not only thanks Agamben, but also says the following about those who wish to guard texts with a philological police, and about the 'mistaken' tradition of reading Diogenes–Aristotle: 'a tiny philological *coup de théâtre* cannot prevail in the venerable tradition which, from Montaigne to Nietzsche and beyond, from Kant to Blanchot and beyond … no orthographic restoration or archival orthodoxy will ever damage this

other, henceforth sedimented archive … no philological fundamentalism will ever efface the incredible fortune of this brilliant invention.' Derrida, *Politiques de l'amitié*, 234; trans., 206. See also Giorgio Agamben, 'On Friendship,' *Contretemps* (December 2004), 2–7. For Montaigne's 'sovereign' friendship, see Derrida, *Politiques de l'amitié*, 201–9; trans., 177–83.

70. Derrida, *Politiques de l'amitié*, 24; trans., 7.

71. Derrida, *Politiques de l'amitié*, 29; trans., 12. See also Aristotle, *Ethics to Eudeme* (London: William Heinemann LTD, 1952), 394–5; 1239a40–1239b1–2.

72. Derrida, *Politiques de l'amitié*, 19, 40, and 183; trans., 3, 21–2, and 158–9.

73. Derrida, *Politiques de l'amitié*, 294 and 309; trans., 263 and 278.

74. Carl Schmitt, *Der Begriff des Politischen* (Berlin: Humblot, 2002), 26–8.

75. Derrida, *Politiques de l'amitié*, 159–92; trans., 138–70.

76. And Derrida is not unaware of Schmitt's complexity, he knows his project is to reconstruct the political. Nature or family are here instruments to counter the baseness of modern life; see Derrida, *Politiques de l'amitié*, 127; trans., 104.

77. Derrida, *Politiques de l'amitié*, 265; trans., 237.

78. Derrida's italics: '*familiarity of election [familiarité d'élection]* which will everywhere remain our theme.' Derrida, *Politiques de l'amitié*, 28; trans., 11.

79. Derrida, *Politiques de l'amitié*, 265; trans., 237.

80. See n. 59, above.

81. Derrida, *Force de Loi*, 94; trans., 272. Better understood if in conjunction with Derrida, *Politiques de l'amitié*, 258–9; trans., 231–2.

82. I mean that the many, the number, the crowd, are not simply excluded in a logic of singular universalization (or finite infinity). The way in which the number suffers is not by means of exclusion, but by means of exploitation and depletion that sustains infinite accumulation and capitalization.

83. The expression 'spacing' (*espacement*) is an attempt to articulate the common undercutting of time and space, the temporalization of every space, even the most immediate, through time, the rupture of space through time. And yet the very affirmation of time also requires a world shaped spatially, an environment (even if such an environment, and in fact most intensely, is that of silence, void and interval). This tension of strange turns and referrals speaks to the restlessness of 'spacing.' Cf. Derrida, *Voyous*, 60; trans., 35. Cf. also Derrida, *De la grammatologie*, 99–108; trans., 68–73.

84. Jacques Derrida, *L'animal que donc je suis* (Paris: Galilée, 2006), 27–8; 'The animal that therefore I am (More to follow),' trans. D. Wills, *Critical Inquiry* 28 (Winter 2002), 379–80.

85. Derrida, *Politiques de l'amitié*, 264; trans., 236.

86. The grammar of the perhaps, Nietzsche's 'dangerous perhaps,' is crucial for Derrida as that which unsettles settled alternatives, opening up leeway for another sociability. See Derrida, *Politiques de l'amitié*, 43–66; trans., 29–48.

87. Derrida, *Politiques de l'amitié*, 259; trans., 232. Notice the complexity that Derrida attributes to this simple expression, 'il faut.' See Derrida, 'Sauf le nom (Post-Scriptum),' 76.

88. Derrida, *Politiques de l'amitié*, 26; trans., 8.

89. Ibid., 35; trans., 18.

90. Derrida, *Politiques de l'amitié*, 87; trans., 68.

91. Derrida, *Politiques de l'amitié*, 152–3; trans., 129–30. This oppositional 'logic' is accurate only if understood in the trivial sense, as reasoning based on established principles and assumptions. If I were to say 'logical' as derived from the *logos*, then an oppositional 'logic' would not even be human, let alone commonsensical. For Derrida, in following Heidegger and Heraclitus, the *polemos* as *logos* is a conflict, struggle or tension that makes common sense and quotidian 'logic' possible. Yet, Derrida wishes to further complicate Heidegger's paradoxical appeal to the hearing of the unheard-of *polemos*. Derrida, rather, emphasizes the equivocations of this strategy, and its failure, its ruin, so that the totalitarian appropriation of this call may be avoided—even though, at the same time, he acknowledges that the thematizations of equivocation and ruin are themselves limited, and the risk of spurious appropriations is never entirely dissipated. Jacques Derrida, 'L'oreille de Heidegger: Philopolémologie (*Geschlecht* IV)' in *Politiques de l'amitié* (Paris: Galilée, 1994), 409–14; 'Heidegger's ear: Philopolemology (Geschlecht IV),' in *Reading Heidegger: Commemorations*, ed. John Sallis, trans. J. P. Leavey (Bloomington: Indiana University Press, 1993), 208–12.

92. An interesting cross-reference that brings us back to *The Other Heading* is Derrida's strong critique of Habermas: 'Under the pretext of pleading for transparency ... for the univocity of democratic discussion, for communication in the public space, for "communicative action", this discourse tends to impose a model of language allegedly favourable to that communication. Intending to speak in the name of intelligibility, *good sense, common sense* [my emphasis] or democratic morals, this discourse tends by that token to, as if naturally, discredit everything that complicates this model. It tends to suspect or repress anything that bends, over-determines, or even questions, in theory or practice, this idea of language.' Derrida, *L'autre cap*, 55–6; trans., 54–5.

93. See n. 59, above.

94. Jacques Derrida, *Positions* (Paris: Minuit, 1972), 56–67; 'Interview: Jacques Derrida—Positions,' trans. G. Scarpetta and J. L. Houdebine, *Diacritics*, 2/4 (1972), 35–43.

95. I do not claim that Derrida disregards deconstruction's social-historical conditions, nor that texts or institutions are passive before the deconstructive operation. This claim appears in Günther Teubner, 'The King's Many Bodies: The Self-Deconstruction of Law's Hierarchy,' *Law & Society Review*, 31/4

(1997), 763–88. The problem lies not in that type of historical disregard; even though one could benefit if Derrida had devised a provisional narrative of pertinent historical events. Derrida does put himself and his discourse in question—Derrida's autobiographical style renders Teubner's contention almost meaningless. As I have maintained, Derrida also promotes, performatively, certain postulations; and that is a subtle way of constructing 'worlds of meaning' (Teubner ignores that at 772ff.). Teubner is not more successful in his more recent sympathetic tone towards Derrida, who is neither an 'external observer,' nor in the business of championing 'particularistic asymmetry, ecological orientation, and the non-rational other of justice,' as Teubner would have him. See Günther Teubner, 'Self-subversive Justice: Contingency or Transcendence Formula of Law,' *The Modern Law Review*, 72/1 (2009), 1–23. Yet, there is a problem in Derrida's lack of thematization of deconstruction's own success in fleshing out paradoxes. What is extraordinary is that institutions (literary, legal, and religious) appear almost impervious to the dissemination of their own paradoxes. Evidently, Derrida means more than consciousness-raising of paradoxes, but he at least takes for granted that such 'consciousness-raising' is necessary. For the use of such an expression, see Jacques Derrida and Lieven De Cauter, 'For a Justice to Come: An Interview with Jacques Derrida,' in *The Derrida–Habermas Reader*, ed. L. Thomassen (Edinburgh: Edinburgh University Press, 2006), 262. For Derrida's markedly historical-biographical commitments, see Jean-Luc Nancy, 'L'indépendence de l'Algérie et l'indépendence de Derrida,' *Cités*, 30 (2007), 65–70.

96. One may contend that the aporia itself should not be necessary; perhaps so. However, the aporia serves to guard against the smooth streamline of causes and consequences that one can so easily fall back to. The aporia is not an opposition; it is rather the encounter with the limit, the limit of saying, of knowledge, and of oneself. An opposition provides guidance. It reduces the complexity of the social world. It imposes upon the differential spaces of sense, a will, or a power. The aporia is rather more careful in working with the limit, a sensibility to power and lack of power. See Jacques Derrida, *Apories: Mourir—s'attendre aux 'limites de la vérité'* (Paris: Galilée, 1993), 49–53; *Aporias* (Stanford: Stanford University Press, 1993), 22–5.

97. Derrida, *Politiques de l'amitié*, 308; trans., 277.

98. Derrida, *Politiques de l'amitié*, 339; trans., 306 and 31; trans., 13–14.

99. Derrida, *Voyous*, 133; trans., 91–2.

100. See also Derrida, *Negotiations*, 36.

101. Jacques Derrida, 'La vérité blessante: Ou le corps à corps des langues—Entretien avec Jacques Derrida,' *Europe* (May 2004), 8–28; 'The Truth That Wounds: From an Interview' in *Sovereignties in Question: The poetics of Paul Celan*, trans. T. Dutoit *et al.* (New York: Fordham University Press, 2005), 164–9. The latter is though only a partial translation.

102. My use of enjoyment here does not pertain to an inherently psychoanalytic discourse, even though it cannot escape entirely a certain psychoanalytic metaphor, which in turn is significant by resonating with

social reality and being real: the psychoanalic metaphor of playing: '*it is playing that is universal*,' says Winnicott (his emphasis), in contradistinction to psychoanalysis as a 'highly specialized form of playing' (56). I refer in particular to Winnicott's attribution of a 'place' for enjoyment in the space of playing between inside and outs ide, subject and object, mother and baby, me and not-me, in transitional objetcs in transitional processes in which 'the paradox must be tolerated' (145). A 'place' incidentally essential to the configuration of the self: 'it is only in playing that the individual child or adult is able to be creative and to use the whole of personality, and it is only in being creative that the individual discovers the self' (73), and a playing which *takes up* time requiring ones attention but not full deliberateness (147). Moreover this 'enjoyment of ourselves' (142) is not merely physical: 'if when a child is playing the physical excitement of instinctual involvement becomes evident, then the playing stops or is aat any rate spoiled' (53). See Donald W. Winnicott, *Playing and Reality* (London: Routledge, 1971). With respect to various ways in which social movements and activists can draw on the insights of Winnicott's psychoanalysis, aware of the limitations of psychoanalytic framework and of the tension between agression and play, see Irena Rosenthal, 'Aggression and Play in the Face of Adversity: A Psychoanalytic Reading of Democratic Resilience,' *Political Theory* 44/3 (2014) 337–62. Rosenthal also underlines the importance of Winnitcott's move from 'the capacity to know to the capacity to play,' in contrast with psychoanalists, such as Klein, who would have privileged the knowledge dimension. Without passing any judgment on the therapeutic aspects of this discussion, in the context of this book, and of Derrida's writing, a hyperepistemic move would be to turn knowing into playing: for that *understanding,* as that which in knowledge saps its own grounds, would be an apt *transitional* term. However, it must be noted that Winnicott's own take on democracy was uncharacteristically unconvincing as he produced direct parallels between subjective conditions and political institutions, without even hinting at taking into account other cogent variables. See Donald W. Winnicott, 'Thoughts on the Meaning of the Word Democracy,' in *The Social Engagement of Social Science: A Tavistock Anthology*, eds., E. Trist and H. Murray (London: Free Association Books, 1990), 546–57.

Chapter 2 Democracy

1. Walter Benjamin, 'Zur Kritik der Gewalt' in *Walter Benjamin Gesammelte Schriften,* Iii, eds., R. Tiedemann and H. Schweppenhäuser (Berlin: Suhrkamp, 1977), 179–203; 'Critique of violence' in vol. 1 of *Walter Benjamin: Selected Writings,* ed. M. Bullock, M.W. Jennings (Cambridge, MA: Harvard University Press, 1996), 241; and Derrida, *Force de loi,* 93–105; trans., 272–9.

2. It may look surprising but the negotiation that Derrida proposes takes place always between two incalculable exigencies or affirmations: 'one negotiates the nonnegotiable.' We shall see several examples throughout this book; see Derrida, *Negotiations,*' 12–14.

3. Derrida, *Force de loi*, 146; trans., 298.

4. Illustrative in this regard is Jürgen Habermas's late reconciliation with Derrida: 'A last farewell: Derrida's enlightening impact' in *The Derrida–Habermas Reader*, ed. L. Thomassen (Edinburgh: Edinburgh University Press, 2006), 307–8. Beyond the earlier gestures of reconciliation, this short text recognizes Derrida's place in the critical tradition, situating him crucially side by side with Adorno—a tradition that many would argue Habermas has renounced. See Pablo Ghetti, *Direito e Democracia sob os Espectros de Schmitt: Contribuição à Crítica da Filosofia do Direito de Jürgen Habermas* (Rio de Janeiro: Lumen Juris, 2006), 176–223. See also, about the enlightenment to come, Derrida, *Voyous*, 165–217 and 132; trans., 117–15.

5. Benjamin, 'Zur Kritik der Gewalt,' 189; trans., 243.

6. Benjamin, 'Zur Kritik der Gewalt,' 189–90; trans., 243. Derrida, *Force de Loi*, 107; trans., 279.

7. In terms of constitutional theory (or 'postmodern philosophy of constitutionality') this issue of the irreducibility of lies is remarkably well discussed in Angus McDonald's 'The Noble Lie: Critical Constitutionalism, Criticised' in *Policentricity: The Multiple Scenes of Law*, ed. A. Hirvonen (London: Pluto Press, 1998), 91. McDonald defends the impossibility of closing the gap between ideals and reality, simply because there is no gap without a process of idealization itself imperative for most 'critical' projects.

8. Benjamin, 'Zur Kritik der Gewalt,' 190; trans., 244.

9. In spite of these very problematic references in the post-scriptum of his essay, Derrida himself notices that Benjamin did acknowledge that pure exigencies would inevitably at some point be brought into a compromise. See Derrida, *Force de loi*, 144; trans., 297.

10. Derrida, *Force de loi*, 111; trans., 281.

11. Derrida, *Force de loi*, 94; trans., 272.

12. Jacques Derrida, 'Remarks on Deconstruction and Pragmatism,' trans. Simon Critchley in *Deconstruction and Pragmatism*, ed. C. Mouffe (London: Verso, 1996), 80.

13. Derrida, *Force de loi*, 94; trans., 272.

14. Johan Van der Walt, *Law and Sacrifice: Towards a Post-Apartheid Theory of Law* (London: Birkbeck Law Press, 2005), 197ff.

15. Derrida, *Force de loi*, 105; trans., 278. It must be added that, with respect to this question of mortality, Derrida is not a Greek, not a Greek Jew. I mean that in political philosophy he is not simply embracing the equality of mortals in their pursuit of earthly immortality, as opposed to eternity, to use Hannah Arendt's distinction in *The Human Condition* (Chicago: The University of Chicago Press, 1958), 26–30. Rather, Derrida attempted not to decide between immortality and eternity or infinity, and not only because the spectres by definition elicit the self-presence of the Greek *polis* or the Jewish synagogue. Derrida explicitly emphasized a logic of survival, a survival of

writing, of the archive, of readership, which is not yet of course the work of eternity (Derrida inaugurated his own archives at the University of California at Irvine). It is as if Derrida had erected for himself, and for philosophy with him, his own pyramid, or his tomb, reverberating ceaselessly his own death in advance, and disseminating his own tomb in life. See for this position the exhilarating book by Peter Sloterdijk, *Derrida, un Égyptien—Le problème de la pyramide juive* (Paris: Maren Sell, 2006), 21 and 36.

16. This take on law in Derrida's work can be grasped in Jacques Derrida, 'Prejugés: Devant la loi' in *La Faculté de juger*, eds. J. Derrida, V. Descombre et al. (Paris: Les Éditions de Minuit, 1985), 122ff.; 'Before the law' in *Acts of Literature* (New York: Routledge, 1992), 204ff. Not only there, however, see also *Force de loi*, 87; trans., 269. See also Peter Goodrich, 'Specters of Law: Why the History of the Legal Spectacle Has Not Been Written,' *UCIRVINE Law Review* 1/3 (2011) 773–812. Despite sharing a number of his views, on the in-visible sources of the law (which requires that kind of apt exposure that Goodrich provides in various pieces) and the adiaphoristic predicament of legal practitioners, I must contend that the scene of 'law as a hierarchical order' does not take into account the democratic transformation of law, the *complication* of a law whose source and purpose ought to be found in the people, which does not simply refer to a a mystical ground but which devolves that mystical force to the people themselves. In the distinction between the sovereign and the *oeconomic* (also legislative and executive, reigning and governing) realms, having both a theological homology, Goodrich (who follows and juristifies an aspect of Agamben's work in this instance) loses sight that the contemporary rise of administration and governance of the living (of which the welfare State and communism themselves are a key elements) is also a function and moves in tandem with the process of democratization. See Claude Lefort, *Complications: Communism and the dilemmas of democracy*, trans. J. Bourg (New York: Columbia University Press, 2007), 185–90. Agamben himself does recognize such a connection (democracy-*oeconomic*), but he subsumes the force of the people to a theological scheme which it, by definition, tries to escape, especially in characterizing democracy as 'the government by consent,' and by acclamation, in a relation father-son that elicits the turn, with all its problems and limitations, but nonetheless a turn, to the government of the brothers or of friends, to democracy as a constitutive exposure of the people themselves to their own finite ability to create together (which to be sure also involves a certain theological-political and Pauline inheritance). See Giorgio Agamben, *Il Regno e la Gloria: Per una Genealogia dell'economia e del governo* (Vicenza: Neri Pozza, 2007), 277–84 and 303–4.

17. Even though he sees the homonymy in relation to exception not in relation to fora (inside–outside); Giorgio Agamben, *State of Exception* (Chicago: University of Chicago Press, 2005), 37–8.

18. Jacques Derrida, 'Fors: Les mots anglés de Nicolas Abraham and Maria Torok' in *Le Verbier de l'homme aux loups*, N. Araham and M. Torok (Paris: Flammarion, 1976), 9–73; 'Fors: The Anglish words of Nicolas Abraham and Maria Torok,' *Georgia Review* 31/1 (1976), 64–116. Here Derrida plays with

the terms forum (French *for* and *forum*, in the sense of environment, forum, private or public, on the one hand, and a political-juridical institution, on the other), force, and forcing (*forçage*), save (archaic *fors*), and fora (*fors*, French plural of *for*, in the sense of forum, internal–external). 'Fors' thus inhabits the dividing and sharing line between interior and exterior, private and public, safe and unsafe, as force does. Indeed one can find another instance of Derrida's work: he also uses the term in an evocative, apparently trivial way (meaning essentially an exception, sauf), 'fors le nom.' See Derrida, *Politiques de l'amitié*, 20; trans., 4.

19. Agamben, *State of Exception*, 32–40. Certainly, though, Agamben did raise a previously neglected dimension of Derrida's work. Yet, it must be said that he moves back and forth in often conflicting interpretations of Derrida. Compare Giorgio Agamben, *Language and Death: The Place of Negativity*, trans. K. E. Pinkus (Minneapolis: University of Minnesota Press, 1991), 39; *Homo Sacer: Sovereign Power and Bare Life*, trans. D. Heller-Roazen (Stanford: Stanford University Press, 1998), 49–62; 'Pardes' in *Potentialities*, trans. D. Heller-Roazen (Stanford: Stanford University Press, 1999), 205–19; and 'Friendship,' *Contretemps*, (December 2004), 2–7.

20. And in a way that resists more strongly the type of over-determinateness characteristic of social formations such as 'nation' and 'empire.' See Peter Fitzpatrick, 'Righteous Empire,' *Unbound*, 2/1 (2006), 12. See also Peter Fitzpatrick, '"What Are the Gods to Us Now?": Secular Theology and the Modernity of Law,' *Theoretical Inquiries in Law*, 8/1 (2007), 184ff.

21. John Dewey, 'Creative Democracy: The Task before Us' in *The Later Works of John Dewey, 1925–1953, vol. 14: 1939–1941, Essays*, ed. J. A. Boydston (Carbondale, IL: Southern Illinois University Press, 1981), 224–30. See also Axel Honneth, 'Democracy as Reflexive Cooperation: John Dewey and the Theory of Democracy Today,' Political Theory, 26/6 (1998), 763–83. For a more recent attempt to move beyond Dewey, less 'holistic,' but still retaining a pragmatic and epistemic approach to democratic theory, see Robert B. Talisse, 'A Farewell to Deweyan Democracy: Towards a New Pragmatist Politics,' August 2007, available at SSRN: http://ssrn.com/abstract=1005645, accessed 15 May 2010.

22. Rather, every exposure is also a form of *intervention*. See Derrida, *Positions*, 57; trans., 36.

23. Derrida, *La dissémination*, 69–198; trans., 69–186.

24. Derrida, *La dissemination*, 166–7; trans., 144–6.

25. Derrida, *Voyous*, 66; trans., 41.

26. Derrida, *Voyous*, 194; trans., 139.

27. Benjamin, 'Critique of violence,' 242; trans., 188. See also Derrida, *Force de loi*, 94; trans., 273.

28. Derrida, *Voyous*, 36; trans., 15.

29. On this 'curving' see Derrida, *Politiques de l'amitié*, 258; trans., 231.

30. See Plato, *Republic*, books VI–VIII, trans. P. Shorey (Cambridge, MA: Harvard University Press, 2005), 284–91 [VIII, 557b558c]. And see Aristotle, *Politics*, trans. H. Rackham (Cambridge, MA: Harvard University Press, 2005), 488–97 [VI, I, 1317b–18a].

31. Derrida, *Voyous*, 44–5; trans., 22.

32. Aristotle, *The Politics and The Constitution of Athens* (Cambridge: CUP, 1996), 154.

33. Derrida, *Voyous*, 47; trans., 24.

34. Derrida, *Voyous*, 48; trans., 25. Translation modified.

35. Derrida, *Voyous*, 48; trans., 26.

36. Derrida plays with the French verbs être (being) and *suivre* (following) to say 'the word *rogue*, what I follow/am here.' He also says that his maternal grandmother used to call him a '*voyous*' (French term for rogue, rascal, or devious). In addition, when engaging with the work of Jean-Luc Nancy, Derrida reproaches him for dissimulating too much, that is, Nancy abuses dissimulation, a dissimulation that Derrida also practices: 'I will not dissimulate [the aporia] or at least dissimulate less than he does.' Derrida, *Voyous*, 96, 115 and 76; trans., 64, 78 and 49 (respectively).

37. See Plato, *Republic*, trans. R. Waterfield (Oxford: OUP, 1993), 296 [557b–d.]

38. Plato, *Republic*, 279 [544d–e]

39. Derrida, *Voyous*, 43; trans., 20–1.

40. Derrida, *Voyous*, 97; trans., 64.

41. For an instance of this regrettable and simplistic option (in spite of its apparent complexity), see Slavoj Žižek, *The Paralax View* (Cambridge, MA: MIT Press, 2006), 37. There Žižek equates democracy with the Master-Signifier. Precisely so, if there is a master-signifier, I wish, with Derrida (in the social position of the weak–strong, see Derrida, *Voyous*, 13; trans., xiv) to keep, to guard, the master. So much so that the 'master' will be overflown with material and symbolic investment—it will be transfigured. This is possible because capitalism itself can only function via the active roguishness of people. 'We' are participants in the capitalist emptiness. What is necessary is to bring that emptiness to the extreme to achieve a true deconstitution. Here, my approach is relational, but not oppositional. And this is not to bring about 'destruction,' as in Baudrillard; see Baudrillard, *Paroxysm: Interviews with Philippe Petit* (London: Verso, 1998), 25ff. It is a relational approach for it occurs in relation to a social meta-code of symbolic and material exposure and suffering. Yet, in this structure, and in spite of all inequalities and injustices, there is one fundamental and general assumption of equality. This is the equality of productive and differential capacity—not of pay—but of production: 'we' can all produce, yielding to the economy of knowledge; animals, dead labour, the entirety of existence is equalized in production. Marx noticed this process: 'The secret of the expression of value, namely, that all kinds of labour are equal and

equivalent, because, and so far as they are human labour in general, cannot be deciphered, until the notion of human equality has already acquired the fixity of a popular prejudice.' See Karl Marx, *Capital* (Harmondsworth: Penguin, 1976), 151. Derrida, and Nancy after him, notice the more general condition of this productivity. Not that this is simply a natural phenomenon (it is in a way, *ex post facto*, a nature surrounding us), but it can only be perceived under certain societal conditions, and these were provided by modernity. What Marx said of Aristotle, Derrida, in his own peculiar way, said of Marx. As Marx privileged the human-equal aspect of production, Derrida privileges the living–dying animal; it is the equality of the survivors, those who experience *différance* that can be experienced today. Nonetheless, such an equality is also the equality in exposure to difference and, in a certain way, freedom. See Derrida, *Specters of Marx*, 125–76 (I shall return to this in chapters 3 and 4). Cf. also Jean-Luc Nancy, *La création du monde, ou la mondialisation* (Paris: Galilée, 2002), 26–7; and Philippe Lacoue-Labarthe, 'Présentation,' in *la pauvreté (die Armut)*, Martin Heidegger, trans. P. Lacoue-Labarthe et A. Samardzija (Strasbourg: Presses Universitaires de Strasbourg, 2004), 5–65. On Nancy's take on Marx, I can also point to a cogent commentary on *La création du monde, ou la mondialisation*: Jason Smith, '"A Struggle between Two Infinities": Jean-Luc Nancy on Marx's Revolution and Ours,' in *Nancy and the Political,* ed. Dejanovic (Edinburgh: Edinburgh University Press, 2015), 272–89. See also Pablo Ghetti, 'World and Waste, or the Law of Liquidity' in *Liquid Society and its Law*, ed. P. Jiri (Aldershot: Ashgate, 2007), 61–77. Despite references to the theory of value, one can neither reduce capitalism to the conundrums of the commodity form, nor expand it to an all-encompassing social ontology, and in this respect I follow Ernesto Laclau, who takes into account other mechanisms, political, symbolic, that will add to the capitalist configuration, even though I do not embrace fully his theory of 'emancipations,' nor his strict distinction between the ethical and the political, or better I endorse so long as I may, in parallel, engage in a hyperepistemic move that will sap the *order* of that distinction and stand in-between the realm of Emancipation (singular) and that of emancipations (plural): *On Populist Reason* (London: Verso, 2005), 232–44; and *New Reflections on the Revolution of Our Time* (London: Verso, 1999), 41–85.

42. Derrida, *Negotiations*, 36.

43. It must be clear that there is no unidimensional system in control of all inclusion–exclusions, exploitation–enjoyment. There are rather several overlapping assemblages of encodings whose inclinations are exploitation and exclusion: assemblages of encoding such as the economic, the state administration, the instances of socialization (family and education), the legal, the political, the religious. Yet, none of them constitute securely delimited encodings, or societal subsystems in the language of autopoiesis. When I say overlapping encodings I mean that each trace in each encoding may have several 'allegiances,' and these allegiances operate strange intra- and inter-coding recursive effects. Furthermore, each encoding, given its iterative nature can universalize itself and attribute for itself an overarching function.

A hypothetical observer—and we all hypothesize ourselves, and tend to lift ourselves outside ourselves in different ways—could easily realize such a development in the way through which the cognition-prone elements (agents) of an encoding pursue to attribute to their operational field a predominant role in the allocation of resources and symbolic power. In that way, an observer of cognition can attribute to itself an even higher cognitive capacity—the capacity to discern the truth of the whole. Even if in terms of power-relations this observer recoils to a position of lesser direct power, the academic for instance, he reinforces the overarching and agonizing tendency of encodings in putatively codifying-unifying all experience through the gathering power of knowledge. Derrida always faces the dilemma of playing the philosopher 'role,' and by doing this reinforcing existing encodings through knowledge—the knowledge of the philosopher-sociologist 'king' or 'god.' Precisely, he can acknowledge the impossibility of this overarching knowledge, the failure of knowledge. But if such an acknowledgement remains on the cognitive level, it can be appropriated in an economy of knowledge-power relations. It is only when observation turns into a practice of exposure, becoming enjoyment, experience, and play that a more disruptive chain reaction can be initiated. For the extent to which a 'system' cannot be an all encompassing compound of exclusion–inclusion, see Peter Fitzpatrick, *Modernism and the Grounds of Law* (Cambridge: CUP, 2001), 222–3. For an approach to systems theory that includes a vicarious moment (traces or elements can belong to different 'systems,' which will endure the impact of one another because of this, depending on the explanations that are pursued), see Gregory Bateson, *Steps to an Ecology of Mind* (Chicago: University of Chicago Press, 1972), 454–71. For Derrida's use of code and encoding, see amongst many other writings, Jacques Derrida, 'Signature Événement Contexte' in *Marges de la philosophie*, 365–93; 'Signature Event Context' in Margins of Philosophy (Chicago: University of Chicago Press, 1985), 307–30. For that vicariousness in philosophy, see Philippe Lacoue-Labarthe, 'Typographie' in *Mimesis des Articulations*, Agacinski, Derrida et al., (Paris: Aubier-Flammarion, 1975), 168–246.

44. Derrida, *Negotiations*, 34–6.

45. Derrida, *Voyous*, 110 and 119; trans., 75 and 168.

46. Derrida, *Voyous*, 37–8; trans., 16–17 (exceeding itself), 105 and 144; trans., 71 and 101 (exceeding time).

47. Derrida, *Voyous*, 211; trans., 153–4.

48. Derrida, *Voyous*, 212; trans., 154. Another instantiation of this discussion is Jacques Derrida, *Without Alibi*, trans. by Peggy Kamuf (Stanford: Stanford University Press, 2002), xix–xx.

49. I shall argue more extensively about this in the next chapter. Let me say for the moment that the use of this expression is both economic and strategic. Pablo Ghetti, 'From the Posthumous Memoirs of Humanity: "Democracy *to Come*",' *Law, Culture and the Humanities*, 1/2 (2005), 208–20. Derrida indeed uses the expression democratic sovereignty, see Derrida, *Voyous*, 110; trans., 75.

50. See ch. 1, section 1.2.

51. Derrida, *Voyous*, 69; trans., 44.

52. Ghetti, 'From the Posthumous Memoirs of Humanity,' 208–20. Derrida indeed uses the expression democratic sovereignty. See Derrida, *Voyous*, 110; trans., 75.

53. Derrida, *Voyous*, 111; trans., 76.

54. Derrida, *Voyous*, 33; trans., p 13.

55. Derrida, *Voyous*, 33; trans., 13.

56. See the role of the walls of the borders of the city, Derrida, *Voyous*, 98–101; trans., 65–8.

57. Derrida, *Voyous*, 41–9; trans., 19–27.

58. Derrida, *Negotiations*, 35.

59. Sloterdijk, *Derrida, un égiptien*, 43.

60. The translation has been slightly modified; see Jacques Derrida, 'Force et signification' in *L'Écriture et la différence* (Paris: Éditions du Seuil, 1967), 34; 'Force and signification' in *Writing and Difference*, trans. A. Bass (London: Routledge & Kegan Paul, 1978), 20.

61. Rodolphe Gasché, *The Tain of the Mirror*, 177–251.

62. Derrida, *Acts of Literature*, 70ff.

63. Derrida, *Voyous*, 63; trans., 38. See also *De la grammatologie* and the explanation of *différance* as the difference/deferral between two movements, two dynamics: 'l'apparaissant et l'apparaître' (literally appearing and appear). The translation of this is extremely difficult, but the solution found by Spivak might have misled many, since if 'apparaissant' can be well translated into 'appearing,' 'apparaître' cannot be translated into 'appearance' without compromising Derrida's whole effort. Other alternatives could be the literal 'appear' or 'to appear'—with which one could suggest movement and folding, the differential folding of the appearing, the sliding imitation of the appearing. Derrida also 'translates' this *différance* as that between the 'world' and the 'lived,' where 'world' imports the already settled or normalized sensed information or perception around oneself, and 'lived,' the very fresh 'sensing' that joins the living dynamism of the perception with unforeseen consequences. *Différance* is also used, in contrast to 'difference' ('*différence*'), for the former is the production of the differing, both as distinction in space and rupture in time. Since, in French at least, the difference between the two spellings can only be noticed in writing, Derrida plays with the plurality, dissemination of writing. Hence, *différance* is conceived against the forgetting of writing, and for the sake of the forgetting in writing, as that which is forgetting of interiority and presence. See Derrida, *De la grammatologie*, 38–40, and 95; trans., 23–4 and 65.

64. Derrida, *Voyous*, 63; trans., 39.

65. Derrida, *Voyous*, 69; trans., 44. See n. 51, above.

66. Derrida, *Politiques de l'amitié*, 128; trans., 105.

67. Jacques Derrida, *Marges de la philsophie* (Paris: Les Éditions de Minuit, 1972), 133–4; *Margins of Philosophy*, trans. A. Bass (Chicago: University of Chicago Press, 1982), 113–14.

68. Derrida, *Force de loi*, 93; trans., 272.

69. For the relationship between force and form see Derrida, 'Force et signification,' 9–49; trans., 3–30. Force speaks for the tension and the intensity, pervasive and unclassifiable, whereas form speaks for the architecture, the structure, the paradigm or the framework. In this text the two are juxtaposed by Derrida precisely to highlight the subaltern position of force, and the necessity to reinstate its consideration, now in a differential way, in fact inextricable from form.

70. Nancy, *The Experience of Freedom*, trans. B. McDonald (Stanford: Stanford University Press, 1993), 96–105.

71. Derrida, *Voyous*, 82; trans., 54.

72. Derrida, *Voyous*, 69; trans., 44.

73. For an example of the paradox of constitutionalism (human rights vs popular sovereignty), see Frank Michelman, *Brennan and Democracy* (Princeton: Princeton University Press, 1999), 4–10. For a more recent recasting of the 'balancing' problem of two distinct exigencies, see Eric A. Posner and Adrian Vermeule, *Terror in the Balance: Security, Liberty and the Courts* (Oxford: OUP, 2007), 15–58.

74. Chantal Mouffe, *The Democratic Paradox* (London: Verso, 2000), 93.

75. John Rawls, *Political Liberalism* (New York: Columbia University Press, 1993), 4–10. Jürgen Habermas, *Between Facts and Norms* (Cambridge, MA: MIT Press, 1996), 82–131.

76. Jürgen Habermas, *The Inclusion of the Other: Studies in political theory* (Cambridge, MA: MIT Press, 1998), 105–28.

77. Habermas, *Between Facts and Norms*, 151–67.

78. For a recognition of this problem internal to Habermas's tradition, see Axel Honneth, 'The Other of Justice: Habermas and the ethical challenge of postmodernism' in *Cambridge Companion to Habermas*, ed. S.K. White (Cambridge: CUP, 1995), 289–324.

79. An issue reworked, for instance, in Jürgen Habermas, 'Constitutional Democracy: A Paradoxical Union of Contradictory Principles?,' *Political Theory*, 29/6 (2001), 766–81.

80. Jürgen Habermas, *The Theory of Communicative Action* (Boston: Beacon Press, 1987), 119–52.

81. Also difficult to dissociate from problems in his consensual theory of truth, which has to make recourse to a community of speakers. See Habermas, *Between Facts and Norms*, 9–16.

82. Derrida, *Voyous*, 71, trans., 45.

83. Derrida, *Voyous*, 59–61, 64, 70–1, 126–7, 130–1, 144, 160–1, and 173;

trans., 35–6, 39, 45, 86–7, 89–90, 101, 114, and 123.

84. Jacques Derrida, *Foi et Savoir—Les deux sources de la religion aux limits de la simple raison* (Paris: Éditions du Seuil, 2000); 'Faith and Knowledge,' in *Acts of Religion*, 42–101.

85. Derrida, *Foi et Savoir*, 75–80; trans., 85–8.

86. Derrida, *Foi et Savoir*, 77; trans., 86.

87. Derrida, *Foi et Savoir*, 78; trans., 87.

88. Derrida, *Foi et Savoir*, 78; trans., 87.

89. See n. 82, above.

90. Benjamin also pointed out the tension between the attribution of a sacred value to life, on the one hand, and the notion of an original sin, its affection of guilt, and the requirement of expiation or salvation. Here perhaps a great example of how the sacredness of the living is marked by the requirement of being sacred in the name of that which overflows life—towards expiation and salvation. Benjamin does not quite see the connection, and rather stresses the paradox and the 'decadence' of attributing such a value to biological life. It must be noted, though, that Derrida does not restrict this tension between respect/sacredness of life and 'sacrificial vocation' to biological life. 'Spiritual' life, or that which is 'greater' than biological life in a form of common life (including the construct of the political community) precisely involves in its constitution the very possibility of destruction, of immunizing itself against itself. See Benjamin, 'Zur Kritik der Gewalt,' 200; trans., 251.

91. Derrida, *Foi et savoir*, 79; trans., 87.

92. So autoimmunity can be distinguished from the risk of an absolute immunity. See Derrida, *Voyous*, 210; trans., 152.

93. Derrida, *Voyous*, 132; trans., 91.

94. For a sustained engagement with speech act theory and the distinction between the constative and the performative, see Derrida, 'Signature Évenément Contexte,' 365–93; trans., 307–30.

95. Derrida, *Voyous*, 132; trans., 91.

96. Derrida, *Voyous*, 132; trans., 91.

97. Derrida, *Voyous*, 126; trans., 86.

98. Derrida, *Spectres de Marx*, 95; trans., 55.

99. Richard Rorty, *Philosophy and Social Hope* (London: Penguin Books, 1999), 87–8.

100. Derrida, *Voyous*, 126–7; trans., 86–7.

101. Derrida, *Voyous*, 128; trans., 88.

102. Derrida, *Voyous*, 128; trans., 88.

103. And I say seem to reject because of the complexities that I have pointed out in Benjamin's text, but also because the contours of the problem

of corruption and its relation to virtue and dignity are indeed intricate. One key author in early modernity 'grounded' his political philosophy on the struggle against corruption, and that is Niccolo Machiavelli, as especially in his *Discorsi*, but not only. Yet, his insistence on the revival of a polities' origin (Book III, chapter I), as a way of keeping it in touch with its dignity, set forth a mad pursuit of grounds at the moment when the possibilities and abilities of Princes were being opened and tested (various chapters of the Prince, but also II, chapter I of the *Discorsi*). The 'changeability of conditions' (III, chapter IX, and 'changeability of Fortune,' I, chapter II), the openness of fortune to the able (the one endowed with *virtù*) was no reason in itself to fear or refrain from the origin (I, chapter XXVI). Here the ruin is not a function of its instability. And if one thinks in terms of a republic (which incidentally he clearly favoured, or of a *commonwealth*), where a return to its 'beginning' is return to the liberty and equality of the citizens, to the limit of their own forces (I, chapter XXI), then from that common lowness and a certain poverty (which he also deems as a cornerstone of the Republic, Book III, chapter XXV) there can be a perseverence in dignity. This is not dignity as indemnity or wholeness, but as openness imprinting on political philosophy and perhaps on philosophy as such, as claims Abensour in following Lefort: the author of *The Prince* does not limit himself to judging tyranny defective in light of the model of the just State. Instead, he welcomes the diversity of situations. Society is seen as in principle open to the event by virtue of the originary division that inhabits it. As a result of this "break"—at once unavoidable and irreparable the conception of being as constant and stable presence is undone. The very idea of degradation vanishes in favor of a new conception of being characterized by the upsurge of the unprecedented.' See Miguel Abensour, *La démocratie contre l'Etat—Marx et le moment machiavélien* (Paris: Editions du Félin, 2004), 181–2.

104. Nancy employed the term extortion essentially as a substitute for exploitation. I understand what he means as a generalized version of exploitation, beyond the economic, in every contact-relation that inscribes the creation of value into a system of production. I prefer to use the more traditional Marxian term, 'exploitation,' on most occasions, and not to endorse Nancy's work entirely by using his term. My approach to the relationship between exploitation and exposure is certainly in the vicinity of Nancy's writings. Yet, his distinction between exposure and exploitation is situated as a struggle of the West against itself. I have in this regard severe questions to pose to Nancy concerning the very concept of the West, the deeply Hegelian philosophy of history behind this notion, and the place assigned to Latin America. See Nancy, *La création du monde*, 60. As to his view on Latin America, I have to thank him for clarifying this in private correspondence. The latter has though only reinforced my impression that Latin America is excluded and included from his concept of the West in a way that is on the one hand slightly romantic, and on the other hand probably inattentive to the true transformative potentials of Latin America in the 'world.' Latin America, and Brazil in particular, should not be seen as the 'other of the West,' given its music, dance, and literature: 'as to Latin America, I am convinced that there is there a marked difference of culture in relation to Europe and North America: the difference of a Christian culture

detached from Protestantism and linked to indigenous [*indiennes*] cultures, which has produced something very original, less theoretical and more sensible, less given to abstract universality and hence also less given to totalitarianism (which is different from dictatorships!); a more literary than philosophical culture, a little bit like the Russian ...' (private correspondence, on file with the author—27.08.2004). Rather I see Latin America's dominant culture as a more thorough affirmation of the West, in a drive of accumulation, a simple, but overarching binary code 'have/not-have' (in some ways more subtle, in others more brutal than in Europe or North America). That is an affirmation that is not detached from Protestantism but which throve on anti-Protestant Catholic syncretism. The widespread 'roguish' capitalism that thrives especially in the developing world, but not only there, devoid of deeply entrenched notions of honour and shame tells more about the ultimate possibilities of modernity and capitalism, and the extent to which a type of sensibility may rejoice in the suffering of the other. See Jean-Luc Nancy, *La communauté affronté* (Paris: Galilée, 2001), 12. Other issues of concern are his rehabilitation of the notion of people as unity in Jean-Luc Nancy, ♩♩♩♩ in *La démocratie à venir,* ed. M.-L. Mallet (Paris: Galilée, 2004), 341–59 (the 'title' makes a reference to the 'Chant du départ,' a revolutionary song from 1794, music by Méhul and lyrics by Chénier, official anthem of the First Empire, heard at the beginning of the presentation). Such question, though, in some sense bears the recognition that the appeal to the people (as in the lyrics discussed in the text: 'le people souverain s'avance,' 'the sovereign people moves forward'), which one might deem romantic, still has a practical cogency and cannot be neglected—and here I think that Nancy would agree that one should not leave such a discourse as the remit of the fascists and ultranationalists, allowing for an opening up of the notion of people). In this sense, it is symptomatic that after the seminar, as Nancy explains later, Derrida has approached him to say he 'would have been able to say everything,' except for the word people: 'j'aurais pu dire tout ce que tu as dit, mais pas avec le mot "peuple".' Nancy replied asking what to put in its place, and Derrida answered: 'je ne sais pas, mais pas "peuple",' 'I don't know, but not "people".' See Jean-Luc Nancy, *La possibilité d'un monde*, entretien avec Pierre-Philippe Jandin (Paris: Petits Platons, 2013), 67–8. It is clear that Derrida is much more reserved about the use of established terms such as people, fraternity, community, etc. And Nancy has agreed in several occasions about that risk and the necessity of a new vocabulary. But he says he does not in relation to people, and as he put in the musically titled piece (342), and I agree: 'the name of democracy is worth at the least, or even designates that: the absolute exigency of keeping opened the wait, the question, the call contained in this word "people." If we forget "people," we forget "democracy".' His recent writings on democracy, in turn, do not fundamentally depart from Derrida's approach to it, even though there are differences. The thinking of and on the borders and limits of democracy is alive here [even though the reference to *droit* is somewhat unsatisfactory]: 'It is necessary to go a step further in order to think how unfounded politics, and in a way in a state of permanent revolution ... has the task of allowing the openness of spheres, which are by right [*en droit*] foreign: the spheres of truth and sense; those that name ... "art", "thought", "love", "desire" or all the other possible names of the relation to endlessness [*l'infini*], or, better saying, of the endless relation [*du rapport infini*].' See Jean-Luc Nancy, 'Démocratie finie et infinie' in *Démocratie, dans quel état?*, eds., G. Agamben et. al. (Paris: La fabrique, 2009), 83. This implies, rightly I believe, that societal spheres should be kept, that it is healthy to define and value them, and distinguish between them, even though their border should always be provisional. Yet, it is more problematic to argue, as he has, that there is a fundamental divide in the nature of democracy between 'metaphysical' democracy, a regime of meaning and sensibility, and absolute openness before the groundless abyss of life, on the one hand, and the 'politics' of democracy that sustains the spaces that allow the experience of such an abyss, without determining its final ends, on the other hand. It is rather the task of a deconstructive political philosophy to bring to the fore the groundlessness of 'normal' politics. See Jean-Luc Nancy, *Vérité de la démocratie* (Paris: Galilée, 2008), 59–63. See on exploitation also the phenomenology of the wheel that appears in Derrida, *Voyous*, 25–43; trans., 6–21 (and 110–1, above). See n. 43 and ch. 2.2 on exclusion.

Chapter 3 Law

1. Even a highly sophisticated theorist such as Badiou falls into this error in his legal-political essay; see Alain Badiou, 'Of an Obscure Disaster,' trans. B. P. Faulks, *Lacanian Ink*, 22 (2004), 58–89. For an interesting approach to legal theory that attempts to rescue something in Badiou's treatment of law see Bruno Bosteels, 'Force of Nonlaw: Alain Badiou's Theory of Justice,' *Cardozo Law Review*, 29/5 (2008), 1905–26. Peter Fitzpatrick has extensively shown how wrong are deterministic approaches to law. See, for instance, Fitzpatrick, *Modernism and the Grounds of Law*, 70–107.

2. Immanuel Kant, *Metaphysics of Morals*, trans. M. Gregor (Cambridge: CUP, 1996), 23–34.

3. This is not to say that such an instability, unconditionality, and incalculability are not at all integrated—or potentially integrated—into a higher order of determinacy. Yet, the role played by these experiences of legal openness cannot be underestimated, including in their capacity to facilitate acceptance or acquiescence of hierarchical social orders.

4. See for instance Jacques Derrida, 'Mochlos. Le conflit des facultés' in *Du droit à la philosophie* (Paris: Galilée, 1991), 409; 'Mochlos, or The Conflict of the Faculties' in *Eyes of the University: Right to Philosophy 2*, trans. Jan Plug et al. (Stanford: Stanford University Press, 2004), 90.

5. Derrida, *Force de loi*. And Jacques Derrida, 'Privilège. Titre justificatif et Remarques introductives' in *Du droit à la philosophie* (Paris: Galilée, 1990), 9–108; 'Privilege: Justificatory title and introductory remarks' in *Who's Afraid of Philosophy? Right to philosophy 1*, trans. J. Plug (Stanford: Stanford University Press, 2002), 1–66.

6. See Jacques Derrida, 'Pour José Rainha. *Ce que je crois et crois savoir* ...' in *Papier Machine* (Paris: Galilée, 2001), 333; 'For José Rainha: What I believe and believe I know' in *Paper Machine*, trans. R. Bowlby (Stanford: Stanford University Press, 2005), 109. See also how the theme of the risk of a 'programme' is pervasive in *Force de loi*, 50, 53, and 61; trans., 251–2, and 257.

7. Much in the same way that he claims the relevance of his quasi-transcendental approach, or the 'necessity of posing transcendental questions in order not to be held within the fragility of an incompetent empiricist discourse.' And in this same line of thought he explains that any 'transcendental questioning' (even though different from 'classical transcendental seriousness') is not incompatible with accidentality, contingency, and above all 'the fatality of the aporia.' See Jacques Derrida, 'Remarks on Deconstruction and Pragmatism,' 81.

8. Derrida, *Force de loi*, 13–63; trans., 230–58.

9. Derrida, *Force de loi* 35; trans., 243.

10. Derrida, *Force de loi*, 25–6; trans., 237. McCormick even argues that the whole essay is a 'defence piece' in light of the accusations against deconstruction in the wake of revelations on Paul de Man's past which would have damaged Derrida by extension. See John P. McCormick, 'Derrida on Law: Or Poststucturalism Gets Serious,' *Political Theory*, 29/3 (2001), 395–423. I am not convinced by McCormick's somewhat overstretched argument, but in any case my concern is not for the immediate context of the piece. On the point of the defence of deconstruction and the alleged 'ethical turn,' it is worth pointing out the work of Jacques de Ville, who denies correctly such claim that there has been a fundamental break in Derrida's work. He also provides an excellent characterization of Derrida's reception in legal circles and his own indebtedness to various philosophical traditions. However, I hold reservations as to his denial of "presence" and appropriation as political engagements or strategies. I understand he means to exclude a fascist use of justice and 'total assimilation,' by those who 'view themselves as marginalized,' but he perhaps encompasses too many political allegiances, including nationalists, for instance. And my point has two dimensions: first, it is not in our hands to say who is or is not marginalized and, as he himself demonstrates, one cannot exclude monstrosity absolutely, in a Derridean perspective, and second, the work of exposure and self-exposure, as shown here, goes a long way in reducing this inevitable risk. It is worth mentioning that the idea of reclaiming and reappropriating the State, and also religion in some form, is one of the key ways in which popular emancipatory agency has taken place in recent years, in light of several movements in Latin America, in Bolivia in particular. The Arab Spring(s), in turn, can also be seen as an attempt to reclaim the State, for the sake of some very basic notions, such as dignity, liberty and the fight against corruption. What is crucial is that these ideas and claims, no matter how 'appropriative' (for they bear resemblance to the realm of the proper—what more dangerously romantic and grounding than 'the will of the people'?), may be fundamentally open to criticism, to criticizability, to self-exposure

and to perfectibility. See Jacques De Ville, *Jacques Derrida: Law as Absolute Hospitality* (London: Routledge, 2011), 164. For my part, I feel no difficulty in employing these terms strategically, but not without voiding them and turning them secretly into shibolleths, coded passwords well known to the initiated (but in this case at least open to becoming public and to shifting current ideas), as in Derrida's response to Negri about ontology. See Jacques Derrida, 'Marx and Sons,' in *Ghostly Demarcations: A Symposium on Jacques Derrida's Specters of Marx* (London: Verso, 1999). A thought that goes very deep in the track of this 'appropriation' of religion is Nancy's latest instalment of Christianity's deconstruction, this time importing Islam and Judaism more explicitly: Jean-Luc Nancy, *L'Adoration (Déconstruction du christianisme, 2)* (Paris: Galilée, 2010), 19–63, whose use of terms such as ontology, people, freedom, fraternity, and even philosophy (perhaps I would have liked to have advanced such a hypothesis) is also secretly a code for what renders these terms *inoperative* in their practical instantiations.

11. And this adds a twist to Derrida's problematic starting point, for it also involves etymology, which is not necessarily instructive here. Derrida is very clear about this etymological debt on a section title of *Du Droit à la philosophie*: 'Of a Popular Tone—or of Philosophy (in) Direct (Style) (Directives and Directions: Straight (*le droit*), Rigid, Rigorous, Rectilinear, Regular),' Derrida, *Du Droit à la philosophie*, 71; trans., 42.

12. Derrida, *Force de loi*, 26 ; trans., 237.

13. Derrida, *Force de loi*, 18; trans., 233. (Modified translation, note that the French term here is *loi*, but one that comes right after the use of *lois*, laws, in the plural; it implies that Derrida still refers to a juridical law, and not law in the generic sense, whose meaning could be closer to justice's).

14. See Carl Schmitt, *The Leviathan in the State Theory of Thomas Hobbes: Meaning and failure of a political symbol*, trans. G. Schwab and E. Hilfstein (Westport, Connecticut: Greenwood Press, 1996), 53–63. Schmitt explains that line of influences by analysing the trajectory of Hobbes's Leviathan as a symbol from Spinoza to Pufendorf, Thomasius, and finally Kant. For Schmitt, Hobbes opened the doors for the rise of the neutral state and the technical era, even though that was not his intention—he had fought tenaciously against divisive powers, and in favour of the unitary order. Schmitt does not explain well Hobbes' reasons for indeed opening that door; he concentrates on the Cartesian mechanicism of the era, and on the consequences of his choosing an 'ambiguous myth' of the 'Hebrew bible.' This blatant anti-Semitism attempts to shift the blame for the origin of the technical, neutral and powerless state (key to the malaise of the times according to Schmitt) from Hobbes himself to Spinoza, 'the Jew.' Schmitt neglects the very practical aspect of Hobbes approach to a private space of freedom which would indeed be further developed in line with the development of private capital and interests: 'for internal faith is in its own nature indivisible, and consequently exempted from jurisdiction.' See Thomas Hobbes, *Leviathan* (Oxford: OUP, 1996), 348 (see also 332). Hobbes not only posits the distinction between obedience and belief, but he also gives reasons for the impossibility of rationally establishing the correct belief. See Hobbes,

Leviathan, 248ff. (see also his explicit distinction between *foro interno* and *foro externo* in relation to natural law obligations, 104–6). Even if this move is clearly designed to safeguard sovereign might, it does expose a structural social dissent that was already in play. Thus is 'force of law,' as I discussed in the previous chapter, one can also hear the challenge to these distinctions and to a restless insistence on the dividing lines of 'forums' of law—between internal and external, private and public, near and foreign, land and sea.

15. Derrida, 'Privilège,' 77; trans., 46.

16. Immanuel Kant, *The Metaphysics of Morals*, trans. M. Gregor (Cambridge: CUP, 1996), 25–6.

17. Kant, *The Metaphysics of Morals*, 25. This is the title of §E. I have modified the translation to use 'law' instead of 'right.' This has the disadvantage of not making a distinction in English when there is a distinction in German, between *Recht* and *Gesetz*. But the two terms are somewhat clarified by translating 'Das Stricte Recht' as 'Strict Law' (*Recht*), where the latter term is distinguishable from 'universal law' (*Gesetz*).

18. Kant, *The Metaphysics of Morals*, 24–5 (§C of the 'Introduction to the metaphysics of right').

19. Kant, *The Metaphysics of Morals*, 24–5.

20. Kant, *The Metaphysics of Morals*, 5 (§D of the 'Introduction to the metaphysics of right').

21. Immanuel Kant, *Groundwork of the Metaphysics of Morals* (Cambridge: Cambridge Uniiversity Press, 1998), 31 (G 4:421, Kant standard quotation). It is difficult to question this derivation of law from morality when Kant explicitly says so in §E (Kant, *The Metaphysics of Morals*, 25–6), as we shall see in the next paragraph of my text. Habermas, for instance, is one of the most significant contemporary theorists who attempt to 'update' Kant, and he seeks to take leave precisely of this element of Kant's thought. For our purposes it is key that 'In the Kantian formulation of the principle of law, the general law carries the weight of legitimation. The Categorical Imperative is always already in the background here: the form of a general law legitimates the distribution of liberties, because it implies that a given law has passed the universalization test and been found worthy in the court of reason. In Kant this results in a subordination of law to morality.' See Jürgen Habermas, *Between Facts and Norms*, 120 (and more generally on Kant, 90–131).

22. Kant, *The Metaphysics of Morals*, 25–6 (§E of the 'Introduction to the metaphysics of right,' 6:232–3). The same text appears also in Derrida, *Force de loi*, 18; trans., 233.

23. Derrida, *Force de loi*, 18; trans., 233. Derrida, 'Privilège,' 71–81; trans., 42–54.

24. Explicitly, for instance, Derrida, 'Privilège,' 77–81; trans., 45–8.

25. Kant, *The Metaphysics of Morals*, 25 (§D of the 'Introduction to the Metaphysics of Right,' 6: 231).

26. Kant, *The Metaphysics of Morals*, 26–7 (Appendix to the 'Introduction to the doctrine of right: On ambiguous right,' 6:234–6).

27. Habermas, Between Facts and Norms, 103.

28. According to Kant, Ulpian's maxim, 'give each his own,' or 'suum cuique tribuere,' is empty standing on its own. Yet, under the state it gains another significance: '*Enter* a condition [society] in which what belongs to each can be secured to him against everyone else.' See Kant, *The Metaphysics of Morals*, 29 ('General division of duties of right,' 6:237).

29. There are countless examples of Derrida's texts that discuss the violence of the as such. Here are some of the most interesting: Jacques Derrida, 'Préjugés—Devant la loi' in, *La Faculté de juger*, eds., J. Derrida, V. Descombre et al. (Paris: Les Éditions de Minuit, 1985), 87–139; 'Before the law,' 181–220; Jacques Derrida, *L'Université sans condition* (Paris: Galilée, 2001); 'University without condition' in P. Kamuf (ed.), *Without Alibi* (Stanford: Stanford University Press, 2002), 202–37. Jacques Derrida, *Séminaire La bête et le souverain, Vol. II (2002–3)* (Paris: Galilée, 2010), 104.

30. On some telling instances of this logic of constitution and suppression see Peter Fitzpatrick, '"What are the Gods to us now?": Secular theology and the modernity of law,' *Theoretical Inquiries in Law*, 8/1 (2007), 161–90.

31. In 'Force of Law' Derrida insists on how 'force' is intense, differential, and consequently it cannot ultimately be so settled—settled by the State—as Kant claimed, even though Derrida does not follow this reasoning explicitly: 'a first precaution against the risks of substantialism or irrationalism is to recall the differential character of force ... it is always a matter of differential force, of difference as difference of force, of force as *différance* or force of *différance* (*différance* is a force *différée-différante*).' See Derrida, Force de loi, 20; trans., 234–5. Moreover, *différance* as a key to force is defined, shortly after this, as 'the displacement of this oppositional logic [between nature and convention, or natural law and positive law]'; Derrida, Force de loi, 21; trans., 235. The combination of these two references should show how the Kantian project is constitutively doomed to fall apart, paradoxically, in its very appeal to 'force.' On force see also Derrida, *Negotiations*, 13–14 and 29–30.

32. Derrida, 'Privilège,' 77; trans., 46.

33. See in this respect Derrida's approach to Kant's strictness and rectilinearity as also a matter of *presentation*—a gesture towards pedagogy, simplicity, and pure intuition (one whose contours are not only about an external or accidental presentation, but even internal to the concept, the essence of law, in its 'popularity,' as opposed to philosophy's inaccessibility). See Derrida, 'Privilège,' 78; trans., 46–7.

34. Jean-Luc Nancy, 'Lapsus Judicii' in *L'impératif catégorique* (Paris: Flammarion, 1981), 43–4. And for a more sustained approach to Kant's inconsistencies in 'exposition' and 'presentation,' see also Jean-Luc Nancy, *Le discours de la syncope* (Paris: Aubier-Flammarion, 1976), 31–55.

35. For a brilliantly concise and perspicacious account of the relationship

between the faculties, see Gilles Deleuze, *La philosophie critique de Kant* (Paris: PUF, 1963), 33–6, 63–6 and 84–107.

36. An accord within judgement which still leads to the prevalence of practical reason: Deleuze, *La philosophie critique*, 95–6.

37. For Kant's own take on the relationships between faculties, see Immanuel Kant, *Critique of Judgement* (Oxford: OUP, 2007), 12–32 (in particular 29–32). For a concise explanation of the terms employed above on Kant's architectural work see Markus Weigelt, 'Introduction' in Immanuel Kant, *Critique of Pure Reason* (London: Penguin, 2007), xxxvii–lvii.

38. Derrida characterizes law, with Kant, as a formal structure of exposure: 'Even when a certain interiority is summoned or called to appear [*comparaître*] ... it is supposed to be exposable.' See Derrida, 'Privilège,' 77–8; trans., 46. Moreover, Derrida refers to his own task in this book as that of exposure—and here one finds a very concrete experience of writing as exposure of exposure. See Derrida, 'Privilège,' 12 and 22; trans., 2 and 9.

39. Derrida, 'Privilège,' 86–7; trans., 52.

40. In many respects Derrida follows Nancy here; in fact the whole text is dedicated to Nancy. See Derrida's key references to Nancy, Derrida, 'Privilège,' 76 and 90–4. In attributing to philosophy the role of a tribunal of reason—one that is not posited but posits itself, 'tribunal of exception'—Kant initiates, or in fact accentuates, philosophy's fall or ruin by virtue of its own *case*. Philosophy's jurisdiction becomes a *case* for itself to the extent that it posits itself absolutely—albeit through the multiplication of its intellectual/mental surrogates: reason, understanding, and judgement. Problems around judgement, in particular, are key to Nancy. For even if one could warrant the formulation of categories (concepts of pure understanding such as causality) it would be necessary still to find ways to bring together categories and experience, to apply empirical data to the understanding (categories are necessary for creating order out of the chaos of our intuitions). The faculty that fulfils this role is imagination in producing schemas, which establish the *a priori* conditions for all knowledge. It is precisely the task of philosophy to establish the conditions under which this work of mediation is possible. Philosophy establishes the general rule, and also in perceiving the risk of application, in noticing the problem of the case, attempts to anticipate all cases *a priori*: 'It is a matter then of eliminating the casualty of the case, and to forge the contradictory notion of a jurisprudence that owes nothing to experience.' See Nancy, 'Lapsus Judicii,' 56. See also Kant's key passage for Nancy: 'As critique [different from 'doctrine'], however, in order to guard the power of judgement against mistakes (*lapsus judicii*) in its use of the few pure concepts of the understanding that we possess, philosophy ... is called upon with all the acuteness and powers of scrutiny at its command.' See Kant, *Critique of Pure Reason*, 175 (B175/A136).

41. Jacques Derrida, 'Préjugés—Devant la loi,' 108–11; trans., 190–4.

42. Nancy, 'Lapsus Judicii,' 56–8.

43. Derrida, 'Privilège,' 90; trans., 199–200.

44. Derrida, 'Privilège,' 90; trans., 55.

45. Nancy puts the problem of law (*droit*) in relation to philosophy and Kant in an effective way. It is a matter of philosophy, in borrowing the language of law from law and the sciences, ending up *falling* upon the problem of enunciation, the *lapsus* 'proper' of law (*lapsus* is Latin for fall, in a sense the problem of the troubling enunciation of law, *juris-dictio*, an enunciation that can never simply repeat the correct formulae of law and decide without recourse to fragile judgements without certainty): 'since philosophy thinks itself—says itself—in terms of right, it inevitably thinks in a way that is structured around (or affected by) *lapsus judicii*, by the slipping and falling that are an intrinsic part of the lack of substance within which jurisdiction takes place.' See Nancy, 'Lapsus judicii,' 55. Despite this reference, and the acute impact of Nancy on Derrida, it must be said that Nancy in the text abstains from addressing Kantian homology between law and morality and from discussing Kantian *stricturation* of law (droit). In his more recent preface to the Italian edition, which appears in English with two extra paragraphs called 'From the Imperative to Law,' in B.C. Hutchens, ed., *Jean-Luc Nancy: Justice, Legality and World* (London: Continuum, 2012), 11–8. Nancy refrains again from dealing such a dimension of Kantian thought. In his short re-reading, which revisits themes that appear conspicuously in *The Experience of Freedom*, 155 (a fragment). It is worth reminding that Nancy defended his thesis, later published as that book, in 1987 and that 'Lapsus Judicii' was published in 1983. Taking into consideration that chronology and the several references to Nancy is Derrida's work on law and democracy, it would be more accurate to point out that Derrida from the late 80s onwards sought to respond to Nancy and their mutual friends (Blanchot, Kofman, Lacoue-Labarthe, and Levinas). Regardless of my interest in Nancy's post-Heideggerian 'ontology,' one needs certain caveats and precautions when interpreting the categorical imperative in the way he does. If I were to agree that Kant 'begins the self-legitimation of existence, and existence as the abyss of this self-legitimation' (22), I would have to add, almost at the self breath, two caveats: the first pertains to the structure of Kant's writing that attempted to wrest, and partly successfully in long hindsight (taking into account post-Modern Jurisprudence), this 'self-legitimation' abyss from law itself for the sake of phisophy and its architectural machinery. So, one can only postulate that he *begins* such a move if it is a beginning for philosophy only. The second point would consider the historical dimension of such a *selfing* moment in modern history and the history of philosophy, being as it is inextricable from a certain mode of subjectivity integral to capital accumulation, namely possessive individualism, in contrast with intersubjective, commonal, social or egalitarian drives that have striven to resist it. Nancy has preempted this type of criticism in his book on Hegel, with regard to views that Hegel would have favoured individualism or egotism, deeming these critiques as 'unphilosophical.' See Jean-Luc Nancy, *Hegel–The Restlessness of the Negative*, trans. J. Smith, S. Miller (Minneapolis: University of Minnesota Press, 2002), 5. For my part, I have no problem with 'unphilosophical' critiques, and incidentally the move that brings back historicity to phenomenology is crucial to Derrida's work (as I shall discuss later in this chapter). In the Continuum book, Christopher

Watkin takes up Nancy's 'social ontology' in order to put forward an engaged form of ethics that departs from Derrida's view of justice. The article presents a superficial understanding of the 'the messianic democracy to come,' a phrase never coined by Derrida, and, more importantly in a boo dedicated to Nancy, fails to note that Nancy's version of 'ontology' is indebted to Derrida's writing as pointed out in various pieces, including in the *Experience of Freedom* itself: the connection between freedom and the 'order and event' of 'come,' 108 and 197. The relation between Nancy's take on freedom and Derrida's *différance* appears here: '*Différance* thus implies freedom, or is implied by it. Freedom *différance*, while *différance* defers freedom, which does not mean that *différance* keeps freedom waiting: it is always already there, but by surprise,' 186. See also Etienne Balibar, "'Possessive Individualism' Reversed, From Locke to Derrida", *Constellations* 9/3 (2002), 299–317.

46. Derrida, 'Mochlos ou le conflit des facultés' in *Du Droit à la philosophie*, 397–438; trans., 83–112.

47. Derrida, 'Privilège,' 90; trans., 200.

48. For the 'history of judgement,' see Nancy, 'Lapsus judicii,' 44–52. For the point in relation to the Roman law tradition see Michel Villey, *Le droit romain* (Paris: PUF, 1945), 9–50.

49. Derrida, 'Privilège,' 84–5; trans., 51.

50. Derrida, 'Privilège,' 88; trans., 53.

51. Derrida, 'Privilège,' 88; trans., 53.

52. Derrida, 'Privilège,' 88; trans., 53.

53. Jacques Derrida, *Marges de la philosophie*, 391–2; trans., 328.

54. Derrida, *Force de loi*, 32–3; trans., 241.

55. Take the crucial example of Siyès's or Schmitt's notion of constituent power. Such an absolute power that has no limitation, and founds for itself a wholly new juridical order, refers always to a higher ground in the pre-established notions of 'the Nation' (Sieyès), and 'the German People' (Schmitt). The notion of a bearer of constituent power is crucial in this regard. For Sieyès, 'the nation,' understood as the social whole is capable of everything—holding a constituent power—as opposed to founded or delegated laws and powers. But even the 'nation' is based on a notion of community, of equal contribution to the general good—so that those who are deemed parasites, the nobility, may be excluded. See Emmanuel-Joseph Sieyès, *Qu'est-ce que le Tiers État?* (Paris: Société de l'histoire de la Révolution Française, 1888), 27–30, 67–8, and 75. In Schmitt, as I have indicated in the first chapter, the people themselves are predicated on this commonsensical distinction between friends and enemies. In turn, in Schmitt's work, this distinction is predicated on a certain vitalism: the existential threat of death of the enemy and the choice for friends and life. On the central character of the risk and threat of death for the legal-political order, see next chapter, 35–48. Cf. Carl Schmitt, *Verfassungslehre* (Berlin: Duncker & Humblot, 1993), 20–8. See also Derrida's approach to the American Constitution, and the role of the founders who had to refer

(in inventing it) to the signature of 'the People,' whose signature in turn was warranted by a final counter-signature which represents the limit, the absolute limit, of knowledge: God—in a certain, Derridean way, already in play here (as the name of a limit of knowledge and radical heteronomy)—is the 'mystical foundation of authority.' See Jacques Derrida, 'Declarations of independence' in *Negotiations*, 46–54.

56. Derrida, *Force de loi*, 34. trans. P. 242.

57. It is very touching and revealing to learn of Derrida's experience, the 'imprint' on Derrida's memory and body of the name 'Jew' (in the impact of its concrete sounds), not simply as in the French *Juif*, but as in J.u.i.f. (to signify that all phonemes are clearly heard and 'imprinted' in his memory). See Jacques Derrida, 'Abraham, l'autre' in *Judéités—Questions pour Jacques Derrida*, eds., J. Cohen and R. Zagury-Orly (Paris: Galilée, 2003), 20.

58. Derrida, 'Declarations of independence,' 50.

59. Michel de Montaigne, *Essais, III*, ch. XIII, 'De l'expérience' (Paris: Garnier, 1959), 320–1; Derrida, *Force de loi*, 29; trans., 240.

60. See ch 1.2 and 2.1. See also Kant, 'Perpetual peace: A philosophical sketch' in *Political Writings* (Cambridge: CUP, 1991), 112–13. See also Fitzpatrick on the exclusion of grounds as a whole from Public Law, Fitzpatrick, 'What are the Gods to us now?,' 161–90.

61. Derrida begins his legal opus with a discussion on title, see *Force de loi*, 13–4; trans., 231. See also Derrida, 'Privilège,' 9–23.

62. 'La déconstruction est la justice [deconstruction is justice]': Derrida, *Force de loi*, 35; trans., 243; see also Derrida, *Force de loi*, 18; trans., 233.

63. Jürgen Habermas, *Justification and Application: Remarks on discourse ethics*, trans. C. P. Cronin (Cambridge, MA: MIT Press, 1994), 60–1.

64. Derrida, *Force de loi*, 40–2, 52–7; trans., 246–7, 252–5. Countless other texts refer to subjectivity—an example that Derrida does not give here in those pages mentioned is Jacques Derrida, 'Désistance' in *Psyché: Inventions de l'autre* (Paris: Galilée, 1987), 597–638; 'Introduction: Desistance' in P. Lacoue-Labarthe, *Typography: Mimesis, philosophy, politics* (Cambridge, MA: Harvard University Press, 1989), 1–42.

65. So much so that very early in the text Derrida refers to law with force as justice that has become law, as law (juridical-ethical-political) that has become legal-strict law: 'it is the force essentially implied in the very concept of *justice as law* [*droit*], or justice as it becomes law [*droit*], of the law as Law [*de la loi en tant que droit*].' See Derrida, *Force de loi*, 17; trans., 233. We will get back to this in the next chapter.

66. See ch. 1.3 (on calculation) and 2.1 and 2.3 (on force).

67. See ch. 1.3.

68. Kant, 'Metaphysics of morals,' 134–6.

69. See Derrida, *Force de loi*, 15 and 18; trans., 232–3. Here Derrida's

references to Bourdieu are crucial, but Bourdieu is not directly cited (there is a gesture in Bourdieu's direction via 'the juridical field,' Derrida, *Force de loi*, 61–2; trans., 257). Later in the text Derrida becomes more reluctant to utilize the term for fears of association with Lacan—and because symbolism here should not be confounded with synthesis or 'logic'; Derrida, *Force de loi*, 91; trans., 271. For explicit references to Bourdieu at the same period, and a critical discussion on Bourdieu's objeticvity criteria in social sciences, see Derrida, 'Privilège,' 25, 73, 102–7. Unfortunately Derrida does not refer at any point to the text to which 'Force of Law' could well be seen as a response: Pierre Bourdieu, 'The Force of Law: Towards a Sociology of the Juridical Field,' *The Hastings Law Journal*, 38 (1987), 805–53 (published originally in 1986, and where 'droit' is translated as 'law': 'La force du droit: Eléments pour une sociologie du champ juridique,' *Actes de la recherche en sciences sociales*, 1986, vol. 64, n.1, 3–10). Despite Derrida's lack of reference to Bourdieu in this particular text, it is worth noting that Bourdieu alludes to 'deconstruction' in his 'The Force of Law': 'Those who refuse to accept (as do Wittgenstein and Bachelard) that the *constitution* of the "community of scholars" [*la constitution* du "peuple savant", translation modified] which is the historical structure of the scientific field, constitutes the only possible foundation of scientific reason condemn themselves either to self-founding strategies or to nihilist challenges to science inspired by a persistent, distinctly metaphysical nostalgia for a "foundation," which is the nondeconstructed principle of so-called deconstruction' (Bourdieu, 'La force du droit,' 5; trans. 819). Here Bourdieu refers to the lower faculties, like philosophy: those that are free to pursue truth and are not guided by the orientations of the State. Here the foundation of philosophy and by extension of all social sciences is predicated on the constitution of its own social field, on its own forces, which in turn tend to be seen as complex replications of wider patterns of power relations and hierarchies. Law enters a scene, a higher crisis also makes foundation its own theme, given 'an acute crisis,' and by means of the 'theoretical' transference to law of a philosophical question (operated supposedly by Kelsen). In this context, the pursuit of the understanding of the conundrums (regularities, 'habituses,' 'postures' and professional practices) of the law as force takes also the function of a revelation of what lies behind a set of beliefs, a 'chain of legitimation,' 'an illusion,' 'a miscognition,' or a 'quasi-magical' operation that grants authority and autonomy to law. It is as if the modern operativity of law were essentially derived from the *constitution* of its field that resists and enters into relations with other social fields. The legal pursuit of a legitimating ground is perceived as an attempt to isolate law and to eschew social realities. And yet, in my appreciation this discourse fails to realize the actual operation of a sym-bolic (a launch of the common, of that which unities in exposure: 'fiction,' 'illusion,' the 'as such') power of law creation that at every turn, through various recourses to its grounds, or to their void, universalizes singular events and experiences (another way of understanding this is through recourse to the hyperbolic, or excessive, dimension of the symbolic: see Derrida, 'Privilège,' 98). An operation all-too evidently displayed in modern democracies and in the democratization of law at issue in juridical-political constitutions (as opposed to constitutions merely political or organizational, of a by-gone era)—a phenomenon wholy forsaken in Bourdieu's approach. On symbolic power see Pierre Bourdieu, *Language and Symbolic Power*, trans. M. Adamson and G. Raymond (Cambridge: Polity, 1992), 163–70. Returning to the example of the faculties, it is worth mentioning that even philosophy, for Kant is somehow 'authorized' by legitimate institutions because its absence would be eventually to the Government's [*Regierung*] own detriment.' See Immanuel Kant, *Conflict of the Faculties*, trans. M.J. Gregor (Stanford: Abaris books, 1979), 28–29. It is also worth retaining the relationship between the legality and wider hierarchies and Bourdieu's inclusion of justice through the aim of justice in the systematizing work of legal theorists, even though in Derridean terms this would be a rather *strict* view of justice. On the violence of language as such, see Derrida, *Force de loi*, 33 and 119–15; trans., 285–93.

70. And as we saw previously, the semantics, homonymy, and pragmatics of 'force' are almost infinite, and comports precisely the French *for*, forum—possibly both private and public, on the border, and *fors*, archaic for 'except for,' to include the issue of an outside that subsists in the inside of the very essence of law, as force); see ch. 2.1.

71. Derrida, *Force de loi*, 17 and 35; trans., 233 and 243.

72. Derrida, *Force de loi*, 17 and 35; trans., 233 and 243.

73. Derrida, *Force de loi*, 17 and 35; trans., 233 and 243.

74. Derrida, *Force de loi*, 17 and 35; trans., 233 and 243.

75. Derrida, *Force de loi*, 17 and 35; trans., 233 and 243.

76. Derrida, *Force de loi*, 17; trans., 233.

77. Most interesting in this regard in relation to law (relevant to themes to be discussed later in this chapter) is Derrida's careful treatment of the actor and director Antonin Artaud. His effort to conceive of a theater of cruelty (of necessity and of life as such), beyond representation, beyond the authority of the author, beyond the distinction between actor and public, beyond writing, beyond repetition and imitation show in an antimetaphysical attempt various metaphysical predicaments: such as the privilege of the proper, of life, of originality, of presence, an absolutely inimitable one – as if these terms did not imply their opposites. Derrida points also to Artaud's recognition of the phenomenon of 'prescription' and of even the 'law' of cruelty—the law of necessity a 'law of the house' to which the new theater will attach itself and which in turn is pacifying: 'at this point, perhaps, cruelty pacifies itself within its regained absolute proximity, within another summary reduction of becoming within the perfection and economy of its return to the stage.' See Jacques Derrida, 'La parole soufflée,' in *L'Écriture et la différence* (Paris: Éditions du Seuil, 1967); *Writing and Difference*, trans. A. Bass (London: Routledge & Kegan Paul, 1978), 192. A crucial element is also the fact that in Artaud 'this law is raised to the level conscience' which does not impede it from conceiling a 'fata complicity': 'the transgression of metaphysics through a "thought" which, Artaud tells us, always risks returning to metaphysics.' Derrida, 'La parole

soufflée,' 194.

78. Another strategy to investigate Derrida's *justice* would be to pursue the meaning of what he calls 'esprit de justice' (*Force de loi*, 39; trans., 245). I thank Johan van der Walt in a conference paper for pointing out the potential problems of 'spirit' in the text—Critical Legal Conference, Kent, Sep 2005, 'Immimanence.' This paper was published, and the question of spirit and spiritual in Derrida's work were referred to in relation to Derrida's reading of Benjamin, but there was no reference to Derrida's own use of the problematic term. See Johan Van der Walt, 'Immimanence; Law's language lesson,' *Law, Culture and the Humanities*, 2/1 (2006), 2–16. I would argue that the context of Derrida's use of the term implies an analysis of the French term 'esprit.' The term in French translates German '*Witz,*' and English 'wit.' The sentence perhaps should be translated as 'without spirits of justice' (in the sense of moods), or better 'without spirited justice,' or even 'without wit of justice' rather than 'without spirit of justice.' There is certainly yet another Kantian element, this time pertaining to the third critique, but not necessarily only to Kant. 'Esprit' refers to a play and fragility/accidentality of discourse in a way that is crucial for instance to Jean-Luc Nancy, who brings a range of other references on the German '*Witz*': 'Indeed, it is always possible to control *Witz*, to dispose it for the production of knowledge and of works that have always assured the finality of *judgment*. But because they reached the culmination of this mastery, the Romantics also saw it dissolve in their hands, in a flash. In their attempt to generate everything by means of *Witz* there recurred what most properly constitutes Witz, or rather what never constitutes Witz, but a *Witz*, what can never be appropriated in any way, what can never be injected in any work (not even, especially not, into *Tristram Shandy*): its uncontrolled birth,' Jean-Luc Nancy, 'Menstruum Universale' in *The Birth to Presence* (Stanford: Stanford University Press, 1993), 264. But Nancy finds this dehiscence of any discourse that appeals to Witz even earlier in Kant, and in particular to the extent that it blurs the fixed lines of law (in this case Kant's own architectonic). Indeed Nancy associates judgment and wit by means of uncertainty and multiplicity. See Nancy, *Lapsus Judicii*, 45–6 (and his n. 10). In Kant himself, and not only in Nancy (who paraphrases it but does not give reference to this passage), one can read that 'it is only a conformity to law without law, and a subjective harmonizing of the imagination and the understanding without an objective one ... that is consistent with the free conformity to law of the understanding ... and with the specific character of a judgment of taste.,' Immanuel Kant, *Critique of Judgment*, trans. J. C. Meredith, rev. N. Walker (Oxford: OUP, 2007), 71. See in that regard how Deleuze would show the general *legal* problem here more clearly: 'aesthetic judgement is reflective [as opposed to determinant and less problematic judgements dealt with since the first critique]; it does not legislate over objects, but only over itself,' Deleuze, *La philosophie critique*, 90. Reflective judgement entails a moment that is at once singular and universal: it always depends on a singular and disinterested experience that claims legislative powers, *claims* universality by the indeterminacy of the concept of the object over which it reflects (Deleuze, *La philosophie critique*, 70–1). In this way, this reflective

judgement that involves the creativity and imagination that Derrida requires of judges is bound to the unity of subjectivity which can only ultimately be attained by an assumption, a claim, or a postulation. If Derrida were utilizing a Kantian notion of taste, or 'spirit' (*esprit*) that would be very problematic. One can only assume, in the absence of much further evidence, that Derrida claimed rather an 'esprit' of the Nancyan variety: that is, one that already assumes the failure of the Kantian, and Romantic, judgements, as self-founding structures.

79. Derrida, *Force de loi*, 21; trans., 235.

80. Derrida, *Foi et Savoir*, 28–35; trans., 59.

81. On the former, see Derrida, *De la grammatologie*, 90; trans., 61. On the latter, Jacques Derrida, *L'Écriture et la différence* (Paris: Éditions du Seuil, 1967), 43; *Writing and Difference*, trans. A. Bass (London: Routledge & Kegan Paul, 1978), 26.

82. Derrida, 'Remarks on Deconstruction and Pragmatism,' 81.

83. Jacques Derrida, 'Introduction' in *L'Origine de la géométrie*, E. Husserl, (Paris: PUF, 1962), 61; *Edmund Husserl's 'Origin of Geometry,'* trans. J. P. Leavy (Lincoln, NE: University of Nebraska Press, 1989), 70.

84. Derrida, 'La démocratie ajournée,' 122; trans., 107. See also ch. 1.2.

85. For a more recent and rigorous attempt to restage the doctrine of the separation of powers in broadly Kantian terms see Habermas, *Between Facts and Norms*, 168–93.

86. Analytical minds may dispute the very possibility of calling Derrida's work a legal theory. On the one hand, there is certainly no doubt today that Derrida's work has a legal relevance, given so many prominent appropriations of his work by legal theorists. On the other hand, it is also clear that Derrida is not only a legal theorist. The question seems to be whether Derrida's work offers in itself an adequate treatment of a given number of venerable legal questions. In this book I am not interested in this type of classificatory question. Yet, I assume that if an author undertakes to research the social role of law or the relationship between law, force and justice, one can safely discuss his findings in the realm of a 'legal theory' without further ado. Quiviger tries to answer the classificatory question, coming to the doubtful conclusion of a 'legal turn' in Derrida. See Pierre-Yves Quiviger, 'Derrida: de la philosophie au droit,' *Cités*, 30 (2007), 41–52.

87. Derrida, *Force de loi*, 38; trans., 244.

88. Michel Villey, 'Préface—La doctrine du droit dans l'histoire de la science juridique' in Immanuel Kant, *Métaphysique des mœurs—Doctrine du droit* (Paris: Librairie Philosophique J. Vrin, 1971), 24.

89. Michel Villey, *Le droit et les droits de l'homme* (Paris: PUF, 1983), 37–54. Also Villey, *Le droit romain*, 9–50. Cf. as well Michel Villey, *La formation de la pensée juridique moderne* (Paris: PUF, 2003), 149–76.

90. Villey, 'Préface,' 9–11.

91. Villey, Le droit et les droits de l'homme, 49.

92. Chaïm Perelman, *Logique juridique: Nouvelle rhétorique* (Paris: Dalloz, 1976), 110ff.

93. Villey, *Le droit romain*, 47. Also Ibid., 36–50.

94. Villey, *Le droit romain*, 44. Here I follow Villey's text, but this is a reference to Ulpian (Digest, book I, title I, fragment 10): '*Jurispudentia est divinarum atque humanarum rerum notitia, justi atque injusti scientia*' ('Jurisprudence is the understanding of divine and human affairs, a knowledge of the just and the unjust'—my translation).

95. Villey, *Le droit romain*, 49–50.

96. Villey, *Le droit romain*, 38.

97. Derrida was aware of Villey's critique of Kant, and he even stated that 'the conclusion of this long preface [Villey's] would appeal no doubt to a long meticulous discussion—and perhaps a general remaking of this immense problematic.' Yet, Derrida does not pursue this further and proceeds as if such a critique of Kant had not been available. See Derrida, 'Privilège,' 73; trans., 198.

98. Surely Derrida has always been interested in history and is not 'naïf' in any vulgar sense at all. His standard approach has indeed been to highlight the problematic nature of history, origin, grounds of philosophy itself, and the extent to which there is a limit to—but also a place for—the transcendental project of suspending judgement and reaching universal conditions of possibility. One can see this since very early in his work: Jacques Derrida, *La genèse dans la philosophie de Husserl* (Paris: PUF, 1991), 247–83 (dissertation completed at the École Normale Supérieure in 1954); *The Problem of Genesis in Husserl's Philosophy*, trans. Marian Hobson (Chicago: The University of Chicago Press, 2003), 153–78. Moreover, technological transformations and key events of his own time were always relevant for Derrida. Just one example is Jacques Derrida, 'La machine à traitement de textes' in *Papier Machine* (Paris: Galilée, 2001), 151–66; 'The word processor' in *Paper Machine*, trans. R. Bowlby (Stanford: Stanford University Press, 2005), 19–32. Derrida is also renowned for his autobiographical approach, of which an example is his 'Abraham, L'autre,' in *Judéités*, 11–42. Moreover, Derrida's notion of historical time is certainly of a very long term perspective, where a more recent example is this boutade: 'we have never left totemism,' Jacques Derrida and Jean-Luc Nancy, 'Responsabilité—du sens à venir,' in *Sens en tous sens—Autour des travaux de Jean-Luc Nancy*, eds., F. Guibal and J-C. Martin (Paris: Galilée, 2002), 199. I do not disagree with Derrida's long term perspective and autobiographical approach, in fact they are extraordinary qualities. Yet, there are shorter term changes that should be heeded and investigated—at least strategically for the sake of making the deeper, more fundamental points. The contemporary question for instance of a shift in modernity, or a radicalization of modernity, and especially in relation to law, cannot be avoided. I recorded Derrida saying that he did 'not know of post-modernity, but of modernity only' (notes of the 3rd lecture of the Conference Cycle on 'Sovereignty and Cruelty,' Rio de Janeiro, Public Planetarium, 9 June 2001, on file with the author). In that context he quite rightly meant that he had nothing to do with

the champions of philosophical 'post-modernism,' and that the fundamental historical transformations with which we are still trying to cope to this day are fundamentally modern ones. Yet, Derrida himself acknowledges in several writings that there is a huge transformation taking place in the history of sovereignty, and in particular in relation to the possibility of its sharing; see Derrida, *Voyous*, 13; *Rogues*, 154–5. Another element of this transformation, which Derrida also acknowledges, is that the individual, subject of human rights, seems to be concentrating a form of un-sharable sovereignty (Derrida, *Rogues*, 128; trans., 88—and ch. 2). These are key factors of which sociologists who employ terms like post/late/liquid/hyper-modernity are trying to 'make sense'—indicating some changes as intensifications of the modern drive. For an early stage treatment of the possible 'post' of modernity, see Anthony Giddens, *The Consequences of Modernity* (Cambridge: Polity, 1991), 45–53; for an approach that reconciles post-modernists and late modernists via 'liquidity,' see Zygmunt Bauman, *Liquid Modernity* (Cambridge: Polity, 2000), 16–52; and for a much less convincing, but still symptomatic view of the radicalization of modernity, see Gilles Lipovetsky, *Hypermodern Times* (Cambridge: Polity, 2005), 29–71.

99. A significant number of legal theorists have sought to make law adequate to new times, and hence have scrutinized societal transformations. In more rare occasions they have also taken advantage of societal transformations to address ingrained social problems or traditional legal-theoretical inconsistencies. But irrespective of motivations, legal theory has for a long time attempted to move beyond Kantian, or more generally legal-architectonic, frameworks. On a superficial level, which is strategically relevant, Derrida's deconstruction comes, as it were, after the party has ended (and here I have to agree with Quiviger about Derrida not being aware of legal technicalities, see Quiviger, 'Derrida: de la philosophie au droit,' 41). A few examples of what I think Derrida has missed out, and which have made his Kantian starting point at least dubious, and I restrict myself to what was available to Derrida in 1989, the time of writing of 'Force of Law' (and this is not say that some form of deconstruction is not due in relation to them, but it would certainly have to start from a different, more oblique, angle): Felix Cohen, 'Transcendental nonsense and the functional approach,' *Columbia Law Review*, 35/6 (1935), 809–49; Theodor Viehweg, *Topik und Jurisprudenz* (Munich: C.H. Verlag, 2000 [1953]); Perelman, *Logique juridique: Nouvelle rhétorique*; Sergio Cotta, *Il diritto nell'esistenza*, 2nd edn (Milano: Giuffé Editore, 1991 [1984]), 35–56; André-Jean Arnaud, *Le droit trahi par la philosophie* (Rouen: Bibliothèque du Centre d'Études Juridiques et Politiques de Rouen, 1977).

100. But there is no doubt that the 'critique of ideology' is still important, and Derrida is explicit about this: 'desedimentation of the superstructures of law that both hide and reflect the economic and political dominant forces of society' (Derrida, *Force de loi*, 32; trans., 241). However, what Derrida really strives to reach is 'a more intrinsic structure ... the very emergence of justice and law' (Derrida, *Force de loi*, 32; trans., 241).

101. Derrida, 'Declarations of independence,' 50. See ch. 3, 153–4.

102. Derrida, *Force de loi*, 34–5; trans., 242–3. That transposition of the foundational act to the normality of legal practice by means of the experience of decision-making appears very clearly in the work of Carl Schmitt. See Carl Schmitt, *Political Theology*, trans. G. Schwab (Cambridge, MA: MIT Press, 1985), 16–35. A more complex association is also possible, in particular by virtue of Kelsen's work on interpretation. See Hans Kelsen, *Pure Theory of Law*, 2nd edn, trans. M. Knight (Berkeley: University of California Press, 1967), 348–56.

103. Derrida, 'Privilège,' 64; trans., 37.

104. On the paradigm shifts in legal history, connected with rights discourse, see Habermas, *Between Facts and Norms*, 388–446.

105. Derrida refers to justice and law on several occasions as intertwined, law itself is referred as justice as law (Derrida, *Force de loi*, 17; trans., 233). And after proposing the more strict distinction between law and justice (Derrida, *Force de loi*, 35, 38, 43; trans., 243–4 and 247), Derrida also stages their differential contamination (Derrida, *Force de loi*, 61–3, and 94; trans., 256–8 and 272).

106. 'The law interdicts in interfering and in differing the "férance", the rapport, the relation, reference.' See Jacques Derrida, 'Préjugés—Devant la loi,' 122–3, trans., 204–5. This other reading of law in Derrida has been pointed out by Peter Fitzpatrick in several texts. See Peter Fitzpatrick, 'Access as justice,' *Windsor Yearbook of Access to Justice*, 23/1 (2005), 3–16. Fitzpatrick has also shown, especially through an analysis of judicial decision, that law itself has to combine moments of determination and responsiveness. See Fitzpatrick, *Modernism and the Grounds of Law*, 70–7. My interest, though, in exposure, and overexposure, with and beyond Derrida, in the language of Fitzpatrick, would strive for a responsiveness of responsiveness; that is, an attempt to enjoy more fully responsiveness itself; and without ceasing to recognize that responsiveness, as exposure, is already happening.

107. Jacques Derrida, 'Signature Événement Contexte,' 365–93; trans., 307–30. See ch. 2.4.

108. See, for instance, François Ewald, *L'État providence* (Paris: Grasset, 1986), 15–45; André-Jean Arnaud, *Critique de la Raison Juridique 2, Gouvernants sans frontières—Entre mondialisation et post-mondialisation* (Paris: L.G.D.J., 2003), 99–182; Fitzpatrick, *Modernism and the Grounds of Law*, 183–218.

109. In Kennedy's work, for instance, many of the problems related to the rights discourse seem to stem from democratic practice, see Duncan Kennedy, *A Critique of Adjudication {fin de siècle}* (Cambridge, MA: Harvard University Press, 1998), 315–76. As to the relevance of deconstruction to the legal discourse, it would be necessary to analyse the impact upon Critical Legal Studies, or legal critique more broadly. For such a history, see Costas Douzinas, Adam Gearey, *Critical Jurisprudence: The political philosophy of justice* (Oxford: Hart Publishing, 2005), 61–76 and 229–58. See also Peter Goodrich, 'Satirical legal studies: From the legists to the Lyzard,' *Michigan*

Law Review, 103 (2004), 397–517. See ch. 2.1.

110. This through taking into account the horizontality of the application of human rights in a judicial review context. See Van der Walt, *Law and Sacrifice*, 70–1.

111. Van der Walt, *Law and Sacrifice*, 71.

112. Van der Walt, *Law and Sacrifice*, 140.

113. Van der Walt, *Law and Sacrifice*, 141.

114. Van der Walt, *Law and Sacrifice*, 196.

115. For Nancy the sacrificial is bound with a certain Western and theological-political operation, currently in dehiscence. And this is the point of contention between Van der Walt and Nancy. See Van der Walt, *Law and Sacrifice*, 138 and Jean-Luc Nancy, *Le Sens du Monde* (Paris: Galillé, 1993), 105 and 141.

116. For a critique of Agamben along the lines I refer here see Peter Fitzpatrick, 'Bare Sovereignty: *Homo Sacer* and the Insistence of Law,' Theory and Event 5(2): 34–67. Moreover, the anthropology of carnival in Brazil, the Brazilian feast, bears witness to a plurality of normativities *in exception*. And evidently Agamben is himself attempting to overcome a form of exception, circumscribed by legality, in order to bring about a true exception. A project that I share, albeit from another angle, for here the zone of indistinction between rule and nonrule would have to be rendered more as a hierarchical and/or exploitative modulation of law itself: a law that exposes itself to its own incompleteness and this is a feature of the whole democratic becoming of law at the same time resisted by law. What I aim to bring about is a new sensitivity to this condition so as to enjoy a fuller democratic experience of law.

117. This is not the space for a thorough rendering of the Brazilian constitutional situation, but it is worth pointing out that the requirement to justify legal decisions (Art. 93, IX and X), the institution of the injunction mandate (Art. 5, LXXI, granting the possibility for judges to create legal norms for the particular case in the absence of a norm), the judicial review for legislative failure (Art. 103, §2) and the demand for legal and administrative transparency (Art. 5, LX, LXXI – today all public salaries and the vast majority of public expenses are readily available for consultation on the web: http://www.portaltransparencia.gov.br/) have been key features of the Constitution of 1988, which have led to a certain direction of exposure. An exposure of its own failure, its own characterlessness, its fundamental contradictions, or its position as 'constitution without decision' (a term applied by Otto Kirchheimer to the German Constitution of Weimar), they all render it a constitutional exposure. And any attempt to make it better, to actualize it, to reverse trends and inevitable exclusionary lines of rupture will be a drive into an overexposure. See Otto Kirchheimer, 'Weimar—And What Then? An Analysis of a Constitution,' in Burin, F.S. Shell, K.L. *Politics, Law, and Social Change—Selected Essays of Otto Kirchheimer*, Columbia University Press: New York, 1969, 33–74.

118. In this particular aspect I am closer to a broad trend in constitutional jurisdiction theory that favours more restraint on the part of judges, more space for politics (within and outside the legal system) and more space for judicial review to the extent that it promotes and enhances public deliberation (understood here as inviting agonistic pluralism) and democracy as such. See my treatment of judicial review in *Direito e Democracia sob os Espectros de Schmitt: Contribuição à Crítica da Filosofia do Direito de Jürgen Habermas* (Rio de Janeiro: Lumen Juris, 2006), 152–76. And on this peculiar deliberation, see Pablo Ghetti, 'Laws of Deliberation: From Audaciousness to Prudence... and Back,' *Law and Critique*, 16/3 (2005), 255–75.

119. This line of reasoning is predicated on Derrida's assessment of the South African situation during apartheid and of Mandela's position. According to Derrida, the foundation that produces, the *coup de force* that creates the law in fact also presupposes its existence, appeals to a higher law, and hence erases this foundation's traces of violence. It occurs that in this case such blow remains a 'bad blow.' The speech act that does not work is predicated on the fact that 'the violence was too great, *visibly too great*, at a moment when this visibility extended to a new international scene, and so on. The white community was *too* much in the minority, the disproportion of wealth too flagrant.' The condition of the apartheid legal order was one in which its justification was far from 'sufficient verisimilitude': This very distance from the truth, from the perceived truth also unleashes more resistance and always more violence. And what happens is a permanent condition of violence supported by 'a pathological proliferation of juridical prostheses.' That is why Mandela, in Derrida's appreciation, did not wish to work within that constitutional framework; he admired another law, not the law of apartheid. Note that in the passages above Derrida refers and emphasizes a matter of degree in visibility. It is a matter of degrees of exposure. And in some respects, with regard to the thought of an overexposure, it is to do with an change of quality, a rupture with a given domain of exposure itself. See Jacques Derrida, 'Admiration pour Nelson Mandela ou Les lois de la réflexion,' in *Psyché – Inventions de l'autre* (Paris: Galilée, 1987–2003), 72–3; "The Laws of Reflection: Nelson Mandela, in Admiration", trans. M. A. Caws and I. Lorenz, in *For Nelson Mandela*, eds., J. Derrida, Mustapha Tlili (New York: Henry Holt, 1987), 18–19.

120. Jean-Luc Nancy, 'Lapsus Judicii,' 43.

121. Jean-Luc Nancy, 'Lapsus Judicii, 58.

122. Jean-Luc Nancy, 'Lapsus Judicii, 58.

123. Jean-Luc Nancy, 'Lapsus Judicii, 43.

124. Nancy, 'Lapsus Judicii,' 39. The constitutionality of law hinges on the factuality of cases, each time exposed to their theatrical accidentality. In addition, it is not surprising, but somewhat disturbing that a text dedicated to philosophical translation may have been so severely affected by errors of translation. Its English version seems to ignore the current expression 'Roman Law' (*droit roman*), adopting the almost bizarre 'the Roman discourse on right.' Even more unintelligible is the translation of 'Canon Law' (droit canon)

into this delusional 'the model established by right' (Nancy, *Finite Thinking*, 156).

125. Nancy, 'Lapsus Judicii,' 38 and 41.
126. Nancy, 'Lapsus Judicii,' 39 and 43–4.
127. Nancy, 'Lapsus Judicii,' 40–3.
128. Villey, *Le droit romain*, 43.
129. Villey, *Le droit romain*, 42.
130. Villey, *Le droit et les droits de l'homme*, 38. With regard to Roman jurists, Villey makes reference, on the same page, to their 'méthode tâtonnante,' which I would translate as 'tactful method,' even though it does not convey the dimension of an attempt, a provisional endeavour, and a form of erring that the French term imports. Various interesting approximations with Nancy could be thought on the basis of a conceivable takes into account a certain sense of touching.
131. Nancy, 'Lapsus judicii,' 42.
132. Nancy, 'Lapsus judicii,' 43.
133. Nancy, 'Lapsus judicii,' 42. Most important here, for my purposes, is neither the composition with a world, nor the composition of a world, but composition itself inasmuch as an enjoyment of 'with' happens in the play of worlds that could be 'real' or 'theatrical' or 'literary.' If we were to hold on strictly to this distinction, we would have to see in Nancy something of Schmitt's depiction of *Hamlet*. In Schmitt, Hamlet's character becomes a truly modern myth, because despite epitomizing indecisiveness and an 'intellectual figure,' it conceals a 'real' tension, a real tragedy that resists the infinite time of the play, the spectral contours of *Trauerspiel* (mourning play), of its *characters* and its fateless time. This is why he brings to bear the historical significance of the play in the context of James I accession to the throne in 1603 and showing how the first folio contained references to Hamlet's grievances as not only for the murder of his father, but also for being 'bereft of the Crown.' Hamlet here is James, son of Mary, Queen of Scots, who was deemed to have plotted her husband's (James's father) death with the actual murderer and married him. Yet, this formulation reproduces an old metaphysical structure according to which time legitimates and gives meaning to the play: the subtitle of his book is suggestive: 'the intrusion of time into the play.' However, as Schmitt himself is aware, even though he does not develop this as such, time itself becomes a play: 'all the world is a stage' (Schmitt restricts this baroque theatricality of the State to European neutral states, whereas England would have remained more 'barbaric'). In fact, in this scheme, more than moving from play to time and time to play, what arises is an absolute subordination, and a domestication of play as sanctioned leisure: 'perhaps some day a legislator, realizing the relation between freedom and play or freedom and leisure time, will establish the simple legal definition: play is everything that one undertakes in order to fill and structure legally sanctioned leisure time' (40). Ultimately, this sanction, which allows for 'clear distinctions' (between the political and the juridical, for

instance), stems from a higher, tragic unity: that of human fate of submission to the same gods, be it in the courts, in theater or in the pulpit: 'that would be bad [the play of the play as amusement], because it would prove that the gods in the theater are different from those in the forum or in the pulpit' (43). See Carl Schmitt, *Hamlet or Hecuba: The Intrusion of Play into Time*, trans. D. Pan, J. Rust (New York: Telos Publishing, 2009). It is thinkable, however, a *composition* that enjoys the variability of spheres, the vicariousness of exposure to the courts, the assembly, the communion and the theater without a higher order of meaning, and that in fact finds a fragile truth in the universality and equality of exposure to the evanescent 'with' in playing variability and be-coming itself. It happens in Benjamin's thought through mourning play, in one register, but also in another through the thought of the horizontality of negotiators 'beyond all legal system,' but the whole question of law for Benjamin hinges on violence/force from a third party, a third that lies above the participants in a given conversation or dispute. See Walter Benjamin, 'Critique of Violence,' 247. In a different register, but conserving the same binary tension, Derrida attempts to com-pose a picture of writing that orientates itself beyond any constraining hierarchy, and thus strives for a certain equality (perhaps as resistance to hierarchy and exploitation) in the exposure of the variability and exchangeability of positions that subverts and under-stands the Hegelian framework: *positions*. From a post-Derridean perspective (as that which comes after Derrida) this exposure becomes an ineluctable truth worthy of trust. In overexposure, there is a move, heralded by Derrida himself, towards a leap that adheres to exposure and raises sensitivity beyond awareness. Despite its resemblance to 'awareness-raising,' overexposure would be more aptly described as 'sensitivity-raising': ready to debunk, deconstitute remnants of underexposure, closures to oneself and closed systems of appropriation. This is the common core of both radical democracy and a certain thought of communism. For the Marxian heritage of this jump or leap of postulation, examine this: 'If revolution has to extract its "poetry from to-come", it is because it will be hetero-historical [*hétéro-historique*, or *alter*-historical] and it will not be sustained without an exteriority, indecisive but radical. Or else, sublated [*récupérée*, recovered to self-revolution, to '*autorévolution*'], it will not be.' See Gérard Bensussan, *Marx le sortant—une pensée en excès* (Paris: Hermann Editeurs, 2007), 188.

134. Nancy, 'Lapsus judicii,' 39.
135. Nancy, 'Lapsus judicii,' 39.
136. Nancy, 'Lapsus judicii,' 44.
137. Villey, Le droit et les droits de l'homme, 48.
138. Jean-Luc Nancy, *La communauté desœuvrée* (Paris: Christian Bourgois Editeur, 1999), 102, 152, 230–1.
139. Nancy, 'Lapsus judicii,' 42.
140. Nancy, 'Lapsus judicii,' 43.
141. Villey, Le droit et les droits de l'homme, 50.

142. Villey, *Le droit romain*, 16.

143. Luis Alberto Warat, *A Ciência Jurídica e seus Dois Maridos* (Santa Cruz do Sul: EDUNISC, 2000), 128.

144. Ibid., 128.

145. Ibid. 134–5.

146. See Stephen Meili, 'Cause Lawyers and Social Movements: A Comparative Perspective on Democratic Change in Argentina and Brazil,' in *Cause Lawyering: Political Commitments and Professional Responsabilities*, ed. A. Sarat (Oxford: OUP, 1998), 487–522.

147. James Holston, *Insurgent Citizenship: Disjunctions of Democracy and Modernity in Brazil* (Princeton: Princeton University Press, 2008), 203–32.

148. Regarding 'characterlessness,' in the background I have prominently Mario de Andrade's invective that 'the Brazilian has no character.' This is the insight that grounds Andrade's formidable book and its anti-hero, Macunaíma: The Hero with no Character (1928, read this together with O. de Andrade's the Anthropophagite Manifesto). This lack of character is not necessarily moral, it is ontological, or, better, sensorial (the lack of engraving, from the Greek charassein). There is no character in the sense of a distinctive mark, a culture, and a dignity. Many have interpreted this as a pursuit of a national character, as denunciation of cultural dependency and such triteness. Andrade, one of best authors of Brazilian modernism in the 1920's was not trying to forge any identity but enjoy the lack of identity itself. Macunaíma is the evil god—it means exactly that in the indigenous languages of Amapá (Makuxi, Wapixana, Taulipang e Arekuna—beware, though, that in today's Brazil only less than 0.2 % speak indigenous languages). However, in the 18th century, protestant missionaries mistakenly used the term to translate the Christian God. And the legend arrived to Andrade through German, in Koch-Grünberg's collection of legends of the Amazon; in fact, it was later found out that the legend originates from the tribes of what is today Venezuela. He is already a colonial product, not a myth of origins. He is not even an anti-hero, rather an anti-(anti)hero, indifferent to being or not being a hero.

149. As to the move of the Brazilian Supremo Tribunal Federal to an activist case-law inspired by post-positivism and in particular by a certain reading of the application of the methodology of balancing, often without due consideration for democratic decision-making, or any account of a democratic sensitivity in courts, see Juliano Zaiden Benvindo, *On the Limits of Constitutional Adjudication: Deconstructing Balancing and Judicial Activism* (Heidelberg: Springer, 2010), 83–134. The grave consequences of this oblivion of democracy and of organized politics in the name of the Constitution or democracy itself have been ubiquitous in recent years. The ethos of balancing and pragmatic activism have produced an indistinction between law and politics under the aegis of the hierarchical place the institution of the Judiciary occupies in Brazilian society. It would be worth exploring this phenomenon as an oppressive inclination to the carnivalization of law, with its conservative conception of justice based on hierarchies and social class, as opposed to

the more emancipatory idea, espoused by Warat, of the carnivalization of democracy itself.

150. A reconciliation or a pacification as says Derrida in relation to the conscience-raising of a certain disaster: the erasure of gaps and writing itself in the originary representation of Artaud's theater: 'the ur-stage is then present, reassembled into its presence, seen, mastered, terrifying and pacifying' and this 'pacification' is obtained through cruelty: 'cruelty pacifies itself within its regained proximity.' Such a regained proximity is not naïve, it can see 'origin and necessity': it is brought 'to the level of consciousness' (Derrida, 'La parole soufflée,' 192–4): 'the theater of cruelty thus would not be a theater of the unconscious. Almost the contrary. Cruelty is consciousness, is exposed lucidity.' Derrida, 'The Theater of Cruelty,' in *L'Écriture et la différence* (Paris: Éditions du Seuil, 1967); *Writing and Difference*, trans. A. Bass (London: Routledge & Kegan Paul, 1978) 242. Despite Derrida's admiration for Artaud this exposure qua consciousness is another form of reducing theater and representation itself to a presentation present to itself.

151. Not in the sense that it has been ultimately revealed as this would prove unthinkable, but as the generalization of a certain softening and curvature of law that is open to its own paradoxes. Furthermore, such a trivialization or *banalization* of law can have a positive and a negative connotation. On the positive side, it is linked to the democratization of law: open to political conflicts and strategizing, open to the questions and calls that have been discussed in chapter two about force and people, as if the legality had to integrate and take into account democracy in a more radical and novel sense, for it challenges borders by definition, than the mere application of democratic will of the legislator. It could also mean the beginning of a dwelling on exposure that paves the way for legal sensibility, solidarity, and emotionality, albeit conceivably on a level of resistance. See in this regard the various attempts in the Portuguese and Spanish languages to integrate, with various degrees of success, a more complex rationality, open to its own *interest*, into law: Verdú, Pablo Lucas, *El Sentimiento Constitucional: Aproximación al estudio del sentir constitucional como modo de integración política* (Madrid: Reus S.A., 1985); Cabo Martín, Carlos de, *Teoría Constitucional de la Solidariedad* (Madrid: Marcial Pons, 2006); Luis Alberto Warat, *Manifesto of Legal Surrealism* (São Paulo: Acadêmica, 1988); *A Ciência Jurídica e seus Dois Maridos* (Santa Cruz do Sul: EDUNISC, 2000); and Barreto, José Manuel, 'Human Rights and Emotions from the Perspective of the Colonized: Anthropophagi, Legal Surrealism and Subaltern Studies,' *Revista de Estudos Constitucionais, Hermenêutica e Teoria do Direito (RECHTD)* 5/2, julho-dezembro (2013) 106–15. On the negative side, though, it is as if a bad cynicism found its way to the legal system: the hypothesis is that a heightened awareness of its deconstitution, and even laughter at it, brought about two shields, most impenetrable, in an individualized form of sovereignty, of the worst roguish type, on the one hand, and in a fearful (re)turn to futurity, on the other. These dimensions of our underexposed constitution will be addressed in the next chapter. But I can advance that partly what is necessary is a more radical cynicism that

challenges *oneself* in a movement similar to that that goes between Saint Just and Sade in the French Revolution: from laughter for Revolution to laugher at the Revolution. See Miguel Abensour, *Rire des Lois, des Magistrats et des Dieux—L'impulsion Saint Just* (Paris: Horlieu, 2004), 11427.

152. See Christoph Menke, 'Ability and faith: On the possibility of justice,' *Cardozo Law Review*, 27 (2005), 595–612. Menke describes eloquently how Derrida deconstructs the philosophical task of making the success of our practices successful, or his deconstruction of '*Könnensbewustsein*' (confidence in ability, or more literally consciousness of ability). My problem here goes one step further in asking whether there is not, in Derrida, a problematic 'consciousness of inability,' which itself is also a power, and does not challenge the power of the 'ability of the "I" to be-having' ('possum' or 'I can'), which from a literal etymology is the very question of the 'pos-sum-ability' of possibility. Certainly Derrida has always adamantly struggled against the order of knowledge and the 'I can' of possibility. See on this, for instance, Jacques Derrida, *L'animal que donc je suis*, 48–50; trans., 395–7. The problem of the limits of fragility will be further developed in the next chapter, which addresses the undesirability of a thought that distinguishes sharply between unconditionality with power and unconditionality without power.

153. Jacques Derrida, 'As if it were possible, "within such limits"' in *Negotiations* 363. Another way of approaching this eventuality is invoking 'the dangerous perhaps,' see Jacques Derrida, *Politiques de l'amitié*, 43–66; trans., 26–48. Yet another way of referring to the localization of impossibility is to use the hyphen to emphasize that there is never impossibility as totally distinguishable and immune from possibility, and more importantly from happening: im-possibility; here the possibility of the impossible shall not be immune from the impossibility of the possible. See Jacques Derrida, 'Une certaine possibilité impossible de dire l'événement' in *Dire l'événement, est-ce possible?*, eds., Soussana, Derrida, and Nouss (Paris: L'Harmattan, 2001), 100–1; 'A certain impossible possibility of saying the event,' trans. G. Walker, *Critical Inquiry*, 33 (2007), 453–4.

Chapter 4 'To Come'

1. Jacques Derrida, *L'Écriture et la différence*, 24, 255, 326; trans., 12, 171, 220.

2. Jacques Derrida, *De la grammatologie*, 14, 270; trans., 5, 191. Unfortunately, Spivak is not accurate when translating à *venir* as simply 'future' throughout the book.

3. Jacques Derrida, 'Pas' in *Parages*, 2nd edn (Paris: Galilée, 1986–2003), 19–116; '*Pace* not(s)' in *Parages*, trans. J. P. Leavey (Stanford: Stanford University Press, 2010), 11–102.

4. Jacques Derrida, *D'un ton apocalyptique adopté naguère en philosophie*

(Paris: Galilée, 2005); 'On a Newly Arisen Apocalyptic Tone in Philosophy' in *Raising the Tone of Philosophy*, ed. P. Fenves (Baltimore: The Johns Hopkins University Press, 1993), 117–71.

5. Derrida, *Force de loi*, 55; trans., 254.

6. 'The Pascal *pensée* that "puts together" justice and force, and makes force an essential predicate of justice—by which he means *droit* more than justice' (Derrida's emphasis). Derrida, *Force de loi*, 31; trans., 240.

7. And the essence of law is not itself just, but 'Whoever obeys them [criminal laws] because they are just obeys a justice which is imaginary and not the essence of the law.' Blaise Pascal, *Pensées*, trans. R. Ariew (Indianapolis: Hackett Publishing, 2005), 20.

8. Derrida, *Force de loi*, 55; trans., 254.

9. Derrida, *Force de loi*, 56; trans., 254.

10. Derrida, *Force de loi*, 55; trans., 254.

11. Derrida, *Force de loi*, 56; trans., 254.

12. Derrida, *Force de loi*, 56; trans., 254.

13. Derrida, *Force de loi*, 57; trans., 255.

14. Derrida, *Force de loi*, 56; trans., 254.

15. Derrida, *Force de loi*, 53; trans., 252. For deliberation, see Ghetti, 'Laws of deliberation,' 255–75. And also Pablo S. Ghetti, 'Às Margens da Deliberação: Por uma politica deliberativa por vir' in *Temas de Constitucionalismo e Democracia*, ed. J. R. Vieira (Rio de Janeiro: Renovar, 2003), 20–39.

16. Derrida, *Force de loi*, 60; trans., 256.

17. Derrida, *Force de loi*, 60; trans., 256.

18. Derrida, *Force de loi*, 60; trans., 256. For the deconstruction of the lines that separate the who from the what, see Derrida, *Voyous*, 126; trans., 86. Cf. also, Derrida, *Force de loi*, 42–3; trans., 246–7. Derrida, *Force de loi*, 60; trans., 256.

19. Jacques Derrida, 'Remarks on Deconstruction and Pragmatism,' 88.

20. Derrida, *Voyous*, 123; trans., 84.

21. Derrida, *Force de loi*, 57–63; trans., 255–8.

22. Derrida, *Voyous*, 168–71 and 184–7; trans., 119–21, 131–4.

23. Immanuel Kant, *Critique of Pure Reason*, 496–502, and 590–604.

24. Derrida, *Voyous*, 168 and 185; trans., 120 and 132.

25. Derrida, *Voyous*, 195–217; trans., 141–59.

26. Jacques Derrida, *Papier Machine* (Paris: Galilée, 2001), 15–31; *Paper Machine*, trans. R. Bowlby (Stanford: Stanford University Press, 2005), 4–18.

27. Derrida, *De la grammatologie*, 14; trans., 4–5.

28. Jacques Derrida, 'Introduction: Desistance' in *Typography: Mimesis*,

Philosophy, Politics, ed., P. Lacoue-Labarthe (Stanford: Stanford University Press), 2.

29. See Derrida, *De la grammatologie*, 142; trans., 93. See also ch. 2.3.

30. See Jacques Derrida, *Le toucher, Jean-Luc Nancy* (Paris: Galilée, 2000), 334 and 346. See also B. L. Keeley, 'Making Sense of Senses: Individuating Modalities in Humans and Other Animals,' *The Journal of Philosophy*, XCIX/1 (2002), 5–28. In Keeley's work one realizes the almost mad philosophical-scientific attempt to find out the right border of sense, between sensor and sensed, inside and outside, organism and environment. When one finds it, here in the central nervous system (CNS), one finds 'something' that has no life of itself, that is entirely dependent on its environment, pressed, and locked in the body. One comes back to an ancient, and so-called Platonic, social technique, the distinction between body and soul. In fact, the relevance of the CNS is in highlighting the self perceiving itself, construing its own border each time differently, and according to a space and a time that it cannot determine alone.

31. For the matter of *presentation* see Derrida, *L'écriture et la différence*, 253–91, and 341–67; trans., 169–95, and 232–50. Also Lacoue-Labarthe, 'Typographie' in *La Faculté de juger*, eds., J. Derrida et al. (Paris: Les Éditions de Minuit, 1985), 168–246.

32. I appreciate that Derrida borrows the notion of weak messianism from Benjamin. Whilst I understand that, for Derrida, such a messianism is not devoid of force, or precisely is at a juncture of force and weakness, hegemony and counter-hegemony, calling it weak messianism is often misleading. I shall not adopt such a language. The 'fixed' ideas of strong messianism are indeed strong, but are only strong as ideas because their bearers have to contemplate hegemonic dissemination; they cannot avoid a degree of wider participation in the hegemonic discourse. 'Weak' must be placed within this context of social forces, and a different relation to the determination of positions of power, exposed to the difference and uncertainty of such 'forces.' Weak messianism must not be taken, as it mostly is, as just a dim form of messianism. See Jacques Derrida, *Spectres de Marx*,' 91–6; trans., 152–155, 180–181. See also Walter Benjamin, 'On the concept of history' in vol. 1 of *Walter Benjamin: Selected writings*, eds., M. Bullock and M. W. Jennings (Cambridge, MA: Harvard University Press, 1996), 389–90. On the challenges of a political philosophy that reckons with a contemporary call to a modulation of action that is both strong and weak, violent and nonviolent, in the Marxist tradition, see Etienne Balibar, *Violence et civilité* (Paris: Galilée, 2010), and especially his essay 'Lénine et Gandhi: une rencontre manqué?,' 305–21.

33. For instance, Derrida, *Force de loi*, 137–46; trans., 293–8.

34. Derrida, *Voyous*, 12–13; trans., 8–9. See also Jacques Derrida, 'Performative powerlessness,' *Constellations*, 7/4 (2000), 467–8.

35. I am in fact even reluctant to use the language of abuse, for the language of abuse implies the necessity of moderation. I do not pose these problems on the level of the arcane but still cogent common sense of what is abusive and what is prudent. On a certain level there must be a certain prudence, in the

sense of care and concern for the 'to come.' Yet, such a care may require almost concomitantly great violence and audacity to materialize itself. Derrida's use of 'the reasonable' may give rise to much confusion in this regard. It is precisely designed to employ something akin to the 'return to practical philosophy' (giving great weight to good arguments, good faith, attention to context and public), without yet renouncing the unconditional drive or faith that underpins the pursuit of any form of understanding. In any case, I reckon that the language of abuse can play into the hands of *reasonableness*, of oppressive common sense that Derrida always attempted to counter. See Derrida, *Voyous*, 208–9; trans., 150–1.

36. See, for example, Jacques Derrida, 'De l'économie restreinte à l'économie générale: Un hégelianisme sans reserve' in *L'écriture et la difference*, 369–408; 'From restricted to General Economy: a Hegelianism without reserve' in *Writing and Difference*, 251–77.

37. Derrida 'University without Condition,' 202–37. Also: Jacques Derrida, *L'animal que donc je suis*, 15–77; trans., 379–80.

38. For the year 2001–2 see Jacques Derrida, *Séminaire La bête et le souverain*, vol. I (2001–2002) (Paris: Galilée, 2008); *The Beast and the Sovereign*, vol. 1, trans. G. Bennington (Chicago: Chicago University Press). For the year 2002–3, see Jacques Derrida, *Séminaire La bête et le souverain*, vol. II.

39. Derrida, 'Pas,' 19–116.

40. Derrida, 'Performative Powerlessness,' 467–8. This passage betrays the additional predicament of a theoretical misunderstanding. Derrida's objection to sovereignty is levelled against Habermas's use of 'popular sovereignty.' In this light this becomes virtually a terminological problem. Habermas's notion of popular sovereignty is a seriously deflated one; purposely crafted to avoid theological or 'romantic' associations connected with the affirmation of anything like a collective identity or subject. Habermas's rejection of a philosophy of consciousness and his distaste for the notion of constituent power (one term that would indeed involve the strong affirmation akin to what Derrida is concerned with vis-à-vis sovereignty) indicate indeed a very different notion of popular sovereignty. In fact, it would be much better described as public autonomy, the 'wild' interactions in the public sphere that slowly allow the rational formation of the will and of opinion, and that underlie the institutionalized processes of democratic decision-making. The problem with Habermas is not one of 'sovereignty,' and the eventually self-defeating excess of the unconditional. As Honig has argued, the problem would be one of the normality of constitutions, the prevalence of a putatively rational and settled institutional frameworks. See Jürgen Habermas, *The Inclusion of the Other: Studies in political theory*, trans. C. Cronin and P. De Greiff (Cambridge, MA: MIT Press, 1999), 105–64. Also Bonnie Honig, 'Dead rights, live futures: A reply to Habermas's "Constitutional democracy",' *Political Theory*, 29/6 (2001), 792–805.

41. On the non-predetermined approach to sovereignty, I can refer here, for instance, to Derrida's *Voyous*, 25–39; trans., 6–18.

42. Derrida, *L'animal que donc je suis*, 38–40; trans., at 388–9.

43. Derrida, *L'animal que donc je suis*, 40; trans., at 389.

44. Derrida, *L'animal que donc je suis*, 38–9; trans., at 388–9.

45. Walter Benjamin, 'Über Sprache überhaupt und über die Sprache des Menschen' in *Walter Benjamin Gesammelte Schriften*, IIi, eds., R. Tiedemann and H. Schweppenhäuser (Berlin: Suhrkamp, 1977), 155; 'On Language as Such and on the Language of Man' in vol.1 of *Walter Benjamin: Selected writings*, 73.

46. Derrida, *L'animal que donc je suis*, 39; trans., at 389.

47. Benjamin, 'On Language as Such,' 74.

48. Derrida, *Politiques de l'amitié*, 325; trans. 292–3. Also Derrida, *L'animal que donc je suis*, 39; trans., 389.

49. Derrida, *Politiques de l'amitié*, 282; trans., 251.

50. Derrida, *Politiques de l'amitié*, 258–9; trans., 231–2.

51. Derrida, *Politiques de l'amitié*, 281–2; trans., 251.

52. Jacques Derrida, *Marges de la philosophie*, 291; trans., 246–7.

53. Derrida, *Politiques de l'amitié*, 281; trans., 251.

54. Jacques Derrida, 'Y a-t-il une langue philosophique?' in *Points de Suspension—Entretiens* (Paris: Galilée, 1992), 235; 'Is There a Philosophical Language?,' trans. P. Kamuf, in *The Derrida–Habermas Reader*, ed., L. Thomassen (Edinburgh: Edinburgh University Press, 2006), 40.

55. Derrida, *Politiques de l'amitié*, 43–66; trans., 26–48.

56. Derrida, *L'Université sans condition*, 76; trans., 235.

57. Slightly modified translation, see Derrida, *L'Université sans condition* 70; trans., 232. On 'profession of faith,' see Derrida, *L'Université sans condition* 11–18, and 76; trans., 202–8, and 235.

58. Derrida, *L'Université sans condition*, 12 and 23; trans., 202 and 208.

59. Derrida, *L'Université sans condition*, 18–19; trans., 206.

60. Derrida, *L'Université sans condition*, 14–18; trans., 204–6.

61. Derrida, *L'Université sans condition*, 19; trans., 206.

62. Derrida, *L'Université sans condition*, 33; trans., 214.

63. Derrida, *L'Université sans condition*, 75; trans., 235.

64. As Derrida explains it may well obey a 'certain grammar of the conditional,' but that is to 'announce the unconditional.' See Derrida, *L'Université sans condition*, 75–6; trans., 235.

65. Derrida, *Voyous*, 146; trans., 102.

66. In *Politics of Friendship*, Derrida does highlight a concealed element of sovereign vacuity often concealed in the history of discourses and practices of friendship, but he does not equate friendship with the unconditional moment.

Rather, he clearly dwells at the very intersection between vacuity and fullness, universality and particularity, the incalculable and the calculable—not to reinforce these distinctions, but to further complicate them in a process of differential contamination.

67. For mode of production of subjectivity, see the extraordinary joint work of Felix Guattari and Suely Rolnik, *Molecular Revolution in Brazil* (Los Angeles: Semiotext(e), 2008), 35–178.

68. See ch 1.3.

69. See ch. 1.2.

70. With regard to democracy, to be sure, Derrida did propose such complex and concrete analyses of existing and exposed aporias. The complexity of social practices should not condone the early simplification that 'deconstruction' allows in order to *intervene* in a particular situation. Such intervention will have to be more interpretatively difficult in order to include a narrative that brings together an open project of transformation, according to exposed normative standards, and an accurate understanding of the situation. This joint effort (normative intervention and pursuit of understanding) should yield greater sensitivity—should raise sensitivity to the situation's problems and possibilities and impossibilities of transformation.

71. Certainly in his emphasis on the sovereign's unconditional tendency to suppress divisions, Derrida is reflecting upon a long-standing tradition that attributes indivisibility to the sovereign. See Jean Bodin, *On Sovereignty*, trans. J. H. Franklin (Cambridge: CUP, 1992), 27, 49–50 and 92. Yet, by doing that, Derrida is not quite felicitous. Given this emphasis and these distinctions, in some of his writings, he ends up turning a blind eye to another tradition which can be traced back to Harrington (but perhaps even to Machiavelli), and leads decisively to Marx, according to which power is shaped by force, material and symbolic, in the accumulation and exploitation of 'social' wealth, of 'property.' See James Harrington, *The Commonwealth of Oceana* and *A System of Politics* (Cambridge: CUP, 1992), 40 and 210. For Derrida's own take on accumulation see *L'autre cap*, 56–8, and 66–73; trans., 56–8, and 64–71. See also Derrida, *Spectres de Marx*, 157–279; trans., 95–176. For a certain political and Machiavellian Marx, see Miguel Abensour, *La démocratie contre l'Etat—Marx et le moment machiavélien* (Paris: Editions du Félin, 2004), 5–26.

72. See Derrida, *Voyous*, 203ff.; trans., 148ff.

73. See ch. 2.3.

74. Derrida, 'Pas,' 31.

75. Derrida, 'Pas,' 29.

76. Derrida, 'Pas,' 29.

77. See ch. 2.3 and n. 29, above.

78. Derrida, *Politiques de l'amitié*, 198; trans., 174.

79. For that type of relation see Jean-Luc Nancy, *L' 'il y a' du rapport sexuel* (Paris: Galilée, 2001), 43ff.

80. Derrida, 'Pas,' 21.

81. Derrida, 'Pas,' 24.

82. It enjoys itself in the announcement of its destitution, and its plurality; that is, the value of this 'coming' rests in a call, in a *postulation* by definition plural and whose 'constitution' is undecidable. The important reference to the apocalypse and to messianism is deconstructed from within the apocalyptic and the messianic genres. This 'coming' becomes an exposure of exposure, a disaster of disaster, an apocalypse of apocalypse, sustained only in the play and the joy of an im-possible relation to the other. Let us pause for a moment to appreciate Derrida's extraordinary reading of John's Apocalypse, and some of its resonances with Derrida's thought: 'And each time the Lamb opens one of the seven seals, one of the four living says, "Come", and it is the continuation of the Horsemen of the Apocalypse. Further on—I mean in John's Apocalypse—in chapter 17, one of the seven messengers with seven cups says, "Come, I shall show you the judgment / of the great whore" [17:1] ... And in chapter 21, "Come! I shall show you / the bride, the wife of the Lamb" [21:9]. And above all, at the end of ends, "Come" launches into or echoes itself in an exchange of calls and responses that is precisely no longer an exchange. The voices, the places, the routes of "Come" traverse the partition [*paroi*] of a song, a volume of citational and recitative echoes, as if it [*ça*] began by responding. And in this traversal or this transfer(ence), the voices find their spacing, the space of their movement, but they nullify it with one stroke [*d'un trait*]; they no longer give it time ... "Come" cannot come from a voice or at least not from a tone signifying "I" or "self", a so-and-so (male or female) in my "determination", my *Bestimmung*: vocation to the destination *myself*. "Come" does not address itself to an identity determinable in advance. It is a drift [*une dérive*] underivable from the identity of a determination. "Come" is only derivable, absolutely derivable, but only from the other, from nothing that may be an origin or a verifiable, decidable, presentable, appropriable identity, from nothing not already derivable and arrivable without *rive* [bank, shore]. Perhaps you will be tempted to call this disaster, catastrophe, apocalypse. Now here, precisely, is announced—as promise or threat—an apocalypse without vision, without truth, without revelation, envois (for the "Come" is plural in itself, in oneself), addresses without message and without destination, without sender or decidable addressee, without last judgment, without any other eschatology than the tone of the "Come", its very *différance*, an apocalypse beyond good and evil. "Come" does not announce this or that apocalypse: already it resounds with a certain tone; it is itself the apocalypse of apocalypse; *Come* is apocalyptic.' See Derrida, *D'un ton apocalyptique*, 88–95; trans., 163–167.

83. See ch. 2, concluding remarks.

84. See ch. 2.3.

85. Derrida, *L'animal que donc je suis*, 46; trans., at 394.

86. Derrida, *L'animal que donc je suis*, 47; trans., at 394. Derrida compares this situation to the holocaust, suggesting it would be as if the Nazi's had started to 'breed' their Jewish scientific 'objects.' Yet, Derrida seems to elude

entirely another historical holocaust that took place in gigantic and systematic proportions—what can also be called extermination 'by means of continued existence and even overpopulation': slave trade and the system of slavery itself.

87. Derrida, *L'animal que donc je suis*, 397.

88. There is a careful proximity here to the work of Artaud. But like Derrida, one must not accept any pure representation concomitant to life. The theatre of law that eschews the spectacular logic (one of vision and distance) is not the end of distance or vision; it is not full presence. It is rather a more enjoyable experience of the divide between public and audience, near–distance, vision–touch, and all the other divides that orientate and disorientate sociability. See Derrida, *L'Écriture et la différence*, 253–368; trans., 169–250.

89. For an apparently instrumental use of law that in fact involves also a certain allegiance to law, see James Holston, *Insurgent Citizenship: Disjunctions of democracy and modernity in Brazil* (Princeton: Princeton University Press, 2008), 203–32. On law and literature: 'Literature can play the law [*jouer la loi*], repeating it while diverting or circumventing it.' See Derrida, 'Prejugés—Devant la loi' 134; trans., 216. On playing with legal theory, the 'theory' that is produced at Birkbeck Law School provides an extraordinary set of examples. For an overview see Douzinas and Gearey, *Critical Jurisprudence*, 229–58.

90. Derrida, *Voyous*, 195–217; trans., 141–59.

91. Derrida acknowledges Schmitt's contribution in the text and is in fact in dialogue with him. See Jacques Derrida, *Séminaire La bête et le souverain*, vol. I, 73; trans., 43. See Schmitt's quote in Carl Schmitt, *The Concept of the Political*, trans. G. Schwab (Chicago: University of Chicago Press, 1986), 52. See also Carl Schmitt, *The Leviathan in the State Theory of Thomas Hobbes: Meaning and Failure of a Political Symbol*, trans. G. Schwab and E. Hilfstein (Westport, Connecticut: Greenwood Press, 1996), 72. In that regard, see also Thomas Hobbes, *Leviathan* (Oxford: OUP, 1996), 147 [XXI, 114] and 475 (Conclusion, 396).

92. Guilt here in the sense of a 'being-in-debt: *in culpa esse.*' See Giorgio Agamben, *Homo Sacer: Sovereign Power and Bare Life*, trans. D. Heller-Roazen (Stanford: Stanford University Press, 1998), 26–7.

93. Walter Benjamin, 'The Right to Use Force' in Bullock and Jennings, *Selected Writings*, vol. I, 232. See also, in 233, the interesting critique of the monopolistic, and self-attributing use of force—in this instance I am closer to him.

94. Derrida, *Séminaire La bête et le souverain*, vol. I, 67; trans., 39.

95. Hobbes, *Leviathan*, 198.

96. Derrida, *Séminaire La bête et le souverain*, vol. I, 70; trans., 41 (I modified the translation, replacing 'future' with 'to-come,' in order to show more clearly the reference to the 'to come' in future itself that the French word '*avenir*' allows).

97. Derrida, *Séminaire La bête et le souverain*, vol. I, 72; trans., 42.

98. Derrida, *Séminaire La bête et le souverain*, vol. I, 36; trans., 15 (this translation has been modified to add 'for a long time').

99. Niklas Luhmann, *Law as a Social System*, trans. K. A. Ziegert (Oxford: OUP, 2004), 14, 148ff., 255ff., 467ff. (for stabilization of expectations). As to survival, which Luhmann says is not guaranteed by autopoiesis, one can still say that it is still the force that drives the self-shaping of the 'system.' According to Luhmann the system does that always in its own terms (I have serious doubts about that because it would imply a sort of absolute immunity; see ch. 2); for survival, see Luhmann, *Law as a Social System*, 191, 231, 267, and 466. What I think is crucial to distinguish is between survival of a drive, which inevitably turns to domination, and survival as an experience, a passion, the passion for and in survival (as survivors that 'we,' the living–dying, all are). With that qualification I subscribe to Johan Van der Walt's distinction between domination and survival. See Van der Walt, *Law and Sacrifice*, 13 and 75.

100. See for instance, on the question of spectres, Derrida, *Spectres de Marx*, 157–279; trans., 95–176.

101. Derrida, Séminaire La bête et le souverain, vol. II.

102. Martin Heidegger, *Fundamental Concepts of Metaphysics: World, solitude, finitude* (Indianapolis: Indiana University Press, 2001), 186–366. Illustrative in that regard is Crusoe's cry 'I that was born to be my own Destroyer.' Daniel Defoe, *Robinson Crusoe* (Oxford: OUP, 1983), 40.

103. Defoe, *Robinson Crusoe*, 153.

104. Defoe, *Robinson Crusoe*, 52–3, 69, 80–2. Derrida emphasizes that if Crusoe always insisted in being alone, he implied that the beasts were not alone, together in their 'howlings and roaring' of the night. Perhaps he is referring to Defoe, *Robinson Crusoe*, 27.

105. Crusoe realizes that those footsteps might be 'a chimera of his own,' his own footsteps. Defoe, *Robinson Crusoe*, 157–8.

106. Derrida, *Séminaire La bête et le souverain*, Vol. II, 215–7.

107. I am focusing here on Derrida's reading of Defoe, but these seminars are equally a reading of Heidegger's seminars of the years 1929–1930, in which Derrida critiques Heidegger's positing of an affirmation of possibility in light of impossibility, an ever-present opening to possibility, see Heidegger, *Fundamental Concepts of Metaphysics*, 364.

108. For that matter see an extraordinary piece by Christoph Menke, 'Ability and Faith: On the Possibility of Justice,' *Cardozo Law Review*, 27 (2005), 595–612. Furthermore, with respect to faith I do not endorse entirely Nancy's posing of the distinction between faith and belief (belief being for him still in the vicinity of knowledge). I do not, in particular, accept that it is possible to derive a political or legal theory out of this distinction. To be sure, I do not wish 'faith' to be circumscribed by the architecture of knowledge, but knowledge itself does not come to stand without faith—there is an element of faith in knowledge, in the drive to knowledge and in the moment at which knowledge fails in its promise of order. If one lives in an economy of knowledge

(economy in the sense of a complex force field), it is precisely from there that one may extract faith; indeed Nancy also refers to this way of thinking. See Jean-Luc Nancy, *La Déclosion (Déconstruction du christianisme, 1)* (Paris: Galilée, 2005), 23–4 and 44–5.

109. See Derrida's seminar on 19 February 2003, in Derrida's informal response to the intervention of students (it has not been the policy of Derrida's editors to publish such discussions, and this seminar day does not appear in Derrida, *Séminaire La bête et le souverain* Vol. II): 'If I explain, if I supply knowledge [*savoir*], for me teaching consists in letting the other as other; I leave to the other the responsibility of sorting it for himself [*se débrouiller*]. Each time that someone sorts something for himself, he takes care of his own ghost, and that is the impossible responsibility of sharing. Each one shall remain alone. This is solitude. When I speak of solitude, of my solitude, you think of yours, and you say to yourself that it may be the same thing—but you are certainly mistaken. That is language though [it brings people together in the mistake of their co-belonging or sharing of passion]. There is a great English poet who elaborated a theory that he called self selving, how a self selves itself, how an I becomes itself. It [the 'I'] does that through what Hopkins calls self-taste, the taste for oneself. It is absolutely indescribable, and unshareable. No one can share the taste for oneself ... [but] in the self-taste there is already the other.' This, however, cannot bridge the difference between Hopkins and Derrida regarding the proximity to God (and the institutional religiosity linked with it) of the I/eye that becomes itself. I have had access to informal discussions, and those of this session in particular, through Zelina Beato's transcriptions (Derrida's course in the EHESS from the academic year 2002–3) <http://www.unicamp.br/iel/traduzirderrida/Ecole_2002.htm#26mar>, accessed 30 June 2004.

110. Derrida, Séminaire La bête et le souverain Vol. II, 244.

111. Zelina Beato's transcription (19 Febraury 2003).

112. Defoe, *Robinson Crusoe*, 26–7, for one explicit example.

113. See Defoe, *Robinson Crusoe*, 33–40 and 279–306.

114. Bennington, *Legislations*, 1–3.

115. Derrida, *D'un ton apocalyptique*, 94; trans., 166.

116. It is worth pointing out here that in French, as opposed to English, there is no direct reference to orgasm or sexual enjoyment, albeit in a vulgar sense. I see no obstacle to embracing the full latitude of the term in English, for the openess of a translation is not outside the scope of a deconstructive endeavour such as this one. Symptomatically, at a Conference of the Association for the Study of Law, Culture and Humanities, in Austin, in 2005, Lee Quinby presented a paper, 'Democracy as Found Art' (unpublished), in which she evoked the sexual connotation in democracy 'to come,' for which she was rebuked by a participant who was familiar with the French language. On the occasion I spoke in favour of Quinby's (and the English language's) 'appropriation' and I argued that Derrida in several texts had meticulously discussed the problematic

connotations of notions of brotherly love, fraternity, and freedom, all of which were impacted by the risk of a type of relationship (friendship) and of freedom (*exousia*, or license) that cannot avoid a certain tension with love and sexual difference. See *Politics of Friendship* and *Voyous*. Yet, this coming of which I speak would not lend itself to a simple naturalization, as physical enjoyment. If one is to find a sexual element, one can search in the *differential* view of the sexual relation espoused by Nancy, in his 'external' (focused on language and enunciation) of Lacan: 'enjoyment is the fact or the being of sex inasmuch as it differs and it differs itself'; and 'duality divides itself (straight/gay, male/female), it replays itself (each time first and second, each time enjoying being infinitely finite)'; '*the sexual is the there is of the relation.*' See Nancy, *L' "il y a" du rapport sexuel*, 30, 34 and 53.

117. Constitutional exposure requires a form of political conversation that opens itself to the provisionality of decision-making and the fate of deconstitution without falling back on the security of the freedom of the subject. It is de-liberated: both in the sense of a debunking of a certain closed freedom, but also in the sense of a launch of a differential/coming freedom itself. In addition, it is the deliberation in the sense of a resolute conversation: so resolute to the point of dwelling at the border of various negotiations that expose people to their coming together apart, in the frail making of their lines of sociability, of their laws. In this sense, democracy, or constitutional exposure, is the spacing of *deliberation* on law. See n. 15, above. See also Ghetti, 'Laws of Deliberation,' 255–75. If this exposed conversation, that requires the discourse and the experience of rights claiming, is brought to radical fruition, one may *come* to different articulations of coming-together-apart that challenge current exploitations: overexposure. Derrida, *Spectres de Marx*, 278–9; trans., 175–6.

Postulating Formalizations

1. This democracy of the true to come should not fail to show its belonging, its family resemblance, to a certain 'true democracy' put forward by the early Marx: Miguel Abensour, *La démocratie contre l'Etat—Marx et le moment machiavélien* (Paris: Editions du Félin, 2004), 123–42. With perhaps a difference that it does not simply move against the State, so much as it instils a 'becoming-democracy' of the State and of wealth, reclaiming the State and common-wealth for the sake of and as its own creation in the joyful clash and perseverance of people to the exposure of their forces.

INDEX

Abensour, Miguel 186, 210, 215, 220
affection(s) 35–8, 40, 44, 119–20, 134, 136, 139, 142–3, 147, 185
Agamben, Giorgio 51, 99, 135, 172–3, 178–9, 188, 204
Aristotle 35–7, 54–5, 92, 104, 106, 124, 172
autoimmunity 17, 48, 68–9, 7–2, 102, 126, 135, 141, 185
autonomy 17, 39–40, 43, 48, 67–70, 105, 124, 131, 136, 197, 213

Benjamin, Walter 47–51, 54, 72, 123, 135, 177, 185, 199, 207, 212
Bennington, Geoffrey 25, 141, 167
Blanchot 113, 131, 166, 172, 194
Bourdieu, Pierre 197–8
Brazil 108–9, 140, 186, 204, 208, 215, 217

Cicero 104
Collège International de Philosophie 32
community 40, 54–6, 68–9, 73, 184–5, 187, 195, 197, 205
compassion 133–4, 139, 142
constitution 15
  of democracy 47
  See also deconstitution; *See also* law
constitutional exposure 11–12, 16–18, 20–1, 44, 46–8, 66, 75–6, 90–1, 96–7, 101, 110–14, 145–6, 165, 204, 220
Critchley, Simon 24, 169

'day'
  of democracy 32
  the question of 27–8
  'today' 26, 27, 29–30, 41, 127
deconstitution 15, 17, 47, 51–4, 61, 65–6, 71–2, 76, 82, 86, 111, 114, 119, 128, 137, 146, 148–9, 180, 209, 220; *see also* law
deconstruction
  of political thought 25
  without deconstruction 64
  without democracy 64
Defoe, Daniel 134, 138–40, 218–19
Deleuze, Gilles 23, 193, 199
democracy
  adjourned 26
  and différance 63
  and fiction 29; *see also* legal fiction
  and sovereignty 58–60
  and voyoucracy 57
  foundation of 50
  Politics of Friendship 34
  universalizing role 17, 21
  See also sensitivity
democracy to come 11, 14, 16–21, 24–26, 29, 31–3, 35, 39, 42–4, 46, 48, 50, 55–6, 58, 64–5, 70, 72–4, 89, 94, 96, 110–11, 113–14, 144, 146, 148–9, 167, 169–71, 195; *see also* 'to come'

Derrida, Jacques
  'Call It a Day for Democracy' 29, 41, 44
  Dissemination 47, 56
  Du droit à la philosophie 43, 76–9, 85
  'Faith and Knowledge' 68
  'Force of Law' 52, 76–9, 85, 87, 114, 117, 192, 197, 202
  Of Grammatology 113, 119
  'Pas' 113, 131
  Politics of Friendship 21, 25, 34, 40, 41–2, 57, 62–3, 130, 165, 172, 214, 220
  Rogues 47, 50, 53–4, 59, 62–4, 68–9, 116, 118, 122, 124, 130, 165, 202
  'The Animal That Therefore I Am (More to Follow)' 122
  'The Beast and the Sovereign,' 122, 135, 138
  The Other Heading 26, 29, 32, 34, 38, 43–5, 59, 63, 129–30, 174
  'The University without Condition,' 122, 124–5
  Writing and Difference 113, 198, 209
différance 63, 119, 131, 183, 192, 195, 216
differential contamination 42–3, 51, 91, 95, 203, 215
Dworkin, Ronald 98

eleutheris 54–5
Europe and memory 30, 31
exclusion 11, 14–15, 17–18, 37, 41, 44, 55, 58, 60–1, 68, 73–4, 91, 99, 101, 121, 134, 136, 142, 143–4, 173, 181–2, 188, 196
exousia 54–6, 220
exploitation 11, 13–15, 17, 18, 22, 26, 34, 37–9, 41, 44, 61, 69, 72–4, 88, 91, 95, 97, 99, 101, 109, 111, 114, 121, 129, 133–4, 140–4, 147–50, 173, 181, 186, 188, 207, 215
exposure
  of law 7
  See also consitutional exposure,

overexposure, underexosure
extortion 73, 133, 186

Fitzpatrick, Peter 52, 179, 182, 188, 192, 196, 203–4
Foucault, Michel 23
founding act 85
freedom see *eleutheris* and *exhousia*
friendship 13, 33–42, 71, 130, 136, 165, 172–3, 214, 220

Gasché, Rodolphe 63, 130, 169, 170

Habermas, Jürgen 67–8, 174–5, 177, 184, 191–2, 196, 200, 203, 205, 213–14
Heidegger 22, 134, 138–9, 166, 168, 174, 181, 218
Hobbes 78, 134–5, 141, 190, 217

intensification, of postulation of democracy 17, 18

justice
  as law 88
  idea of 114–15
  undeconstrucitbility of 88

Kant, Immanuel 74–83, 85–7, 90–3, 95–6, 102–4, 110–13, 118, 120, 172, 190–4, 198–9, 201
Kelsen, Hans 197, 203

Lacoue-Labarthe, Philippe 22, 166, 181–2, 194, 196, 212
law 12
  and constitutionality 148–9
  and justice 91
  as calculation 94
  constitution and deconstution of 52, 54, 76
  Derrida and Kant 78–81
  fictionalized grounds of 82

Lefort, Claude 21–4, 45, 178, 186
  empty place 23
legal fiction 104
legal theory 18, 50, 75–6, 92,
    94, 97–8, 107, 112, 134,
    188, 200, 202, 217–18

Machiavelli, Niccolo 186, 215
Marxist tradition 147, 212
Marx, Karl 166, 180–1, 185–6, 190,
    207, 212, 215, 218, 220
messianic 115, 195, 216
messianicity 69–70
messianism 120, 212, 216
Montaigne 36–7, 84–5, 172–3
Mouffe, Chantal 67, 167,
    171, 177, 184
mystical foundation of authority
    84–86, 94, 196

Nancy, Jean-Luc 12, 18, 22, 64,
    76, 81–2, 85, 97, 99, 102–7,
    110, 112, 166, 170, 180–1,
    186–8, 190, 192–5, 199,
    201, 204–6, 218–19, 220
Natural Law 92

overexposure 11–12, 15, 44, 47,
    59, 73, 75–6, 90–2, 101,
    109–12, 114, 137, 142–3,
    145–9, 203–5, 207, 220

Pascal 84, 114, 211
Plato 53–7
poiesis 105
postulation (*postulatio*) 13

right 25–6, 28, 31, 36, 39, 43, 45,
    51, 53, 56, 71, 76, 77–81,
    85, 92, 95, 98, 100–4,
    110, 169–70, 172, 187,
    190–2, 194, 205–6, 212
rights 66–7, 71–2, 78, 81, 95, 97,
    102–4, 107–10, 112, 127,
    135, 184, 202–4, 213, 220

Robinson Crusoe 134, 138–40, 218
Roman Law 103–4, 110, 205

Schmitt, Carl 37–8, 40–1,
    134–5, 173, 177, 190,
    195, 203, 205–7, 217
self-foundation 32–3, 90, 96, 110
sensitivity 11, 17, 62, 107,
    109, 132–3, 139, 143,
    204, 207–8, 215
  democratic 107, 208
  -raising 207
signature 15–16, 20, 25, 196
Sloterdijk, Peter 62, 178
sociability 12, 39, 40, 44–5, 48,
    52–3, 57, 61, 66, 70, 72,
    74–6, 97, 105, 121, 127,
    134, 144, 149, 217, 220
sovereignty 12–14, 17–18, 47, 58–61,
    63–4, 66–7, 70–3, 75, 102,
    109, 112–14, 120–36, 138–44,
    182, 184, 202, 209, 213

theory, suspicion of 15, 16
  See also legal theory
the political 25
Thomson, Alex 21, 22, 24,
    25, 26, 167
'to come' 12–13, 17–18, 26, 46, 50,
    59, 64–5, 73, 75, 112–17,
    119–21, 126, 128, 130–2,
    134, 140–4, 149–50, 217;
    see also democracy to come
totalitarianism 21, 106, 187

unconditionality 12–13, 18, 60, 64,
    93, 113, 118–26, 128–30,
    139, 141–2, 144, 188, 210
underexposure 44, 59, 75, 90, 91–2,
    97, 102, 106, 111, 114, 128,
    133, 142–3, 144, 147–8, 207
universality/universalization
  and exemplarity 30
  and singularity 31, 42
  enjoyment of 45
  logic of 35
  of nation 45

the universal 31

Valéry, Paul 29–31, 170
Van der Walt, Johan 12, 18,
    50, 76, 97–102, 107,
    109, 199, 204, 218
Villey, Michel 18, 76, 91–3, 102–7,
    110, 195, 201, 206
violence
  groundless 112
  law-making 50
  law-preserving 50
  of the polity 100

Warat, Luis Alberto 108, 109–10, 209

www.ingramcontent.com/pod-product-compliance
Lightning Source LLC
Chambersburg PA
CBHW071341080526
44587CB00017B/2914